# THE FOUNDING OF
# THE ROMAN EMPIRE

BY

FRANK BURR MARSH

SECOND EDITION

CAMBRIDGE

W. HEFFER AND SONS, LTD.

1959

 BARNES & NOBLE, Inc., New York

Publishers · Booksellers · Since 1873

SECOND EDITION: 1927 (Oxford University Press)

Photographically reprinted by permission,
without alteration, for W. Heffer & Sons, Ltd.: 1959

Printed in Great Britain by Lowe & Brydone (Printers) Ltd.
London, N.W.10

# PREFACE

THE first edition of this work was published in 1922 by the University of Texas as the first number of the University of Texas Studies. In preparing a new edition for the press I have taken advantage of the opportunity to correct a few errors and to make a number of verbal changes, but the substance of the work has been modified in only a few details. The first chapter was originally read as a paper before the American Historical Association and was printed in their Annual Report for 1913. As it stands in the book this paper has been extensively revised and in part rewritten. Several tabular appendixes included in the first edition have been omitted as unnecessarily elaborate and their place supplied by additional foot-notes. In the last chapter some changes have been made in the statistics based on these tables. These represent no change in my classification of the consuls, but only an attempt to make the categories mutually exclusive, a thing which, in the absence of the tables, seemed necessary to avoid confusing the careful reader. A new appendix has been added on ' The Intentions of Caesar and the Diarchy of Augustus,' which consists mainly of portions of an article published in *The Classical Journal* in 1925 entitled ' The Roman Aristocracy and the Death of Caesar.' For permission to use this material I am indebted to the editors of the Journal.

My general purpose is, I hope, sufficiently clear. I have not attempted to write a complete history of Rome during the period, but simply to trace the causes of the breakdown of the republic and the steps by which the imperial institutions were developed. Many events have, therefore, been entirely omitted, or mentioned only in passing, which would call for more extended treatment in a work of wider scope. In the notes I have aimed at giving my authority for all statements not easily verified by reference to standard works.

There are a few other matters to which I wish to take this opportunity of calling attention. My quotations from Cicero's letters are all taken from the excellent translation of Shuckburgh, because it seemed to me that his rendering preserved the style and flavour of the Latin better than any version that I could make. Had Winstedt's translation been complete a choice between it and Shuckburgh's might have been difficult. In the quotations I have made only a few trivial changes to adapt them to my purpose.

On a number of disputed points I have adhered to the conventional view without comment. Thus in the matter of the *imperium* of Augustus between 27 and 23 B. C. I have disregarded Pelham's theory (in his *Essays on Roman History*) because Hardy's criticism (in his *Roman Studies*) seems to me to leave the question, at the very least, *sub iudice*. I am also aware that there has been some controversy as to the province assigned to Caesar by the senate. It has been contended that the charge of forests and roads in Italy was not a consular province, but as the senate could declare any department of public business a province, I cannot see the force of the objection. In any case the province was an insignificant one, and was, therefore, one not usually consular. Gelzer in his monograph on the Roman nobility has maintained that the Romans only applied the term noble to the consular families. That these families formed a class apart from, and sometimes hostile to, the praetorian families I have recognized, but, as the praetorian families were certainly not on the same level with the knights, and as they shared such privileges as the *ius imaginum* with the consular houses, I have adhered to the commonly accepted usage. The difference between Gelzer and myself seems to me chiefly one of terminology.

Since this book appeared several works have been published dealing with the period. I have tried to take these into account and have added a few notes referring to them. The only one that need be mentioned here, because not referred to in the notes, is Dessau's *Geschichte der römischen Kaiserzeit*, the first volume of which is devoted to the reign of Augustus. On one vital point I remain entirely at variance with the German scholar, who regards the diarchy as a modern fiction, and holds that the principate was a despotism from the beginning. The following pages will make clear my chief reasons for rejecting this view, and in this place I only wish to call attention to the fact that my conception of the principate as developing and changing its character was that held by the Romans themselves, as is shown by the language of Tacitus (*Annals*, i. 2).

I feel that my grateful acknowledgements are due to the authorities of the University of Texas for their generous and sympathetic attitude both in connexion with the first edition and with this as well. I desire also to thank several of my colleagues on the faculty, particularly Professors E. C. Barker, F. Duncalf, W. J. Battle and P. M. Batchelder, who kindly read the original manuscript, for many valuable suggestions.

F. B. M.

Austin, Texas,
   *March* 29, 1926.

B

# TABLE OF CONTENTS

## APPENDIXES

# I. THE ADMINISTRATIVE PROBLEM OF THE REPUBLIC

NO part of Ancient History has fascinated men more than the story of the rise of the Roman republic from an insignificant town of Latium to a position of world empire and the destruction of the civil liberty of the Romans in the moment of their triumph. That the two things were intimately connected is obvious upon the surface, and historians have agreed that it was Rome's conquest of the Mediterranean world that proved fatal to her republican institutions. Two main explanations have been advanced of why this should have been the case. One of these is that, assailed by the new temptations which the empire brought with it, the Romans themselves deteriorated in character; the other is that, having begun her career as a city-state, Rome found her machinery of government inadequate to perform the work which world dominion imposed upon her. Both these explanations are quite obviously true and quite as obviously insufficient. The corruption and degeneracy of a people do not always lead to a change of government, and it should be shown why they did so in this instance. That a city-state could not govern an empire may be true, but it leaves open the question as to why it could not. In what precise ways was the Roman republic unequal to its task ? Just where and why did the machine break down ? When the government finally collapsed why did not the entire fabric go to pieces ? If the degeneracy of the Roman people will explain the fall of the republic, how shall we account for the fact that this same people continued to rule the world ? How did it happen that the Roman world emerged from the chaos of the civil wars, transformed indeed into an empire, but as dominantly Roman as before ? By what steps did the empire develop out of the republican machine?—for it is surely incredible that it had no more solid foundation than the astute hypocrisy of Augustus. A brief survey of the last century of the republic ought to provide some definite answer to such questions, and such a survey is the purpose of the present work. Its object will, therefore, be to show in some detail just how and why the republic failed and fell and in what way the empire was gradually evolved to meet the imperative needs which the old system could no longer satisfy.

It was not entirely because the Roman state was municipal in its origin that it proved unequal to the task of governing a widely extended empire; the peculiar character of the Roman constitution had much to do with its failure. The Roman republic possessed a very intricate and delicately adjusted organization wherein each part was fitted to every other, and this complexity was one of the causes which led to the breakdown of the machine. At the beginning of Rome's extra-Italian conquests difficulties arose. The problem which the administration of the provinces presented had a marked influence on the foreign policy of the republic —an influence generally ignored, but one which will repay a brief consideration because the problem, in one shape or another, lasted throughout the last century of the republic and exerted a transforming influence upon the institutions of the early empire. It will be well, therefore, at the start to see clearly the precise nature of this problem for which Roman statesmen strove in vain to find a satisfactory solution.

A glance at the history of the growth of Rome's imperial power will at once reveal some curious features. The first of these is the intermittent character of Roman expansion. A brief table will make this clear. From 241 to 197 B.C. Rome annexed four provinces; from 197 to 146 B.C. no new territories were acquired; from 146 to 121 B.C. four more provinces were annexed; from 121 to 63 B.C. there was no further increase of the Roman dominions. Thus it will be seen that the Roman empire expanded rapidly for forty-four years, then stood still for fifty-one years, then advanced again for twenty-five years, then remained stationary for fifty-eight years.

A second peculiarity is that in the periods of rest, if they may be so termed, the republic not only did not annex new provinces but strove earnestly to avoid doing so. It was not that opportunities were lacking but that Rome refused to take advantage of them. One or two illustrations will suffice to make this evident. As has been said above, in the fifty-one years between 197 and 146 Rome acquired no new territory. Yet, during this time, Rome carried on several successful wars. From 200 to 196 she was engaged in the Second Macedonian War, the result of which was to place Greece and Macedon completely at her mercy. On this occasion Rome contented herself with curtailing the power of Macedon and withdrew her forces. Hardly had the Roman legions departed than in 192 Antiochus of Syria invaded Greece, and Rome was forced into a war with him. The result of that war was to leave Rome mistress of Greece and Asia Minor. Again she gave up her conquests and withdrew her army without adding even a single district to her empire. In 171 Perseus, king of Macedon, began a war of revenge on Rome. He was crushed at the battle of Pydna in 168, and, instead of annexing Macedon, Rome contented herself with abolishing the Macedonian monarchy, divided the country into four republics, and retired across the seas. When nineteen years after Pydna the Macedonians revolted under a pretender, Rome finally yielded to the inevitable, and, as there was no other way of keeping Macedon quiet, she annexed it as a province at the beginning of the second period of expansion.

Another instance of this same aversion to conquest is furnished by the province of Transalpine Gaul. After Rome had acquired possessions in Spain it was inevitable that she should seek to gain a land connexion between them and Italy. In ancient times the Mediterranean could only be navigated at certain seasons and it would thus be unsafe for Rome to rely wholly on the sea for her communications with the Spanish provinces. All modern historians have felt the force of these considerations. What has not been explained is why Rome remained blind to them for seventy-six years. This, however, seems clearly a part of the general anti-expansionist policy which prevailed from 197 to 146. As soon as a forward policy was resumed Transalpine Gaul was promptly annexed and land communication with Spain assured.

As has been pointed out, this second period of expansion lasted for twenty-five years and came to an end in 121 B.C. Of Roman policy after this time Professor Tenney Frank has admirably said :

A careful examination of the behaviour of the home government . . . reveals the significant fact that a complete indifference to expansion, at times verging upon a positive aversion, existed at Rome. The Asiatic province and Cyrene constitute the only considerable territorial additions, and these were gifts, accepted in both cases with certain restrictions. In Africa, Gaul, and Cilicia, Rome took charge of the least rather than the largest possible portion of territory at her disposal. The senate was, of course, the centre of the anti-imperialistic sentiment, discouraged, it would seem, by its experiences in Spain, and wholly out of sympathy with the military developments necessitated by foreign possessions.[1]

The facts here stated are entirely correct, but the explanation of the senate's attitude seems hardly adequate. Another explanation that has been offered of this attitude is that the senate was jealous of the power of the provincial governors and found them difficult to control.[2] This motive was doubt-

[1] Frank, *Roman Imperialism*, 274. Of the two provinces here mentioned the annexation of Asia really dates from the preceding period since it was then that the first steps were taken for making it a Roman dependency ; the other, Cyrene, seems not to have been administered as a separate province for a considerable time.

[2] For example, Heitland (*The Roman Republic*, ii. 187–8) says : ' That the senate was anything but eager to annex provinces is clear enough, and was no doubt mainly due to the known difficulty of controlling distant governors.' He also points out some other considerations such as the

less present, yet it can hardly be the whole explanation, since such jealousy would be likely to grow steadily with time, while the opposition of the senate to new annexations is clearly greater at certain periods than at others. Why should the senate have been more reluctant to extend the territories of the republic before 146 B.C. than after that year?

If we turn to the constitutional problem which the administration of provinces presented to the Romans, an explanation is readily forthcoming. Previous to 146 this problem involved greater difficulty than after that date, owing to certain new developments in constitutional usage. This explanation, moreover, will apply equally at another point. The growth of the empire was again arrested in 121 B.C., but it so happens that the administrative problem again became difficult of solution at about that time.

The key to the senate's attitude may, perhaps, be found in its composition and its position in the Roman state. In early times the duty of making out the list of the 300 senators had been entrusted to the censors. Very soon, however, their freedom of choice began to be limited by custom. The ex-magistrates came to be regarded as having a moral, if not yet a legal, right to be placed upon the roll. This right seems to have been established by the Ovinian law, which probably directed the censors to fill the vacancies in the senate by designating the most worthy of the ex-magistrates, including the tribunes and quaestors.[1] The number of these last two classes must have been more than sufficient for the purpose, so that under ordinary circumstances the censors

influence of the 'old Roman' party and the wealth or poverty of the province in question, but he seems to regard the reason quoted as the chief cause of the senate's attitude. Mommsen has also emphasized the fear of the vast power which must have been entrusted to the governor as the reason for the refusal of the senate to accept the gift of Egypt under the will of one of the last Ptolemies. *History of Rome*, iv. 319.

[1] The exact provisions of the Ovinian law have been disputed. The arguments in favour of the view taken in the text are very strong and are fully set forth in Willems, *Le sénat de la république romaine*, i. 153–73.

would have little, if any, opportunity to go outside their ranks. Whatever the provisions of the Ovinian law, the account which Livy gives of the filling up of the senate after the disastrous battle of Cannae shows that by 216 B.C. the rule was clearly established in practice that the ex-tribunes and ex-quaestors should be preferred to citizens who had not held office.

When the problem of administering dependencies first presented itself it was easy of solution. The earliest provinces acquired by the Roman people were Sardinia and Sicily, which were taken from Carthage after the First Punic War primarily for the purpose of keeping her at a safe distance from southern Italy and securing control of the Italian seas. Having annexed them, Rome was obliged to provide in some fashion for their government. A brief experience sufficed to convince the Romans that the tranquillity and safety of these islands required the presence in them of a Roman governor armed with the *imperium*,[1] that is, one of the higher Roman magistrates. But all the magistrates were then fully occupied in Italy, and Rome had none to spare for her extra-Italian possessions. Under these circumstances the obvious course was to increase the number of magistrates with the *imperium* and send the newly created ones across the seas. As it was out of the question to increase the number of the consuls, the praetors were selected for this purpose and their number was raised from two to four. At the same time, as every magistrate holding an independent command was accompanied by a quaestor, the number of the quaestors was increased to meet the new demands. This successfully solved the problem for the time being, and when, at the close

---

[1] The term *imperium* signified the power of command. It was applied to the sum total of the powers conferred upon the higher magistrates. The Roman made no clear distinction between civil and military, executive and judicial functions, but included them all in the one term. In a broad sense the *imperium* thus meant the power of governing, and whoever had received it from the people could act as an executive magistrate, sit as a judge, or command an army. The only regular magistrates possessing the *imperium* were the consuls and praetors.

of the Second Punic War, Rome annexed two new provinces in Spain, the same method was again resorted to in order to secure governors. The number of the praetors was now raised to six and that of the quaestors to twelve. At this point, however, a halt was called, and for the next fifty-one years a steadily anti-expansionist policy was followed by the senate. One reason for this lay in the fact that there existed definite obstacles to any further increase of the magistrates, and hence that it was difficult, or impossible, to administer more territory. The precise nature of these obstacles will repay a brief consideration.

During the period of Roman history that closed in 197 B.C. two important developments had been taking place. In the holding of the offices a definite sequence was gradually established by which it was customary to hold the quaestorship before the praetorship and the praetorship before the consulship. The quaestorship thus became the first step in a Roman's official career, even the tribunes being usually ex-quaestors. While this was happening there had been another development of great importance going on. Little by little a new aristocracy took shape, growing steadily more clearly defined and more powerful. From the earliest days of Rome there was a close association between nobility and the holding of office. One of the outstanding marks of the old patrician aristocracy had been their monopoly of office. When the long conflict between the patricians and the plebeians ended in the victory of the people and the magistracies were thrown open to all the citizens, much of the old feeling still remained. Thus those plebeian families whose members had been elected to the higher offices took their place side by side with the old patrician families to form a new nobility. As early as 217 B.C. one of the tribunes denounced this tendency, saying that the new plebeian nobles had begun to despise the people the moment they had ceased to be despised by the patricians. The denunciation was without effect and the new nobility continued to develop without check. This new aristocracy was composed of all those

families which had attained to any of the curule offices.[1]  As
the holding of these offices thus came to confer distinction,
not only on the man who held them but on his descendants
as well, it was entirely natural that the families so ennobled
should feel themselves a class apart and should seek to keep
the offices in their own hands as far as possible.  Such an
attempt coincided far too well with the aristocratic and conservative temper of the Roman people not to meet with a
large measure of success, and the outstanding fact about the
Roman republic, from the end of the Great Wars on, is the
contrast between its theoretical and its actual government.
In point of law, the republic was a democracy and its offices
open to all citizens without distinction of birth, while in
point of fact, they were almost entirely monopolized by a
ring of noble families.  After 197 B.C. it may reasonably be
assumed that this nobility was so far developed and had become sufficiently class-conscious to begin to view the broad
problems of Roman policy from the standpoint of aristocratic interests.

It is evident that a nobility like that of Rome could not
regard with indifference an indefinite increase in the number
of the offices.  If this were permitted a point must ultimately
be reached when the number would become too great for the
existing aristocracy to fill ; and, since the holding of the
higher offices conferred nobility, an undue increase in their
number was equivalent to a creation of peers.  An aristocracy tends naturally to exclusiveness ; the English House
of Lords has twice preferred surrender to the cheapening of
their rank that must come with a large addition to their
number.  A similar attitude on the part of the Roman nobles
may safely be inferred.  They would, therefore, seek to
check any increase in the number of the offices as soon as it
threatened to bring about any considerable augmentation of

---

[1] The curule offices were the censorship, consulship, praetorship, and two
of the four aedileships.  Of the aediles two were known as curule aediles and
the other two as plebeian aediles.  The curule offices were those which had
once been exclusively patrician and were distinguished by certain special
marks and privileges.

their class. By 197 this point had actually been reached, and consequently the increase of the magistrates was checked. But if this were done it was evident that the state could not be permitted to assume new administrative responsibilities, and thus the Roman nobility adopted an anti-expansionist policy abroad partly as a means of securing its exclusiveness at home.

So satisfactory was the existing system to the nobility that they prevented any alteration in the number of the magistrates for over a century and contented themselves with strengthening those features of it which worked most directly to their advantage. In regard to the magistrates a brief consideration will show that any change must have injured the aristocracy. There were during this time six praetors and twelve quaestors. Custom, if not positive law, had imposed the rule that the quaestorship should be the necessary preliminary to all other offices—even the tribuneship. In the case of this last office the quaestorship seems never to have been required, but it was very generally held and it is probable that few of the tribunes who had not held it were admitted to the senate. Thus the quaestorship became the path that led, not only to all the higher offices, but to the senate as well. As the traditional number of the senate was fixed at 300 it would seem that the number of twelve quaestors a year would somewhat more than fill its ranks.[1] It was quite clearly to the interests of the nobles

[1] Willems (i. 161–4 and 404–6) has attempted to fix the average duration of life of the ex-quaestors and has estimated it at thirty years or slightly less. The size of the senate as reorganized by Sulla was certainly between 500 and 600, which, based as it was on twenty quaestors a year, would give the average life at from twenty-five to thirty years. On the basis of twenty-five years twelve quaestors a year would give 300, while with thirty years the number would be 360. Before the last increase in the number of the quaestors they probably numbered ten, which, on the basis of thirty years average life, would give 300. It may not be unreasonable to infer that very probably before this last increase the quaestors were not quite numerous enough to fill the vacancies in the senate and that after the increase the number was slightly larger than was required. The nobility, in that case, would seem to have stopped the increase as soon as the number became obviously too large to serve their purpose and this was, perhaps, as soon as

to maintain this office as an indispensable first step in an
official career and not to permit an undue increase in its
numbers.  It must have served as an excellent means for
maintaining the supremacy of the aristocracy at once in the
magistracies and in the senate.  It was almost always held
at an early age, at thirty or thereabouts, and under the
conditions of Roman public life so young a man was rarely
given any opportunity to impress his personality on the
voters, unless, perhaps, in the law courts.  In general the
candidates for the office would be comparatively unknown
men and the nobles would have little difficulty in securing
the return of the members of their families who might stand.
Now and then a new man might be chosen, but the Roman
voter called on to decide between two candidates of whom
personally he knew little would nearly always vote for the
one who bore an historic name.  The quaestorship would
thus serve the purpose of the aristocracy if the senate and
the higher magistracies were made to depend upon it.  The
greater the number of the quaestors in proportion to the
number of the noble families the less efficiently it could be
so employed.  The stationary number of the quaestors seems
therefore readily intelligible.  To increase the number would
simply have meant admitting inconvenient rivals for the
higher offices from outside their ranks.

The objections to any change in the number of the praetors are even more obvious.  The holding of this office in
itself conferred nobility and six was quite as large a number
as the aristocracy desired to have.  It was, indeed, upon this
office that the size of the nobility ultimately depended.  It is
true that both the consulship and the curule aedileship ennobled their holders, but the praetorship invariably preceded
the one and almost invariably followed the other.  In the
earlier days of the republic this had not been true.  In former
times there had been but two consuls, two praetors, and two
curule aediles, so that at this period the offices must have

the position of the nobility became sufficiently strong and well defined to
enable them to act successfully.

been held more or less independently of each other. There were, therefore, at first six offices which conferred noble rank. It may be only a coincidence, but it is, at least, suggestive that the Roman aristocracy stopped the increase in the number of the praetors at precisely this same number. Apparently they had no great objection to the increase so long as it kept within the limits of the already existing noble families. When that point had been reached and any further increase must result in the creation of more noble families, a halt was promptly called. Yet if new provinces were to be governed it was necessary to increase the number of the praetors. Experience had clearly shown that the governors must possess the *imperium*, which meant that they must be either praetors or consuls. Their class interests as an aristocracy, therefore, impelled the Roman nobles to set themselves against imperialism and foreign conquest.[1]

A simple solution of the difficulty would have been to create a new office which should not confer nobility, or a seat in the senate, and to use this new magistracy for the government of the provinces. This would have meant the direct election of the provincial governors in the assembly, since only the people could confer the *imperium*. This plan, which would seem so obvious and natural to a modern mind, was open to grave objections from the standpoint of the senate and of the nobility who used that body as an instrument of government.

In the first place, a large part of the power of the senate

[1] Ferrero has stated this point in general terms but with great clearness. ' On a aujourd'hui de la peine à comprendre pourquoi Rome, même à l'apogée de sa puissance, hésita si souvent à étendre ses conquêtes et à agrandir son Empire. Mais une aristocratie est un corps fermé, qui ne s'improvise ni ne se développe à volonté comme peut s'improviser et se développer une bureaucratie recrutée dans toutes les classes et dans toutes les nations ; c'est pourquoi Rome dut veiller toujours à ne pas étendre l'Empire de telle sorte que le nombre d'administrateurs et d'officiers supérieurs que pouvait fournir son aristocratie devînt insuffisant ; et c'est également pourquoi elle s'efforça toujours d'administrer l'Empire avec le moins de fonctionnaires possible.' Ferrero, *La ruine de la civilisation antique*, 120-1. My own conclusion had, however, been published before this book appeared.

sprang directly from the fact that it concentrated in itself the whole official experience of the Roman world. Consuls and praetors must inevitably treat with respect the deliberate judgement of a body in which sat every Roman who had led an army or governed a province. Once let official knowledge and experience accumulate outside the senate and much of its prestige would be gone. Such a consideration was vital to a body which, like the senate, ruled far more by influence than by legal right.

Indirectly, too, such a proposal would have been injurious to the nobles. In the Roman mind there was a very close association between the magistrates, the senate, and the nobility. Office-holding and a seat in the senate were among the badges of the noble. Once create important offices which did not confer nobility or a senatorship and there was bound to arise a new order to rival the existing nobles. Such a development could not but appear dangerous to those nobles and could not be expected to find favour at their hands.

Still further, a considerable part of the senate's control over the provincial governors lay in the fact that they were *ipso facto* senators, and the opinion of their order, spoken through a body of which they were members, could not but weigh heavily with them. Break this connexion, let the people name governors who had no direct interest in the supremacy of the senate, and a blow would be struck at its power. If the senate already found its control over the provinces too weak, it would not be likely to consent to a change which would have weakened it still more.

Thus the problem of providing more governors for new provinces seemed impossible of any solution agreeable to the nobles. It is, therefore, not surprising that the senate, which was dominated by the aristocracy, determined that there should be no new provinces to require governors, and that it directed the foreign policy of Rome with that end in view. The senate permitted the extension of the empire as long as the existing system could be so expanded as to meet the urgent needs of government. When that point was reached and when any new annexations would require extensive readjustments, the senate called a halt.

Yet, although the expansion of Rome was checked for some fifty years, the existing system could not be maintained. On the one hand, new annexations could not be forever avoided, and on the other, the system broke down from within.

The growth of judicial business at Rome ended by demanding the retention there of more than two praetors, especially after the establishment of the standing court *de repetundis* in 149 B.C. ; and the senate's Macedonian policy having ended in utter failure, that turbulent country was finally annexed at the same time that the destruction of Carthage placed Africa in Roman hands. Thus the number of the provinces was increased to six, while but three praetors were available as governors. Faced by this situation, the senate threw the system of governing by praetors overboard and worked out a new plan. This was rendered possible by a new and significant development in the Roman constitution, namely, the rise of the promagistracy.

The origin of this institution was simple. In early days, when the number of the magistrates with the *imperium* was very restricted, the state occasionally needed a larger number than was regularly provided. Under these circumstances the *imperium* of some one of the magistrates who were about to quit office was prolonged, and he continued to exercise his powers after he had laid down his magistracy. As he was no longer consul or praetor, but was yet exercising the powers of that office, he was said to be acting *pro praetore* or *pro consule*, that is, in place of a praetor or a consul. The right to prolong the *imperium* in this fashion belonged at first to the people in their assembly, but during the period of the Great Wars the senate assumed it, as it assumed so many other powers of government.

The convenience, and even the necessity, of this power for the conscript fathers in arranging for the administration of the provinces was obvious from the start. Indeed, without it the government could not have been carried on. The Roman republic had only eight magistrates with the *imperium*—the two consuls and the six praetors. Normally two praetors were kept in Rome and four sent to the four provinces then existing. But it often happened that a magistrate with the *imperium* was imperatively needed elsewhere. In this case the senate dispatched one of the praetors, and to replace him left one of the provincial governors in office for a second year as a propraetor. This usage was the easier to establish as it was a regular rule that a governor remained in charge till his successor arrived to take over the government. Now, as each year the senate settled what provinces should be distributed by lot among the praetors, if they failed to designate one of the four regular provinces for this purpose, the praetor there in charge could not be superseded for another year. Thus the right of the senate to continue in office at its discretion a consul or a praetor beyond his regular term supplied the element of elasticity required to make the rigid system workable. Since it was clearly a necessity, no serious objection seems to have been made to this assumption of power on the senate's part. Once established as a legitimate part of the machinery of government to meet exceptional emergencies it came to be employed with increasing frequency. The more the steadily growing needs of the Roman state pressed upon the heavily burdened magistrates, the greater the temptation to relieve the pressure by making use of the promagistracy.

By the year 146 B.C. the promagistrate had come to be a familiar figure in the Roman government. But up to that time the use of a proconsul or propraetor had been looked upon as a temporary expedient to meet an unusual situation. About 146 the senate solved the problem of governing the increased number of provinces by turning the exception into the rule. Henceforth the promagistracy, instead of being a special device to meet an emergency, was a regular part of the ordinary constitution, and the provinces were governed not by magistrates but by promagistrates. The new system

was not, of course, introduced abruptly, nor was the old
system given up at once. What happened was that after
146 the magistrate became rarer in the provinces and the
promagistrate more frequent. We now begin to meet with
instances of a praetor who, having served his year of office
in Rome, was sent out as a provincial governor in the following year. Those praetors who had gone directly to a province
were more and more often left there for a second year. It is,
however, likely that the new system of using the promagistrate as a governor did not become a fixed rule until the time
of Sulla.[1]

This new method of administering the provinces had, from
some standpoints, little to recommend it. It made directly
for poor administration, since, if a man is elected to fill a
given office, he can be chosen with some reference to his
fitness for that office. But if he is elected to fill one position,
and is then sent to fill another and quite different one, this
becomes impossible. Every year the Roman people elected
praetors to serve as judges in Rome ; after their year of
judicial service, the senate shipped them off to govern provinces and command armies. They were necessarily chosen
with but slight reference to their qualifications for these new
duties. Of course some of them, like Julius Caesar, were men
of so versatile a genius that they could do almost anything
and do it well ; but such men were rare, and it inevitably
happened that a very large number were ill-adapted to the
posts which the fortunes of the lot assigned to them. As a
result the provincial administration and Rome alike suffered.

Yet, whatever the demerits of the system from the standpoint of political science, from that of the nobles it had
signal advantages. It solved all the problems of administration and solved them in a way agreeable to the senate. Its
advantages may be summed up as three in number. It
enabled the senate to relieve the congestion of business at
Rome by keeping most of the six praetors there during their
term of office. At the same time it furnished enough

---

[1] For a discussion of this point, see Willems, ii. 566-7.

governors to meet the increased demands, as all six, together with the two outgoing consuls, were available for provincial governorships. It did both these things without increasing the number of the magistrates, and without disturbing any of the existing rules and regulations.

The year 146 B.C. may be taken, then, as marking the beginning of a new form of provincial administration. Henceforth the consuls and praetors were to serve their year of office in Italy, and afterwards to go out for a second year as proconsuls and propraetors to govern the provinces. But the year is significant for another reason. It marks the beginning of a second period of expansion, and this, in part at least, because of the new system. If we have been justified in concluding that from 197 to 146 B.C. the senate was opposed to annexing new provinces because it had no governors to put in charge, after 146 this reason ceased to apply. While, under the old system, the senate had at most only four praetors to send out as governors, under the new there were at least eight promagistrates available for service. As after 146 there were only six provinces the senate had no longer the same motive for resisting expansion. Yet the expansion which was possible under the new arrangement was distinctly limited. The new system would provide for the government of eight provinces, and then a halt must be called or the system would break down.

Yet the new limit of growth imposed by the number of available governors was not quite so rigid as in the case of the former system. The same power which extended the *imperium* of a magistrate for one year could extend it again. If some of the governors were allowed to serve for two years in their province instead of one, a number of provinces somewhat in excess of eight could be provided for. Yet such an extension of the governor's term must have appeared, from the senate's standpoint, to involve some danger. Two years' service in a province might give time for a bad or incompetent governor to do serious mischief and for an able one to become unduly strong. In a single year a governor could hardly inaugurate and carry far a policy contrary to the wishes of the senate, whereas in two he would be in a more independent position and might irrevocably commit the state. Moreover, it tended directly to make him less responsible for his actions. It was an established principle of the republican constitution that a magistrate could not be called to answer for his conduct while he remained in office. It was, therefore, a sound constitutional principle which insisted upon an interval between offices so that the magistrate should become again a private citizen, and as such liable to prosecution for any illegal acts. To secure this the rule had grown up that two years must elapse before a man who had held one office should be eligible for another. If he spent both years as the governor of a province this rule would be practically annulled. A month or two in Rome, canvassing for the next office, would not be sufficient, since his province was at a considerable distance from the city and it would, therefore, require some time to collect the evidence and forward it to Rome. This work, moreover, could rarely be begun until the governor had left the province, and consequently, unless he remained in private life for a considerable time, it would in most cases be impossible to bring him to trial for anything he might have done. If the governor remained only one year in his province ample time would be secured for any prosecution, but, if he were allowed to stay for a second year, this became very doubtful.

From these considerations it will appear that, while the senate might consent to an increase in the number of the provinces to eight, it would be unwilling to see that number exceeded. Whatever its motive may have been, this was actually its policy. Though not exactly imperialistic, the conscript fathers offered little opposition to expansion between 146 and 121 B.C. During these years, besides the two provinces of Macedon and Africa, annexed at the beginning of the period, two other provinces, Asia and Transalpine Gaul, were acquired. At this point the limits of the new system had been reached, and from this time on the senate was again strongly opposed to expansion and for the fifty-eight years following the annexation of Transalpine Gaul the growth of the empire was practically arrested. Yet once again the senate found itself unable to resist the pressure of events. Neither Cisalpine Gaul nor Cilicia seems to have been regarded at first as among the regular provinces, yet they ended by making themselves such. A word concerning them may not be out of place.

The conquest of Cisalpine Gaul was a long and gradual process. It was begun as far back as 200 B.C., but the Gauls offered a prolonged, though somewhat intermittent, resistance. The surviving books of Livy furnish fairly complete information as to the regular annual assignments of provinces from 198 to 167 B.C. The regular method at that time of governing a province was by a praetor, yet during these thirty-one years praetors were sent to Gaul only five times, with three years for which Livy gives us no information. On seven occasions consuls were dispatched to Gaul, so that in all there were not more than twelve or fifteen years during which a regular magistrate was stationed in the province. The inference from this would seem to be clear. When Gaul was quiet it was not thought to require a special governor, and when it was turbulent a praetor or consul was sent to deal with it. This was probably rendered easier by the troubles in Liguria, which called for the presence in the north of Italy of one or both of the consuls with a good deal of regularity. If there was a consul in Liguria, he could doubtless keep an eye on the Po valley and see that all went well. This was the case in eight years at least when no magistrate was sent to Gaul itself. Thus we may reasonably doubt whether the senate viewed the Cisalpine province as a regular charge on its supply of governors

The province of Cilicia presents a somewhat similar case. In 103 B.C. the Romans established a military post in this region. Probably at that time they had no idea of acquiring a province, since the territory was very restricted in extent. Yet here, too, it gradually became evident that conditions were such as to make the presence of a governor necessary during the greater part of the time.

If Cisalpine Gaul and Cilicia were made part of the regular provincial empire, the limits of the promagistracy were already exceeded. This difficulty was removed by Sulla, who, during his dictatorship, increased the number of praetors to eight, thus making the number of promagistrates available each year balance the number of the provinces. This policy of increasing the number of the magistrates was possible to Sulla since, in the first place, he was clothed with irresistible power, and in the second, because, disregarding the feelings of the nobility, he created peers wholesale by increasing the size of the senate.

In spite of Sulla's masterful recasting of the republican constitution the same problems continued to confront it. The whole policy of the senate, as he reorganized it, was anti-expansionist. No doubt the career of Sulla himself made the senate more suspicious than ever of the military power, but the old motives had by no means disappeared. The state lacked governors to send out to new provinces, and hence the senate was resolved not to assume new burdens. Yet in spite of the senate's resistance new responsibilities could not for ever be evaded. A series of complications which the conscript fathers failed to deal with satisfactorily led to the intervention of the Roman people. Their method of solution was to confer sweeping powers on some popular general. For such action by the assembly the incompetent administration which was the necessary result of the existing system of provincial administration furnished an ample excuse and even a direct provocation. Thus with the death of Sulla we enter on the period of the great commands extending over several provinces and assigned for a term of years to some prominent leader of the day. This system ended, and could end, only in the empire, which in its essence was simply the adoption of the great command as a regular part of the republican machine.

From what has preceded it will be seen that for the

Roman republic the task of governing provinces outside of Italy presented serious constitutional difficulties. This was not chiefly because the institutions of Rome were municipal in their origin, but rather because of their peculiar character and the way in which nobility, the magistracy, and the senate had become associated. It has been shown that the problem of administering extra-Italian territory had first been met by increasing the number of the magistrates with the *imperium*. As long as this method could be followed without disrupting the governing machine the Roman dominions expanded somewhat rapidly, but when this limit had been reached there came a pause. Then the senate successfully opposed all further expansion, until finally such expansion could no longer be resisted. By that time, however, the promagistrate had become so far familiar to the Roman mind that his use as a regular part of the machinery of government was possible. This device of substituting the promagistrate for the magistrate opened up another period of expansion, and for a time the senate ceased to offer any very serious objection to it. But when the new system had in its turn been carried to the limit which the rigid rules of the constitution imposed, the senate sought to call a halt and to avoid all further annexations. When, at length, a new policy of imperialism was forced upon the state the problem of administration could only be met by means that proved speedily fatal to the republic. As long as the complex republican institutions could, in some fashion, be adjusted to meet the crying needs of the day they could continue to exist. When, however, such adjustment had become impossible, or at any rate too difficult for the statesmen of the time, the republican government broke down, and, in spite of the protests of idealists and patriots, a new system of government was inevitably evolved to take over the burden which the republic could no longer bear and yet from which it was unable to escape.

# II. THE DEVELOPMENT OF THE MILITARY SYSTEM

I F the administrative needs of a world empire proved embarrassing to the Roman government, the military demands of such an empire presented a difficulty no less serious. The two problems were very closely bound together, since the Roman made no clear distinction between military and civil affairs and was accustomed to deal with both through the same agents. Nevertheless, although the two were thus united, it will make for clearness to consider them separately, bearing in mind that they presented themselves to the Roman as different phases of a single complex problem.

In early days Rome was essentially a city-state, and, like the city-states of Greece, fought her battles with a citizen militia. The so-called Servian constitution reveals the army as practically identical with the whole body of Roman citizens. The muster of the people for war was, at the same time, the assembly of the people for political purposes and the whole matter had a primitive simplicity. The citizens assembled at the call of a magistrate to decide upon all questions of peace or war. If the decision was in favour of war, the people who had voted it marched forth at once under the command of the magistrate who had presided over their deliberations in the assembly, or of his colleague. The battle over, the soldiers returned to their customary occupations, in the case of the majority to their farms. The campaigns were neither carried on at any great distance nor did they last for any great length of time. Aggressive wars, at any rate, were usually so timed as to fall within the slack season of agriculture when the farmer could leave his land to the care of his wife and children for a week or two, and the whole campaign was generally finished before serious harm had been done by the neglect of the daily work. Nor was the absence of the magistrate from the city a matter of much consequence in these rude and simple days. If the courts of justice were closed for a week or two, or if the ordinary work of the government was suspended for a short time, no great amount of damage could result. In case of need the number of magistrates with the *imperium* was sufficient so that one could usually be left in Rome to act, if action was imperatively called for by the circumstances.

Thus, at first, the military and political machinery was entirely adequate to the needs of the small city-state. The army was the citizen body, leaving its routine work for a short time and campaigning in the near neighbourhood under the command of the ordinary magistrates of the city. Such a system could not long continue in the face of changed conditions. The very success of Rome in conquering her enemies soon led to alterations in her methods of warfare. Once master of the immediate vicinity, her armies were compelled to march farther afield and the burden which was imposed upon the soldier became greater with each added mile. Nor was it only the soldier who felt the increasing burden ; the longer the march to and from the fighting, the longer the magistrate was obliged to be absent from his post in the city. Thus the success of Roman arms, coupled as it was with the steady growth in the size of the city and the extent of territory subject to its authority, imposed an ever-increasing burden of civic business on the officials of the state ; and while the armies were forced to make longer and more distant campaigns with each advance of the eagles, the inconvenience caused by the absence from Rome of the magistrates would be felt with a steadily increasing force. Another factor should also be noted in this connexion : as the boundaries of the state expanded, the length of the frontier to be guarded increased in proportion. In the beginning of the republic Rome probably did not often find herself engaged in more than one war at a time. When all central Italy had come under Roman control the occurrence of several simultaneous wars must have become more and more frequent, and this fact imposed another and heavy burden upon the machinery of the state.

The increasing demands of the army were, no doubt, very gradually felt, and for a considerable time the primitive system could bear the added strain. Moreover, in those early days the republican machine possessed considerable elasticity, and it was no very difficult matter to adjust it to meet the new needs whenever they had made themselves sufficiently felt. Such readjustments are found from a very early period, although, in the accounts we have of them, they are connected rather with the early political and social struggle between the patricians and plebeians than with the increasing demands of the growing state. Still it may well be suspected that these had their part in the early changes that were made. When the republic was first established its constitution provided for but two magistrates with the *imperium*, namely the two consuls. But in the course of the struggle between the orders, the patricians suspended the appointment of the consuls and replaced them by a board of six consular tribunes. The motives for this change were, doubtless, chiefly to be found in the political exigencies of the struggle with the plebeians, yet, whatever the motive, it served to increase the staff of officials available to meet the needs of the state and of the army, and this fact may have been one reason for the rather protracted use of this somewhat clumsy political evasion.

In time the pressure on the dominant patricians became irresistible and they were finally forced to restore the consulship and to admit plebeians to that office. It was, however, clear that the old arrangement no longer provided an adequate staff for the management of affairs. When, therefore, the consular tribunes were replaced by the two consuls a new office, the praetorship, was invented which increased the number of the magistrates with the *imperium* to three.[1] No doubt the patricians were intending by this device to diminish to some extent the scope of the concession which they had

[1] Heitland, i. 99.

been forced to make, but it may be confidently surmised that it was the obvious and undeniable needs of the state that induced the plebeians to accept this lessening of the completeness of the victory which they had won by the passage of the Licinian laws.

With the internal conflict settled Rome found herself equipped with three magistrates with the *imperium*. To an increase in this number there was, at first, no serious objection, and by the close of the First Punic War a second praetor had been appointed. As a result of the war Rome annexed the islands of Sicily, Sardinia, and Corsica. Annexation was soon found to imply government, and to meet the new requirements the Romans, as was shown in the preceding chapter, increased the number of the praetors to four, two to act as provincial governors and two to serve as judges in Rome. This proved sufficient for a time, but events soon compelled further changes.

The Second Punic War led directly to two important developments in the Roman governmental machinery. In the first place the acquisition of two new provinces in Spain forced a new increase in the size of the praetorian college, this time to six members, which number remained unaltered until the reorganization of the constitution by Sulla. In the second place the terrible struggle with Hannibal, which taxed to the utmost the stern pride and unyielding patriotism of the Romans, gave rise to a new and most significant institution. When the great invader had been turned from central Italy into the south and stood there at bay, Rome found herself compelled to resort to warfare of a kind and on a scale which she had never yet attempted. It was no longer a question of one or two armies for a short campaign. A number of armies operating continuously were now necessary to wear out and overcome the revolted people of southern Italy and the mighty Carthaginian who had induced them to rise against the Roman supremacy. Little by little Rome succeeded, but to do so called for more commanders than the state possessed in its annual magistrates and this made

necessary the expedient of the proconsulship. The device
was not a new one, but the circumstances of the war against
Hannibal made it a regular part of the machinery of the
state. The Romans had no leisure in the midst of such a
struggle to undertake elaborate constitutional adjustments,
and the use of the proconsul met the immediate needs of the
hour with the least possible change in the formal requirements of the law.

Originally a proconsul was simply a consul who remained
in charge of his army after his year of office had expired.
Such a practice was probably rendered easier of adoption by
the obvious impossibility of insisting that a general should
lay down his *imperium* at the precise moment when his term
as magistrate terminated, since this would often happen
before his successor had come to take over the command.
It was only natural to avoid such a lapse in responsible
leadership by allowing the man in charge to continue to
act until the new general arrived. But since the senate had
the power to determine what functions, of a special sort,
should be assigned to the annual magistrates, it might
happen that, if the new consuls were employed elsewhere,
one of the retiring consuls would be left at the head of the
army which he had been commanding and that no successor
could arrive to supersede him. When he was expected to
remain in charge for any length of time it was, at first, felt
necessary that the people should extend his *imperium* by
a formal vote. Since, however, the senate created the
situation and the commander could continue in his functions
for a time without such formal action, the senate soon
assumed the right to prolong the *imperium* for another year
without consulting the assembly. What was done in the case
of the consul was equally possible in that of the praetor, and
the senate thus acquired the right to prolong indefinitely the
*imperium* once it had been conferred by the Roman people.
This made it possible for the senate to increase its staff of
officers with the *imperium* without adding to the number of
the magistrates.

While these changes were taking place in the command of the armies, their character was also being modified. In early days, when the campaigns were short, the Roman citizen could leave his work and serve without serious inconvenience. When circumstances required a longer time of service this was no longer true, and it became necessary to make up to the soldier in some way the losses which he must now incur. Livy expressly tells us that at the siege of Veii the length of the operations first made the payment of the soldiers necessary. It is quite probable that at first this was regarded as a very exceptional thing, but as the range of Rome's military action grew constantly wider it was not long before it became a regular custom.

With the introduction of pay into the army it became possible to lengthen the time of service without serious difficulty, and this seems to have been done without particular protest. When, as a result of the victory over Hannibal, Rome found herself involved in the task of conquering and holding Spain, the term was of necessity extended far beyond anything that had previously been known and the citizens conscripted for the Spanish armies were expected to serve with the legions for six years.

By the time of the Spanish wars, then, the military system of Rome had changed in almost every particular. Instead of citizens serving without pay, as a part of their civic duty, under the annual magistrates of the city, we have paid soldiers serving for years at a time, and often under the command of a proconsul or propraetor rather than one of the regular magistrates. The use of the promagistrate as a commander was not as yet regarded as regular, but, once introduced, it rapidly extended itself, becoming constantly more common as the needs of the administration grew relentlessly greater and the difficulty of providing more regular magistrates began to be felt. Why this difficulty should develop has been already shown and likewise why the difficulty, once it began to make itself apparent, was met by the rapid development of the promagistracy. At first a special expedient to meet an exceptional case, the promagistracy became gradually a normal and regular part of the constitution.

From a purely military point of view the use of the promagistrate had real advantages in that it made possible a greater continuity of command. A competent general could now be left in command of an army for two years—one as magistrate and the second as promagistrate—and in case of special need for an even longer time, since if the *imperium* could be held beyond the legal term for which it was conferred there was no reason why it could not be indefinitely prolonged. Moreover, as has been seen already, the new system relieved the pressure on the regular corps of magistrates and provided governors to meet the increasing demands of provincial administration.

There can be small wonder, therefore, that the Roman state resorted with increasing frequency to a device so simple, and at the same time so well adapted to meet the growing demands of the state with so little disturbance to the formal constitution. No sweeping changes were necessary, only a slight modification of existing and established practices which, having gradually grown up, were now an accepted part of the governmental machinery.

Could the expansion of Rome's empire have been restricted within the narrow limits which Rome originally set for herself, the new machinery might have worked with little difficulty or change, but this was quite impossible. Whatever the desire of the senate and the ruling statesmen, the fall of Carthage had made Rome a world power. Sooner or later she would be forced to meet the obligations of her new position. Her reluctance might make her slow and half-hearted in assuming these responsibilities but could not enable her to escape them. That Rome lusted for conquest and sought the empire of the Mediterranean, no one who views the actual circumstances of her history can believe. Rather her empire was a penalty imposed upon her by the defeat of Hannibal, a penalty which she strove desperately to avoid paying, but which fate inexorably enforced despite her struggles.

While Hannibal stood at bay in the south of Italy he had striven by every means in his power to find the resources which he needed to crush Rome by drawing into the conflict some outside power. To prevent this Rome had been obliged to interfere in both the East and the West. She had dispatched armies to Spain to keep her foe from using the resources of that peninsula against her, and she had met his attempts to get help from Macedon by entering into close alliances with the various states of Greece.

When the war ended in the destruction of the power of Carthage, Rome found, to her dismay, that she had in effect signed a number of blank checks which others had the power of filling in and which she was bound in honour and in prudence to redeem. The ambitious schemes of Philip of Macedon and his partner, Antiochus of Syria, forced her to reluctant intervention in the East, while, at the same time, her fears of a possible revival of the power of her vanquished rival, Carthage, involved her in the formidable task of conquering the warlike Spanish tribes.

Instead of bringing peace, the end of the long contest with Hannibal served merely as a starting-point for a whole series of wars. Yet few peoples have shown themselves less anxious for conquest than the Romans. After the fierce struggle for their very existence as a state the people of Rome were passionately longing for an end of battles and campaigns, a chance to cultivate their fields and pursue their ordinary avocations in quiet and tranquillity. So intense was this desire for peace among the common people that the senate was only able to induce the popular assembly to vote the declaration of war against Macedon by the false pretence that Philip intended an actual invasion of Italy. Deceived by this misrepresentation, the citizens, weary as they were of war, allowed the constitutionally necessary vote to be wrung from them. The war thus brought about was, indeed, necessary, though not for the reasons that the senate alleged. It was impossible for Rome, without dishonour for the present and danger for the future, to abandon the Greek allies who had served her so well during her time of deadly peril. Doubtless when the senate first dispatched the legions to the East, it was both hoped and believed that it was only for a single brief campaign. But fate overruled the will of people and senate alike and the war with Philip proved to be but the first of several Eastern wars. In the West, as well, the annexation of Spain was found to be the beginning of many years of hard fighting. Thus the defeat of Hannibal was very far from bringing peace to Rome, and the wars which followed it were fought under such new conditions as to affect profoundly the military system of the republic. Hitherto the wars of Rome had been waged in Italy or near at hand in Sicily. The legions had, indeed, crossed over into Africa and Spain, but these expeditions had been too brief to leave any permanent effects. Now for the first time the Romans found themselves engaged in long wars at a great distance. Under these circumstances they began to develop the system of the great commands. This called for three distinct innovations in the military system of the republic. In the first place, armies of exceptional size were now sent out, and in the second place, they were entrusted to the command of a single general who remained in charge for the entire war, and in the third place, the theatre of operations was so far from Italy that any real control by the Roman government was impossible. No one of the three was altogether new, but the frequent combination of all three is only met with after the Second Punic War. That such powers as the great command implied were a possible danger to the republic was as obvious to the Romans as it can be to-day, yet they had little or no choice. It is difficult, if not impossible, to see how Rome could have defeated Antiochus and conquered Macedon and Spain without entrusting her generals with exceptional powers. Whatever the potential dangers which such powers might involve, men could devise no alternative that promised any hope of victory and success.

While thus the Roman generals were growing stronger to the possible danger of the state, a social and political crisis

C

was developing in Italy which intensified the peril. As the empire expanded abroad Italian agriculture underwent a profound transformation, and in many parts of the peninsula the small farms practically disappeared, being replaced by ranches and large estates worked by slave labour. For this change there were many causes, one of which was the introduction into Italy of cheap grain from Sicily. Hitherto this crop had been the chief reliance of a large number of the small farmers who now found themselves exposed to a ruinous competition in many places. That grain could be grown more cheaply in Sicily than in many parts of Italy was by no means the whole difficulty; other factors contributed to make the matter much more disastrous than a simple economic competition need have been.

When first the Romans took control of Sicily they found a revenue system in existence which collected the taxes levied on the inhabitants of the rural districts in kind—chiefly in grain, which formed the staple product of the island. This system the Romans retained and merely adapted to their own immediate needs. The farmers of Sicily were still to pay their tribute as they had been accustomed to do, only now to the Roman government instead of their former masters. Since Rome had no machinery at hand for collecting her revenues, she resorted to the simple expedient of selling the right to collect the taxes to the highest bidder. As a consequence of this the Roman capitalist found open to his enterprise a new field for investment. Thus, too, it came about that there were in Rome influential capitalists with quantities of grain to dispose of, which they had acquired, not by purchase from the producer, but by purchase from the Roman state. This grain they could afford to sell without reference to the cost of its production, but solely on the basis of the bargain they had made with a government in which the influence of wealth was such that they were likely to have made a very easy contract. Hence when, as usually happened, the Roman capitalist bought cheaply, he could afford to sell at a price utterly ruinous to the Roman farmer. The state itself made matters worse. A considerable part of its revenues was paid in grain and such portion of this as was not needed for the army was thrown upon the market to be disposed of for whatever it would bring. Moreover, since it was considered a duty of the government to keep down the cost of living, the state usually met any serious rise in the price of food by selling its surplus stock of grain at a low figure. Thus the annexation of Sicily meant to many Italian farmers a permanent lowering in the price of their chief crop.[1]

The cheap grain, however, was only one cause of the agricultural crisis. The war against Hannibal had been fought mainly in the south of Italy and had resulted in the devastation of a large part of that region. During the struggle the farmers had been forced to seek refuge in the nearest strongholds, and, when the invader was at last driven out, they found their land in a state of utter ruin  Buildings, domestic animals, and tools were gone, and to make a new beginning there was no resource but debt. Under the existing conditions, however, the remedy was all too often fatal. The cheap grain had killed the market in some places, and in many others the decline in the population of the towns, which was the result of the long war, was almost as disastrous.[2] The natural consequence was that the small farmers as a class rapidly disappeared, and, instead of returning to the land,

[1] I cannot agree with Salvioli, *Le Capitalisme*, 170 ff., that the cheap grain affected only the market in Rome and the farmers in the immediate vicinity. The Roman *publicani* collected the tribute in grain and not in money, and it seems to me incredible that they should have sold this nowhere but in Rome where the price was lowest when they could ship it even more cheaply to many towns along the southern and western coasts of Italy. Neither is it likely that no trader thought of buying grain in Rome and selling it at points along the coast, north or south of the city, where the price was higher. It seems to me that we must either maintain that the Sicilian corn had no effect upon the price in Rome previous to the corn law of C. Gracchus, or that it had a corresponding effect in many towns along the coast. I entirely agree with Salvioli, however, that it could not travel far inland, nor go too far by sea, without the low price being neutralized by the cost of transportation.

[2] Frank, *Economic History*, 89.

they began to drift to Rome where food was cheap and where a precarious livelihood might be picked up out of odd jobs, the largess of the candidates for office, or as clients and dependants of some wealthy family.

The small farmer had still other troubles. The dominions of Rome were growing, and, as they grew, called constantly for more soldiers. Nor could the soldiers any longer be sent home after a brief campaign. The wars now being waged by Rome were far across the seas and the men who went out in the service were obliged to stay for years. The drain of these new military needs must have been a serious matter to the agricultural class of Italy.

In considerable degree the very causes which were pushing the small farmer to the wall were, at the same time, preparing a substitute for him. Both the speculations of the capitalist in the grain of Sicily and the wars of the republic abroad brought in a flood of wealth to those individuals or classes so placed as to take advantage of the opportunities. Thus while many landowners were ready in despair to sell their property, much surplus wealth was seeking investment. At first glance it might seem strange that capital should go into agriculture under the existing conditions, but there were some causes at work which made the situation of the large landowner very different from that of the small farmer. The wars had glutted the Roman market with slaves with the natural result that their price had fallen very low. A rich man, therefore, who could acquire a large tract of land for a trifle, could also provide himself with the slave labour necessary to cultivate it cheaply. Large-scale farming made possible various economies, and the slave labour available was by no means crude or unskilled. The eastern wars of Rome had resulted in a flood of slaves drawn from the Orient, which was the home of scientific and improved agriculture, and the Carthaginian captives were of much the same character. Thus it happened that large-scale production could often be carried on by new and better methods than the small farmer knew, or could employ if he did know.

In addition to this the capitalist was less hampered in the matter of his crops. He did not need to confine himself to raising grain, but could turn to olives or the vine, a thing less possible to the small farmer since they were not immediately productive. When no form of agriculture could be made to pay, there was ranching to fall back upon. The ships of ancient times, though they could carry grain with ease and could do so cheaply as compared with the cost of transporting it on land, were unable to handle either animals or meat on a commercial scale. Hence sheep and cattle raised in Italy had no competition from abroad to fear, and all through southern Italy ranching began to take the place of agriculture. So rapid was this change that one man's life witnessed its beginning and completion. The elder Cato as a young man practised farming for profit, but in his old age confessed that it was an amusement rather than a gainful occupation. Asked what was the best form of investment for capital, the old man promptly answered, ' Good ranching land '. When the questioner inquired what came next he replied, ' Fair ranching land ', and, when pressed still further, he gave as the third most profitable investment, ' Poor ranching land '.[1]

The First and Second Punic Wars had, therefore, produced a striking change in the economic aspect of the peninsula. In the North, in Etruria especially, great plantations worked by slave labour had replaced the small farms of earlier times. In passing through this region, Tiberius Gracchus was horrified at the dearth of population and the absence of free labourers.[2] While this transformation had taken place in the North, the South was given over in a similar manner to great livestock ranches whose herds of cattle and sheep were tended by slaves. In both quarters the small proprietors had largely disappeared and gone to swell the idle rabble in the towns, especially in Rome.

These changes did not, of course, affect the whole peninsula equally and in many places they were hardly felt at

[1] Cicero, De Officiis, ii. 25.          [2] Plutarch, Tiberius Gracchus, 8.

all.  Hannibal's ravages had fallen most heavily on the South.  The cheap grain from across the seas, while easily transported by water, could not travel far by land, and was unable to disturb the market prices in the mountainous parts of central Italy.  In Umbria and Samnium conditions remained much the same as in the past, and the rich and fertile valley of the Po was very slightly affected.

Yet, making all allowance for the regions where the new conditions were felt but little, if at all, the change was far-reaching, and, in the eyes of thoughtful Romans, sinister. This was inevitably so for many reasons.  The Roman mind was hard and practical in its texture, and was stubbornly conservative in type.  Not readily did the conqueror of the world take in a new idea, and all the old traditions which he cherished taught him that the small farmer, tilling his little plot of ground by his own labour and that of his family, was the very backbone of the state.  Hence the Roman could not view without the gravest misgivings the rapid decay of the class which he regarded as of such vital importance.  Even had the Roman's mind been free from any preconception on this point, the military system would have brought the problem home to him in a manner at once plain and un-avoidable.  Service in the legions had always been bound up intimately with the ownership of land.  It was the landowner who had hitherto furnished the recruits for the army, and Rome, therefore, depended on the small farmer for her soldiers.  The landless rabble in the city, the urban mob, played little part in the conscription which was used to fill the ranks.  Now, at the very moment when the state was calling for soldiers to an extent unknown before, the class from which, by all established usages and customs, they were drawn was shrinking every day.  With each new war the task of filling up the legions grew more difficult, and the class who gave no military service to the state grew visibly larger. Here was a problem which no Roman could entirely ignore. No candidate for office could shut his eyes to the rapid growth of the city rabble, and no general could fail to perceive the increasing difficulty of recruiting. Neither could avoid the conviction that, while Rome was victorious abroad, things were alarmingly out of joint at home, and that, although the empire grew and flourished, the state was dangerously sick at its very heart.

Yet it was easier to see and feel the malady than to devise a remedy. The mind of the ancient world had given little thought to economic causes. In this sphere the Greek saw but dimly, and the Roman, with his slower wits and duller imagination, was most unlikely to discover truths which the subtle Hellene had not been able to perceive. Even had the Roman been more clear sighted than he was, his vision would have been of little use, since the character of the Roman government forbade the application of an effective cure. The Roman assembly was so constituted as to give a disproportionate weight to that part of the citizen body which dwelt within the city. The small farmer who relied on the cultivation of grain could only be restored in many districts by some form of protection, and this was something which the mob of Rome could never be induced to accept, since it would have increased the cost of living and thereby threatened the daily bread of a large number of the voters. This being so, no Roman statesman ventured to suggest the measure which to us would seem so obvious. Yet, though they could not reach the root of the evil, the Romans were not without remedies of their own, although it may be questioned whether, in this case, the cure proposed was not worse than the disease.

It was Tiberius Gracchus who first tried seriously to solve the problem. As has just been implied, it is no reflection upon his sagacity that he failed to grasp the economic factors in the case. What he saw was the simple fact that Rome was suffering from a decrease in the number of small farmers ; and the remedy which he proposed was simply to increase the class whose threatened disappearance constituted a danger to the commonwealth. The problem which arose from too few farmers he would solve by making more.

His plan for accomplishing this was to distribute land in small allotments to the poor. For this purpose he required a large amount of land, and, as it happened, the Roman law furnished him with a good technical pretext for obtaining it. While the conquest of Italy was in progress the state had declared great tracts of land in every part of the peninsula the property of the Roman people. From it the people had not hitherto received much benefit. Owing to the policy of the wealthy nobles who controlled the government, this land had passed in practice into the hands of private individuals who held and used it, although the title remained vested in the state. The state, however, dominated by the class who had the land in their possession, had allowed many years to pass without making any effort to assert its ownership. As a result the possessors had come to regard the land they occupied as theirs, but, as the Roman law in this matter had no statute of limitations, it was still within the legal rights of the government to revive its claims and act upon them in whatever way it chose. Whether such a course was consistent with equity is open to question, but it was undoubtedly within the strict letter of the law. Tiberius now proposed that the state should reassert its rights and should eject the possessors from the bulk of the public land they held and that the land so acquired should be distributed in small allotments to the poorer citizens, thus breaking up many of the large estates and replacing them with small peasant holdings. How the new farmers were to make a living where the old had failed Tiberius did not stop to ask himself, though some faint suspicion that here might be a difficulty seems to have crossed his mind, since he proposed to make the new holdings inalienable. This feature of his proposal may well have been intended to prevent his new peasants from giving up their farms and returning to the city.

The success of such a scheme must be considered doubtful, though, lacking precise information as to the location of the lands to be distributed, we cannot pronounce a positive judgement on the plan. There were certainly many parts of Italy where agriculture was as profitable for the small farmer as it had ever been, but, even making allowance for this, we may still doubt whether the bill could accomplish enough good to compensate for the strife and confusion which it was sure to cause. Tiberius, however, seems not to have anticipated the violent storm of opposition he encountered. The possessors practically dominated the government and the well established usage of the constitution gave them the power to block the reform at the very outset. The senate, by the letter of the law, had no power to do more than advise the magistrate in case he called upon it for advice. Its decrees when passed had only an advisory force and might be ignored by the magistrate, while the people possessed the constitutional right to legislate regardless of the wishes of the conscript fathers. However, the actual practice of the constitution had for many years required that every bill should be brought first before the senate and that, if it failed to gain the approval of that body, it should quietly be dropped. Yet this was a matter rather of usage than of law, and if the magistrate dared to disregard this custom, there was no legal obstacle to hinder him from bringing a bill directly before the people. In Tiberius Rome found at last a magistrate so confident of his own righteousness and wisdom that he was ready to set tradition at defiance and to use his legal prerogative to the uttermost. Ignoring the senate he introduced his bill in the assembly. But the conscript fathers, though they could not interfere directly, were by no means powerless. Few constitutions have ever been better provided with the means of obstruction and delay than that of Rome. If Tiberius, as tribune of the people, had a legal right to lay his bill before the people, any one of the nine other tribunes had a legal right to stop its progress by the interposition of his veto. The occasions were few and far between when the senate could not find one among the ten who was willing to take its side and stop obnoxious legislation. On this occasion such a

tribune was promptly found and Tiberius was confronted
with the veto of his colleague Octavius. Opposition from
this quarter seems to have been quite unexpected by the
reformer, and in face of it he lost his head. Determined at
all costs to pass his bill immediately, he had the assembly
remove Octavius from office and then proceeded to enact his
agrarian law. He seemed for the moment to have succeeded
in his aim, but the deposition of Octavius was of very doubtful legality, and the passions he had roused by his legislation and by the methods he had resorted to in order to pass
it were violent. The natural, if not the inevitable, end was
the outbreak of a riot in which the bold reformer perished by
violence.

But, though Tiberius Gracchus died, his work survived.
His great agrarian law was not repealed, and under it a commission set to work to seize and redistribute the soil of Italy.
In the next few years more than 70,000 of the poor received
allotments of land. In so far as Tiberius Gracchus had
aimed simply to create more farmers, his law was a success.
How far this result was permanent is, of course, another
matter. The economic causes that lay at the root of the
problem were untouched and must soon have brought about
the ruin of the new farmers as they had that of the old.[1] No
doubt there were many of the new allotments that accomplished the reformer's purpose, when they chanced to fall
in some region of the peninsula into which the cheap grain
did not penetrate, or where other forms of agriculture were
possible besides the cultivation of grain. But such partial
success as may have been achieved failed to relieve the
situation for any length of time.

But, if the social and economic effects of the agrarian bill
were temporary, it was otherwise with its political results.

---

[1] The right to sell the allotments was soon given to the new farmers,
about the time of the overthrow of Gaius Gracchus. Greenidge, *A History
of Rome*, 285. For the number of new farmers see the census returns
given in the Epitome of Livy. These figures have generally been interpreted in the sense in which they are here taken. See, for example,
Greenidge, 150, and Mommsen, iii. 335.

In carrying his law the reformer had violated the usages and traditions of the Roman government. He had given a conspicuous demonstration of what a magistrate who dared to stand upon his legal rights and to defy the senate could accomplish, and this lesson was not lost upon his contemporaries. It was the less likely to be neglected because of the changes in the popular assembly which resulted from the economic crisis. The success of Gracchus was visible evidence that the people were no longer dominated as they had been in the past by the ring of noble families who controlled the senate. Each of these families gathered round it a group of voters, clients or freedmen, of whose votes it could dispose at pleasure, and collectively they seem to have been able for a long time to keep the assembly well in hand. Now, however, the growth of the urban rabble, due, in large part at least, to the decline in agricultural prosperity, had greatly weakened their influence. The crowds who came to the city were too great to be absorbed into the groups of dependants of the aristocratic houses, and, as a consequence, the assembly was escaping from the control of the governing oligarchy. From this time on the people became more and more unmanageable until their power perished with the republic itself.

The death of Tiberius Gracchus left the senate master of the state, but its supremacy did not remain long undisputed. In a few years the younger brother of the reformer took his place as the leader of the party of opposition and protest. The career of Gaius Gracchus as a reformer and popular leader need not be considered in detail, since the constructive part of his programme was largely unfulfilled. Two things, however, he did that should be noted. He set the capitalist class, or knights, against the senate, and by the enactment of his corn law, he still further released the mob of Rome from the domination of the oligarchy. While he defied the senate and courted the knights he found enthusiastic support, but when, confident in his popularity, he attempted to carry through some real reforms, his supporters turned against him, and, like his brother, he perished in a riot. After his death the senate resumed its control of the government, but its power was weakened and undermined. The antagonism which Gaius had striven hard to create between the senate and the knights deprived that body of the support of a large and increasing part of the propertied class, while the corn law, by making the poorest voters depend directly on the state instead of on the great aristocratic families for their daily bread, weakened the influence of the senate over the assembly.

The measures of the democratic party under the Gracchi failed to solve the military problem. The agrarian bill may have augmented the number of the small land-owners, but it did not do so on a scale that would relieve the pressure. The state still needed armies and still found it difficult to raise them ; and, since political reform was powerless to meet the difficulty, it only remained to try the effect of a direct reform of the military system itself, and especially of the methods of recruiting. This change the war against Jugurtha was destined to bring about. This war, in and of itself, was trivial enough; but circumstances combined to give it an importance far beyond its military merits. The manner in which the senate drifted into the war in the first place created a universal suspicion of corruption. Starting thus, the senate's generals failed to fulfil the popular expectation of a speedy victory over the petty African king. No doubt the Roman populace ignored the difficulties of north African geography, but in any case the dragging out of the war year after year exasperated the mob. If the senate could not, or would not, end the war, the people resolved to take matters into their own hands ; and if the generals of the senate were incompetent or corrupt, they were ready to try what a popular general could accomplish. Under such conditions a blunt soldier, C. Marius, unconnected with the ruling oligarchy except by marriage, came forward as a candidate for the consulship, and was triumphantly elected on a pledge to end the Numidian war with a speedy victory.

In the election of Marius the senate had sustained a serious defeat, since he had won on the plain platform of taking out of the senate's hands the conduct of a war which they had shamefully mismanaged.  The conscript fathers would not, however, accept the adverse verdict of the assembly.  It was still their prerogative to determine the provinces for which the magistrates drew lots and they sought, by the use of this power, to retain their general, Metellus, in command in Africa.  But Marius and his supporters were not to be so thwarted.  The war against Jugurtha was what Marius wanted and what the people were determined he should have.  When the senate would not yield to the people's will, the assembly, on the motion of a tribune, passed a law conferring the command in Africa upon their favourite and superseding Metellus.  But Marius had still to provide himself with an army and the senate hoped that in attempting this he would make a shipwreck of his sudden popularity. As soon as he resorted to conscription to obtain his soldiers a revulsion of the popular feeling might be expected.[1]  But Marius met the situation with a measure at once simple and daring, and accomplished a revolution in the military system of Rome of which he did not in the least foresee the consequences.  Instead of forcing the reluctant farmers into the ranks, he called for volunteers, and forthwith found himself with all the men he needed without trouble.  Nothing could be more simple in appearance, yet few measures have been fraught with larger consequences.  By thus making the Roman army a volunteer force, instead of one resting on conscription, Marius changed its character fundamentally. Hitherto the soldier had been a man possessed of some property, but those who flocked to join the new consul were almost all men who had nothing to lose.  Henceforth the legionary owned only his weapons, his plunder, and whatever his general could obtain for him from the state.  Before this time the men were drafted to fight under whomsoever the republic might place in command of the army ;  now

---

[1] Heitland, ii. 355.

they were men who had come forward to serve under a particular man, and who had chosen to serve because of the confidence which they felt in the man and his ability to lead. Henceforth, too, their fortunes were intimately bound up with his. If, when the campaign ended, their leader failed to remain a power in the state, he could not procure for them the rewards to which they looked forward. From this time on, therefore, the army was bound to its commander by a tie that replaced the former loyalty to the state and to its constitution ; and an army could no longer be transferred from one general to another at the pleasure or convenience of the government. If the power of the men who led the legions had already grown to a degree that was ominous for the future by the development of the proconsulship, this change in the composition of the army increased the peril many times and led straight to the predominance of the soldier in the state.

To all of this it is quite probable that Marius was blind. He needed soldiers and he wished to get them without loss of popularity. By taking volunteers he accomplished both his objects and he could do so in no other way. His success went far to justify his innovation, nor is it easy to see how the change could have been long postponed. If Marius had never lived, some other man would surely have met a pressing need by a method so obvious. A state which needed soldiers must soon have been forced to abandon an unpopular conscription when volunteers were to be had for the asking by any man who had the reputation of a competent commander.

The volunteer army of Marius achieved a rapid victory in Africa, and he returned to save the state from a much more serious danger. While he was occupied with finishing the war against Jugurtha, two mighty hordes of barbarians were menacing Italy from the north. The incapable generals whom the normal working of the constitution had put in charge, instead of averting the peril, had contrived to make it worse by leading the Roman armies to overwhelming disaster. The people turned naturally to their favourite and re-elected Marius consul on his return and sent him out to save the state.  Again he justified their confidence and the Cimbri and the Teutons were completely crushed.  After this victory it might have been expected that the rough soldier would retire ; but his own vanity and the character of his army alike forbade this course.  To attract the necessary recruits to his standard he had given a promise that the soldiers should be rewarded with lands at the close of their service.[1]  The time had now come to fulfil his pledges to his men.  As he could hope for no assistance from the senate, which had been steadily hostile to him from the start, he turned of necessity to the mob who had been throughout the basis of his power.  He formed a close alliance with the ruling demagogues of the moment and tried his hand at politics. Unluckily for him his partners, Saturninus and Glaucia, were violent and reckless, and he himself, efficient as a general, was quite incapable in the struggles of the forum.[2]  The almost inevitable result of such a combination was a swift and utter failure.  Marius supported his allies till their proceedings had goaded the conservatives to fury, then, frightened by their wild career, he abandoned them, to the unbounded rage of the democrats.  Thus in a short space of time he fell from the summit of glory to complete political insignificance.  Yet he had done great things for Rome in the field and he had taught his contemporaries two lessons which were not forgotten.  He had shown that a popular soldier could obtain the men he needed for an army simply by asking for them, and also that a leader with the assembly at his back could, by a law of the people, take command of any

---

[1] Frank, *Roman Imperialism*, 270.  See also his article in the *American Journal of Philology*, xlvii. 55–74.

[2] In several respects there is an obvious likeness between the career of Marius and that of Pompey.  Both were good soldiers but neither was a capable politician.  Both were forced by the character of their armies to take a hand in politics and neither was successful.  Pompey, however, had better fortune and his partners, Caesar and Crassus, were men of a very different stamp from Saturninus and Glaucia.  This was Pompey's luck rather than his merit, however.

war or any province that he pleased, regardless of the wishes of the senate.

With the fall of Marius the senate was again in control in Rome. It was not he but another who first grasped the meaning of the military changes he had made. The twelve years that followed the retirement of Marius were filled with agitations ending in civil war. This war, due to the demand of the Italian allies for full Roman citizenship, involved all Italy and brought back Marius once more to the command of a Roman army, but brought also to the front his formidable rival, Sulla. The Italian uprising, suppressed more by concessions than by arms, served as a prelude to a crisis which revealed for the first time, but once for all, the essential character of the new army. While Rome was paralysed by the Italian revolt, war had broken out in the East. The King of Pontus, Mithridates, taking advantage of the situation, had overrun all Rome's possessions in that quarter, and, as soon as the crisis in Italy had passed, she found herself forced to dispatch a large army under a competent commander to recover the lost ground and punish the bold oriental who had made use of her difficulties. For this new task there were two rival candidates, Marius and Sulla. By the normal working of the constitution the task was assigned to Sulla, one of the consuls for the year. But Marius was not disposed to acquiesce in his defeat. Once before he had deposed a general of the senate from his command by virtue of a law passed in the assembly, and he now determined to repeat his performance. With the help of the leading demagogue of the moment, a certain Sulpicius Rufus, he procured an enactment of the people transferring the command of the war with Mithridates to himself. But he had overlooked the change he had himself made in the army. Sulla had no thought of submitting to the law, and Sulla's soldiers belonged no longer to the state, but to their general. Realizing this the consul gathered up his forces and marched rapidly on Rome. The mob were powerless to back up their decree by force, and Sulla occupied the city and undid at pleasure the acts of his opponents.  For the first time a Roman general had turned the swords of his soldiers against his country and his government, and for the first time the army had over-ruled the decision of the forum.  Horror and consternation must have reigned in Rome at such a sacrilege, but power was with the daring general, and for the moment, at any rate, his will was law.  For the time being he was content to impose on Rome the supremacy of the senate, to which he owed his command, and this done, he departed to fulfil his Eastern task.  He must have known when he set sail from Italy that what had been accomplished by violence could be undone by the same means.  He may have thought that he had left the senate with sufficient force to meet its enemies, but if so he miscalculated.  Perhaps he did the best he could and trusted to his luck.  In any case, he was scarcely gone when the reaction came ;  the democrats seized possession of power as violently and lawlessly as he had done, and after a short struggle gained control.  As Sulla had outlawed Marius and Sulpicius Rufus, so now he was in turn declared a public enemy.  His friends were murdered, or sought refuge in his camp in Greece, and Marius and Cinna reigned in Rome.  But the democrats had learned the lesson that possession of the government was nothing if not sustained by force.  In Italy there was no power to challenge their supremacy, but in the East were Sulla and his army who, once released from the clutches of the war with Mithridates, were likely to turn their attention to their enemies in Rome. That Sulla's soldiers would follow him none could doubt, and the entire time of his absence was a long nightmare to his foes in Italy, haunted for ever with the question of what he would do when the time came for his return.  The largest army in the Roman world belonged to him, and their sole hope of safety lay in getting a stronger army to protect them from the reckoning he would, late or soon, be in a position to exact.  They, therefore, spent the years which his campaigns against the King of Pontus gave them in desperate attempts to form an army to support their government.

But unfortunately for them they were wofully weak in generals who could make a strong appeal to the common soldier.  They were unable to provide themselves with any force which could hold its own with Sulla's veterans, and when he did at last return to Italy, he rapidly beat down their forces, and once again, at the head of his legions, occupied the city.

For the second time Sulla was the armed master of Rome, but now his position was quite different from what it had been on the first occasion.  Then his soldiers had probably followed him chiefly in order that the Eastern war might remain in his hands.  Of this they were as desirous as he could be himself.  The war against Mithridates promised rich spoil and plunder, and Sulla was a general under whom they were confident of victory.  If the command had been transferred to Marius, other soldiers might have reaped the rewards which were the certain fruits of success.  Now that they had returned victorious, they backed their general because, if he were proscribed, they could not hope to get the land allotments he had promised them.  They were well pleased to see him master of the state, since the greater his power the more easily he could fulfil his pledges.  Nor was a temporary control enough to safeguard them.  They could only hope to keep what he might give them if his enemies, and theirs, were rendered powerless, for if the defeated democrats should get the upper hand again they might reasonably be expected to undo all Sulla's acts.  His army was, therefore, willing to see him made dictator, and to have him protect them by a thorough reorganization of the constitution.  And Sulla, on his part, dared not stop short of this.

So in 82 B. C. Sulla was named dictator with full power to amend and change the laws.  Whether public opinion would have acquiesced in a permanent autocracy may be questioned, but Sulla had no desire for such a role.  He meant to reorganize the republic so as to secure his own safety, and, to accomplish that, the steps to take were clear and unmistakable.  The irresistible pressure of circumstances had bound him to the senate by ties he had no power to break.  Between him and the people no accommodation was possible, even if he had desired it.  The only course left open was to reorganize the state under the sole control of the senate, and to destroy every power that might threaten that control.  No doubt such convictions as he had pointed this way and made the path of interest coincide with that of duty.  His constitutional reform, therefore, took the shape of a senatorial restoration.  His purpose, through all his legislation, stands out clear and plain—to reorganize the senate so as to secure the control of that body to his friends, and to make it absolute master of the Roman government.

If Sulla had but little choice in the work, at any rate he did it as well as circumstances rendered possible.  He enlarged and increased the senate, and chained down every power that could interfere with its supremacy.  The tribunes and the assembly he completely gagged.  No more should the turbulent mob-leaders be permitted to use the legislative power of the people to modify or to upset the arrangements of the conscript fathers.  No law could be submitted to a vote of the Roman citizens until it had received the sanction of the senate.  That body was thus left in unchallengeable control of laws, provinces, wars, and armies.  Never again should a Marius intrude himself where the conscript fathers did not desire his presence ;  no more should tribunes of the people dispose, as Sulpicius had tried to do, of armies and of provinces.  Whatever arrangements the senate might see fit to make should stand.

But if the senate was to govern, it must have at its command the means of government.  So Sulla provided it with a staff of magistrates adequate to deal with the affairs of the empire.  He increased the number of praetors, so as to give the senate a supply of promagistrates sufficient to administer the provinces and to dispatch the business of the state at home.  Besides this he gave the senate the exclusive right to try governors accused of maladministration.  That Sulla, in transferring this function from the knights to the senate, aimed principally to weaken the influence of the capitalist class upon the administration is no doubt true, but the change would, nevertheless, strengthen the hold of the senate on the provincial government both directly by making the governor effectively responsible to the senate, and indirectly by shutting out all possibility of outside interference.

The senate was thus placed in a position of supreme authority and fortified on every side. From a purely legal point of view there was only one weak point in the senatorial fortress. That was that the magistrates, who were still the executives of the state, were chosen by the vote of the people. Thus the senate might find itself compelled to carry on the government through officers who were politically hostile to it. This Sulla could not prevent without an almost unthinkable breach with Roman customs and ideas. Nor is it likely that he regarded the danger on this side as serious. The interference in the past had come mainly from the tribunes, who were now effectually silenced. Consuls and praetors had not usually given the senate much trouble. Nor were they likely, under Sulla's constitution, to be strong enough to do much harm. Even if a democratic consul should be elected, Sulla had tied his hands effectively and he would find himself so restricted and confined that he could accomplish nothing of importance.

When Sulla, having finished his reforms, retired to enjoy the fruits of his successful Eastern war, he left the senate in a position that was legally impregnable. No move could be made against it without a violation of the law. But could the law be trusted as an adequate protection ? If the military system by which Sulla had risen to the dictatorship remained unchanged, what guarantee was there that others might not follow his example and that what he had set up with the sword might not be overthrown by it ? Yet Sulla left the military system as it was, either because he did not fully appreciate the danger, or because he could devise no substitute. He seemed uneasily aware that here was the weak link in the chain by which he sought to bind the

Roman people, but he was unable to strengthen it.[1] The armies must still be commanded and the provinces governed by the promagistrates, and the state must find its soldiers where it could. If in the future ambitious proconsuls should find themselves in conflict with the senate and with powerful armies at their backs, the conscript fathers must meet the situation as they could. While Sulla lived the danger was not likely to arise, and by his temperament he may have been disposed to anticipate Louis XV, and say, 'After me the deluge!' At any rate, when Sulla died in 78 B.C., the new military and the new political systems stood side by side in harmony. No sooner was he gone, however, than his elaborate constitution fell crashing to the ground.

[1] He enacted strict laws against a governor who defied the senate, but with his own career in mind he can have had little faith in their value.

## III. THE SUPREMACY OF POMPEY

AT this point it may be desirable, even at the risk of some repetition, to sum up the outstanding features of the administrative and military system of the Roman republic. The government of Italy itself need not detain us now. Here, in the environment which had created them and shaped their early growth, the institutions of the city-state could work after a fashion, and had Rome's power been limited to the peninsula, she might, perhaps, have gone on indefinitely under her ancient and traditional forms. It was in attempting to govern provinces across the seas and under the burden of the wars that came inevitably with the empire of the Mediterranean world that the republic actually broke down.

In Italy the government remained vested in the people, magistrates, and senate as before. The older theory of the constitution had placed these powers in this order, but Sulla in his reforms had changed it to senate, magistrates, and people. The citizens in their assembly still chose the magistrates each year and they, under the direction and by the advice of the senate, administered affairs at home. When the year was up the senate dispatched those possessed of the *imperium* abroad as governors in the provinces. It was here that serious difficulties arose.

When Sulla reorganized the state he estimated the number of provinces requiring governors at ten, namely: Sicily, Sardinia and Corsica, the two provinces of Spain, the two Gauls, Africa, Macedon, Asia, and Cilicia. To provide for them he gave the state two consuls and eight praetors every year, making the ten promagistrates required. Each year the senate fixed the provinces for the ensuing year, specifying which should be consular and which praetorian, and the outgoing consuls and praetors then distributed the provinces among themselves by lot. To each would normally be assigned a term of one year as governor in some part of the empire outside of Italy. In unusual circumstances the senate could meet the case in either of two ways. As it had the sole right to determine what the provinces should be, and, as it had long since assumed the right to prolong the *imperium* after it had been conferred by the vote of the assembly, it could, by simply omitting one of the ordinary provinces from the list, leave in control for another year the governor whose province was omitted, since, as no magistrate could draw the province, no successor could appear to supersede the incumbent then in office. The magistrate who was not assigned one of the ordinary provincial commands remained, under these circumstances, available for service elsewhere, and could be given an extraordinary command put down for that particular occasion in the list of provinces submitted to the chances of the lot. The same result could be attained if at any time the senate should see fit to unite two provinces, should send, for example, but one governor to take charge of both Spains or of both Gauls. Sulla might reasonably have thought that he had thus provided the senate with an administrative staff equal to its needs and that it had ready at hand the means for such readjustment as might be rendered necessary by temporary circumstances. This, indeed, was true, but only on the assumption that the extension of the Roman empire was to cease and that Rome was henceforth to pursue a purely defensive policy. Such a policy the senate was willing and even eager to adopt, but fate willed otherwise and the machine which Sulla had made broke down in consequence.

The military system likewise was built upon the theory of peace as the normal state of things, and it also broke down under the strain of constant and serious warfare. It may seem strange that a people so continuously engaged in war as the Romans should have constructed their whole army for the day of peace that never came. Such is, nevertheless, the fact. The Roman republic had no standing army. It persistently refused to regard war as a normal condition, but looked on each campaign as an exceptional necessity to be met by measures of a temporary character. It is, of course, too much to say that the Romans expected perfect peace and complete tranquillity. Hostilities with barbarous peoples on the frontiers were, no doubt, a thing which they anticipated and provided for, but prolonged and serious wars requiring large armies the Roman world did not contemplate as a thing likely to occur at frequent intervals. Hence the standing army, the force that stood in constant readiness for action, was extremely small. Adequate for the ordinary needs of frontier warfare, it was quite unequal to a campaign upon other than a petty and restricted scale. This standing army consisted of the small forces stationed in the provinces under the command of the provincial governors, a force not larger than was absolutely needed to maintain order and protect the frontier from the restless border tribes. If the republic found itself at war with any foe of greater power than these tribes it raised a special army for the campaign in question. Once the Roman arms had triumphed the victorious army was disbanded, since the state had now no further use for it. Thus the real military power of Rome rested wholly upon armies raised for each occasion and disappearing as soon as the need had passed away. The idea of maintaining a great force under arms in time of peace was wholly alien to the Roman mind. Why burden the state with legions for which there was no immediate use ? If circumstances required, a new force could always be raised, though this took time and the republic was like to have paid dear more than once for its persistent unreadiness to act.

When all was tranquil, therefore, the Roman world had no soldiers under arms in Italy, and only small forces in the provinces. Where there were no dangerous neighbours, as for example in Sicily, these forces amounted to little more than a handful. Where a turbulent frontier, or restless tribes within the border, made a more dangerous situation, as in

Spain or Gaul, a larger force was stationed, yet in no case
did the governor have at his disposal an army capable of
taking the field against a really formidable enemy.[1]

Insubordination from the ordinary governor was not,
therefore, a danger which was greatly to be feared.  He had
no force sufficient to enable him to march on Italy, or overawe the government, without a risk far greater to him than
to the state.  Nor were his troops likely to be willing to
follow him in any perilous adventure.  Appointed as he was
by lot, he had no close or vital connexion with either his
province or his troops, and his term of office was normally
too short to permit him to acquire a dangerous popularity
with either.  When his successor arrived he could do nothing
but surrender his command and return to Rome as a private
citizen liable to be called to account before the courts for
any act of his that might have overstepped the law.  The
court before which, in such a case, he must appear for trial
was, after Sulla's dictatorship, composed exclusively of
senators, and, while they might be careless, or corrupt, if
the charge related only to the plunder or oppression of the
provincials, it can scarcely be supposed that, if he had been
guilty of insubordination to the senate, his judges would
have been disposed to leniency.  Thus it would seem clear
that the independence from control on the part of the
ordinary provincial governor was not a serious peril to the
state, nor one that needed to concern the senate overmuch.
If dangerous men were chosen by the people to be consuls
or praetors, they could do little during their year of office
and the senate might sometimes by manipulating the provinces for the following year contrive to eliminate them as
factors to be dreaded.[2]

---

[1] When Caesar went to Spain as propraetor, he found there a force of
two legions (Dodge, *Caesar*, 44).  When he assumed command of the two
Gauls, he found at his disposal four legions or about 20,000 men (Rice
Holmes, *Caesar's Conquest of Gaul*, 42).  In both cases his first measure
was to increase his forces.  With a force of four legions only he could hardly
have ventured on the civil war.

[2] An illustration may be found in the case of Caesar.  The senate re-

The danger to the state arose from those extraordinary conditions, as the Roman viewed them, which kept recurring with such frequency. It was when a war arose calling for one of those *large* armies which the state only raised in time of need and for a specific campaign that the military system involved an element of real and serious peril. When there was need of a force greater than was normally under arms in the provinces, the Roman policy of never meeting a danger in advance made the peril all the more intense. An army must be improvised, and, since the state usually delayed its preparations as long as possible, it must be improvised at once and in hot haste to meet the crisis which statesmen had refused to see afar. When this was the case the state, depending as it did after the reform of Marius on volunteer enlistment, found itself obliged to have recourse to the men of established military reputation who could attract recruits. Thus arose a small group of indispensable generals, the men who could raise an army, whenever it might be required, by virtue of their reputation and personal popularity.

With armies thus brought together by the prestige of a successful general, a change in the commander was no easy or simple matter, and the character of the wars which called such generals to the front would have made frequent changes dangerous, even if the character of the army had not rendered them impossible except under very unusual conditions. Not only did the state find itself compelled to call upon the popular general in order to obtain an army for its wars but, once selected, it had no real choice except to leave him in command until the war was finished and *his* army could be

garded him as dangerous and foresaw the probability of his election as consul. The conscript fathers, therefore, named as the consular provinces for the year of his proconsulship the charge of the roads and forests in Italy. Caesar was not to be thus put aside, however, and, as the assembly had by that time been freed from the restrictions which Sulla had put upon it, he succeeded by its help in setting aside the arrangements of the senate. In addition to its power of fixing the provinces, the senate had also the right to determine the number of the troops and the amount of the funds at the disposal of a governor.

dispensed with. Thus practical permanence of command was grafted on the Roman system, and that command was more and more disconnected from the annual magistracies. It would rarely happen that a crisis would arrive at the precise moment when one of the few who, under the new conditions, was capable of taking up the task chanced to be among the men ready to depart for their provincial duties, and, even if he were, the lot by which these duties were assigned gave no assurance that he could be employed where he was wanted. It necessarily follows that the normal machinery could not be used in case of any serious war and that, whenever the state was confronted by such a war, it was driven to create an extraordinary command in order to meet it. That is to say, the constitution of Rome, while adequate to meet what Roman statesmen regarded as a normal situation, would not work in a case of greater difficulty. The annual magistrates were average Roman leaders and politicians and the annual governors of the provinces were necessarily the same and such men were unequal to a grave responsibility. That the great commands were fraught with danger to the state was clear enough to men of very moderate foresight, but to realize this was useless unless a remedy could be provided, and this the Romans were unable to supply. Whenever the senate attempted to carry on a serious campaign by means of the ordinary machinery, disaster followed promptly as a result and a great command had to be resorted to in order to retrieve a situation which delay had only made more critical. Whatever the reluctance of the senate, the state could wage successful war on a large scale only by this means, and such wars it found itself unable to avoid.

It was this fact that caused the failure of Sulla's work of reorganization. All that he was able to do was to entrench the senate in control of things so that it could govern in relatively tranquil times. His really vital failure lay in this, that he was unable to create a world in which the military and administrative machine, such as he found or made it, could work successfully. For this failure he was not responsible. He was dictator of Rome but his autocracy stopped at her frontiers. He could not rule at once his country and the rest of the world. He had been forced to leave his eastern enemy, beaten but still unconquered, while he fought for mastery at home. Once master in his own house, he reorganized the state as best he could, but he could not give it power to meet the difficulties which arose once he was gone. As soon as he was dead his constitution broke down because the mechanism was unequal to the work the world required. The senate which he left was, perhaps, adequate for peaceful days but dangerously weak for stormy weather. This weakness has sometimes been laid to the charge of the successive massacres which had decimated the governing nobility. While these contributed their part, the essential weakness was not that the average senator lacked courage or conviction for the task of holding the fortress which Sulla had ingeniously contrived to fashion. That many senators did lack these qualities is true, but what really mattered was the dearth among them of men of established military reputation who were at the same time thoroughly loyal to the constitution which Sulla had devised. Some there were, indeed, but not enough for the troubled times the state had to confront, and this could only mean that sooner or later the senate would find itself driven by necessity to place strong armies in the hands of men it could not trust and take the chance that they would show an unexpected loyalty to those who had reluctantly entrusted them with power.

With Sulla gone there remained but four really competent generals, namely Lucullus, Metellus, Pompey, and Crassus. The first two were devoted partisans upon whose loyalty the senate could rely; the others had been regarded with suspicion by Sulla himself. If he had not wholly trusted them, the senate could have even less confidence, for the awe which the dictator inspired and the thought of his veterans would probably have kept them loyal to him, while the senate was much less likely to inspire a salutary fear. Upon the military side, therefore, the senate was ill equipped for storms, and even in Sulla's lifetime the clouds had been gathering upon the horizon. In the East a renewal of the war with Mithridates was an obvious possibility, while the civil war in Italy had led directly to a new and serious war in Spain. In this last region Sertorius, the governor appointed by the democratic régime which Sulla had overthrown, had rallied the remnants of his party that had escaped the vengeance of Sulla and was waging open war against the government at Rome. So grave had the situation become in Spain that the dictator had dispatched Metellus to take charge and crush the rebels. This task soon proved to be no easy one and the war dragged on with varying fortunes. Thus, at the moment of Sulla's death, the senate, which he had restored to power, had ready at hand in Italy only one general, Lucullus, in whom it had entire confidence. Unfortunately for the conscript fathers his reputation as a commander was yet to make, for, though he had done good service in the East, he had borne no part in the civil war in Italy and his Eastern service had been chiefly with the fleet. He was probably but little known at home, and in spite of his capacity as a general, he never possessed the gift of making himself popular with his men. In an emergency which called for instant action he was likely to be of little use, and the senate might be forced to fall back upon the services of Pompey and of Crassus, however little it might trust them.

Scarcely had Sulla's death occurred in 78 B. C. than the senate found itself facing a crisis. Lepidus, one of the consuls for the year, began an agitation which threatened to undo all Sulla's work. Taking advantage of the discontent then seething throughout Italy, he made a bargain with the democrats and sought to repeat the revolution that had placed Cinna and Marius in power after Sulla's departure to the East. After some preliminary skirmishes in Rome he put himself at the head of an open rebellion in Etruria. We need only to recall what Sulla had done to realize that Italy

was full of combustible material.  He had confiscated immense
quantities of land and penalized numerous Italian munici-
palities that sided against him in the civil war.   Add to this
the children of the proscribed, the discontented democrats,
and all the other classes who were injured by his reforms and
it is evident that a revolt had excellent chances of getting
strong support.  The advantage of the senate lay in the fact
that Sulla's victory had been so recent and so crushing that
many who sympathized with the movement were inclined
to wait till it should be well started before they joined it
openly.  The best hope, if not the only one, of averting
a dangerous civil war lay in prompt and vigorous action.
Of these things the senate was well aware and it was clear
enough to the conscript fathers that their safety required
that Lepidus should be suppressed before his insurrection
had a chance to spread.  If time were given him to arouse
and organize the elements of unrest, all Italy would soon be
in flames.  To save itself the senate had to act at once, and
that it might do so, it required a man whose name would be
enough to call in volunteers.  One such man there was ready
to hand and whatever their opinion of his soundness in the
faith, the conscript fathers had no choice but to place
Pompey in actual command of their forces.  This they did,
and the rebellion of Lepidus was swiftly crushed : but the
victory left the state facing a new peril less menacing, indeed,
but not less real than that which had just passed harmlessly
away.

The youth to whom the senate had been forced to turn
for safety, although not yet thirty years of age, was already
a well-known and popular soldier.  His father had been
a general more distinguished for his dubious loyalty than
for any striking military achievements.  At the time of the
elder Pompey's death the son had been too young to attract
the attention of the dominant democrats and so had lived
to witness the return of Sulla from the East.  Then, boy as
he still was, he had hastened to join Sulla at the head of
a considerable body of volunteers.  In the civil war he

rendered services of importance to the future dictator and displayed a military capacity which led to his being entrusted with the task of destroying the remnants of the Marian party in Africa and Sicily and so securing the food supply of Rome. For his victories, which, though of vital significance to the dictator, were scarcely wonderful in themselves, he demanded the unprecedented honour of a triumph, something never before conferred on any one not a regular magistrate of the republic, and the right to use the title of Magnus, or the Great, as a family name. Sulla, although astonished at his presumption, granted his demands, but, having done so and thus disarmed his vainglorious lieutenant, retired him forthwith from public life. It seems clear that this retirement was due to the dictator's understanding of the man and to a perception of the fact that he could not be relied upon to put the interests of the senate before the promptings of his own vanity and ambition. Still Pompey had contrived to impress his contemporaries with a sense of efficiency and to acquire the reputation of a general who could win the hearts of his men. When Lepidus menaced the state with a counter-revolution the senate in its terror called upon him to use his popularity to crush the rebel. His success in this task was rapid and complete. His name brought men to fill the ranks and his real gifts as a commander, joined to the incompetence of his opponents, did the rest.

The danger from Lepidus once averted, the senate found itself confronted with the problem of dealing with its own general. The victorious Pompey was at the head of a strong force in Italy which he refused to disband and the senate had at hand no soldiers to resist him. As it happened, what he desired at the moment was not very distasteful to the senate. The war in Spain was still dragging on and Metellus, the general in charge there, was calling loudly for reinforcements. Pompey requested that he and his army might be employed on this mission and the senate yielded its consent. He and his troops departed for the Sertorian war and for the next few years he was too far away and much too busy to cause further trouble to the government he served. Still the first downward step had been taken, and the armies of the state were no longer in the hands of men thoroughly loyal to the new constitution.

Pompey had hardly departed for Spain when war blazed up again in the East. For this the senate itself seems to have been largely responsible. Nicomedes, the king of Bithynia, died, and by his will bequeathed his kingdom to Rome. The conscript fathers, probably under the pressure of the knights, accepted the legacy, although they must have known that this would mean a war with Mithridates, who could not accept the annexation of Bithynia by Rome without abdicating his place as an independent sovereign. Lucullus, at the moment, was one of the two consuls and after considerable manœuvring and intrigue he succeeded in having himself dispatched to take charge of the war.[1] With his departure for the East the senate was left without a single loyal general of established reputation in Italy. The danger of such a situation was not long in making itself felt in the peculiarly sinister form of a great servile insurrection in the peninsula. A band of gladiators under the leadership of Spartacus, breaking from their barracks, raised the standard of revolt and speedily aroused the country districts of Italy which were crowded with slaves whom the hard conditions of their life had rendered desperate. In a short space of time the original band of gladiators had grown into a formidable force and seemed to the Romans to menace, not this party or that, but organized society itself. The danger was made worse by the incompetence of the ordinary annual magistrates to deal with it. Consuls and praetors were driven from the field in headlong disgraceful flight by the revolted slaves till the lesson was at length fully learned that the average Roman politician could not handle one of

---

[1] Reinach, *Mithridate Eupator*, 318–20. Lucullus obtained the command by resigning the province that had already been assigned to him by lot under the Sempronian law of C. Gracchus. Having done this, the senate had the legal power to appoint him, without the use of the lot, to a new command.

the new armies with any prospect of success. When, at length, the senate dared no longer trifle with the situation, it reluctantly called in the help of yet another general of tried capacity but doubtful loyalty to anybody except himself. With the support of the oligarchy Crassus was named as praetor for 71 B.C., and given the command against Spartacus and his servile rebels. Like Pompey he had been one of Sulla's able lieutenants, and like him had been retired from command. Now, once more at the head of an army, he speedily restored discipline which had gone to pieces in the inefficient hands of his predecessors and soon was pressing his foes with energy. For a time he seemed unable to crush the uprising completely, and in spite of his successful campaign the gladiators still kept the field. As Pompey had now brought the war in Spain to a triumphant close, the senate called him home with his victorious army to help their praetor finish the rebellion once for all. Before he could arrive, however, Crassus, furious at the thought of dividing the glory with one whom he regarded with an envious jealousy, had made an end. Nevertheless, obeying with alacrity the summons of the senate, Pompey arrived in Italy with his devoted soldiers at his back.

Thus by the inexorable pressure of necessity the senate had been forced to place in doubtful hands two armies, both of which were now in Italy itself. The loyal generals were powerless to help. Lucullus was absent in the East and Metellus was unable or unwilling to offer any serious assistance. Ready to hand there was no force that could oppose Crassus and Pompey, and the senate was quite helpless to resist them if they should unite. If they should fight each other there might be a chance of safety for the conscript fathers, yet this they did not do, although for a time men seem to have anticipated some such event. The two quite cordially and sincerely disliked each other, yet neither was prepared to pay too high a price to gratify his feelings. Pompey had the stronger army, and if it came to open war would probably have won. This Crassus knew and con-

D

sequently he was desirous to come to terms with his rival
rather than to fight him.  Pompey, even with victory
probable, had no wish for a civil war, if he could gain his
ends without it.  So, setting aside their private feelings,
they came to terms.  The senate, which Sulla had thought
to make the supreme power in the state, could only look on
helplessly and humbly ratify a bargain in whose making they
were not consulted and of whose every stipulation they
strongly disapproved.  The elaborate safeguards with which
Sulla had surrounded the conscript fathers were useless
because the Italy he left behind could not be managed by
the average politician, even though he came of an old family.
Such a politician might be an able speaker in the forum and
a skilful vote getter, but he could not in a time of stress
command the kind of soldiers on whom Rome now relied
to fight her battles, and thus the power inevitably passed to
the exceptional men who could raise and lead the armies
that the state required.

The terms on which Pompey and Crassus formed their
combination were dictated in the main by vanity and personal ambition.  Pompey desired the consulship and Crassus
wished to stand as high as he.  Pompey preferred Crassus as
a colleague to a civil war with him.  They, therefore, speedily
agreed that they should be the consuls for the ensuing year
although by Sulla's laws neither was eligible for this dignity.
Pompey had never held the minor offices required of a candidate for the highest post in the republic, while Crassus was
actually praetor and an interval between offices was demanded
by the law.  But legal technicalities were nothing to men
with armies at their backs, since what they asked could
hardly be refused.  Moreover, such elections were not unknown in Rome.  From time to time the Roman people had
exempted some favoured candidate from the requirements
of the law and made him magistrate though legally dis-
qualified.  This Pompey and Crassus now demanded for
themselves, and the senate, menaced by the swords of their
armies and having no means of meeting force with force,

saw itself compelled to yield a sullen consent to their joint candidacy.

That consent given, the path of the two ambitious generals seemed clear. They deemed it wise, however, to take ample precautions against possible obstacles. With the senate and its partisans overawed, the only chance of trouble was that the people in their assembly might refuse to do their part. To obviate this danger they struck a bargain with the democrats and thus made all secure. The demand of the democrats was that, once in office, they should undo Sulla's work and put the constitution back where it had been previous to his dictatorship. To this they agreed, Pompey desirous of popularity and Crassus perhaps approving, but in any case unable to resist and probably quite content with the satisfaction of his personal ambition. For the senate, whose exclusive control they pledged themselves to destroy, neither cared at all. They must have known that it distrusted them and that it had called on them for help only because necessity had left no choice. For the future they could hope for little from the conscript fathers, except under such pressure, but the mob stood ready to applaud and trust. There seems no reason to suppose that any qualms of conscience troubled them at tearing down what they had recently fought valiantly to raise. Certain elements in the character of each of the two men will go far to explain the apparent contradiction.

Pompey was by no means destitute of scruple, but throughout his life he was quite unable to perceive the larger aspects of a political problem. He was capable of sacrificing his personal ambition to the interests of the state, only he was too short-sighted to discern a conflict between the two unless it was particularly glaring. Thus it came about that, in spite of good intentions, he struck deadly blows at the republic without realizing it, and set invaluable precedents for an empire of which he did not dream. In this particular case it is not necessary to charge him with real inconsistency. It was true that he had fought for Sulla, but, when he joined his standard, the policy of the future dictator was still involved in much uncertainty. That Sulla, if victorious, would favour the senate and the aristocracy was obvious to all ; but it was by no means clear what precise measures he would take or how far he would go in this direction, and at the beginning of the civil war he used language of studied moderation. Pompey may very well have seen in him the only hope of delivering Rome from the tyranny of the discredited democratic régime then in power ; but such an alliance did not bind him to approve of the violent and drastic fashion in which Sulla used his victory. It is not impossible that Pompey, like many other men of moderate views, supported Sulla in the civil war only to be disgusted by many of the laws which, as dictator, he enacted in his endeavour to entrench the senate securely in power. If this were so, he might, without conscious inconsistency, now use his opportunity to repeal some of the measures to whose too narrow partisanship he had always been opposed. The oligarchy which the dictator had set up might seem too weak and founded on too sudden a break with the traditions of the Roman constitution to hope for permanence. An attempt at some sort of compromise by which, while it retained all its ancient rights and its former position in the state, the senate should be deprived of its recently acquired monopoly of power, might seem to Pompey a wise precaution against future violence and to involve no surrender of the principles for which he had fought in the past.

Crassus was less scrupulous, and since Sulla's disfavour had forced him to retire from politics he had been busily engaged in amassing wealth. In this pursuit he was naturally drawn into close and active relations with the equestrian class who were the financiers and capitalists of Rome. Sulla, in his reorganization of the state, had striven systematically to weaken the knights and consequently the destruction of some parts of his work would be pleasing to a class with whom Crassus had come to be on intimate and cordial terms. The chief role in the task to which the two had pledged them-

selves fell outwardly to Pompey, but Crassus may have had
no wish, except the promptings of his personal jealousy and
dislike, to thwart the work.

The triple combination of Pompey, Crassus, and the democrats proceeded to undo the constitutional reforms of Sulla.
The new consuls, for 70 B.C., could not legally bring any bill
before the people without the approval of the senate, but,
while their armies remained camped without the city on the
pretext of their triumph, that body dared not refuse its
consent.  Their first important act was to restore to the
people the powers of which Sulla had deprived them.  The
requirement of the senate's preliminary consent to bills was
thus annulled and any magistrate, with the support of the
assembly, could once more legislate at will, regardless of the
wishes of the conscript fathers.  This was the really vital
point because the cancelling of the control of the senate over
legislation made possible all manner of changes in the future.
The rights and privileges of the tribunes were also restored
and the courts remodelled so that the knights recovered, if
not the complete monopoly which Gaius Gracchus had conferred upon them, at least a powerful influence which
amounted to practical control.  Thus the hold of the senate
over the provincial governors was weakened and the capitalist
class was given a weapon with which to push their interests
in the empire at large.

Beyond these two great measures, great if tested by their
influence upon the future, Pompey and Crassus accomplished
little in their consulship.  But what they did, although it fell
short of a complete repeal of Sulla's laws, destroyed their
essential meaning and purpose and thus pulled down the
edifice their author had constructed.  The senate's exclusive
power and control over the state, as established by the
dictator, had fallen under the stress of military necessities
which he had been unable to foresee or to avert, but for the
moment this overthrow seemed to make little difference with
the working of the government.  The people were too ill
organized to exert continuously their newly recovered power

of interference, and at this moment, perhaps because of the grim thoroughness of Sulla's bloody proscription, they were lacking in strong and purposeful leaders, capable of heading an attack upon the clique of noble families who still continued to monopolize the offices. It was also true that just then there seemed no adequate reason for any interference. Few Roman democrats had ever imagined that the machinery of the state could run without the nobles as the usual holders of the offices or had dreamed of the democracy as capable of more than an occasional intervention when things went seriously amiss. Gaius Gracchus seems, indeed, to have cherished the design of substituting the assembly for the senate as the constantly directing and controlling power of the state, but no other leader can be found to whom such large and far-reaching designs can reasonably be ascribed. The others had put forward individual reforms or attacked this or that detail of the administration of the senate but without giving any indication of a broadly conceived plan of replacing it. When no grievance was acutely felt it seemed to most Romans that there was no occasion for popular action, and in the year 70 B.C. there were no leaders on the democratic side of such influence as to be capable of making their ambition a sufficient excuse for legislation. Thus it came about that when the popular party had demolished the essential work of Sulla, a pause ensued as if, with that accomplished, there remained no more to do.

The two consuls, once they had fulfilled their pledges to their supporters, allowed their personal dislike for each other to dominate their conduct. Crassus, as the weaker of the two, could hardly venture on any initiative himself, but was content to thwart his ambitious colleague whenever possible. Pompey, on his side, cast longing eyes toward the East, where he desired to supersede Lucullus in the expectation of winning new laurels for himself. Such a design met with little favour from Crassus, who was bitterly opposed to anything that promised additional glory for his rival. In alliance with the senate he succeeded in checking Pompey, and the latter, disdaining an ordinary proconsulship, announced that at the close of his year of office he would retire into private life. Crassus promptly followed the example thus set, partly, no doubt, for financial reasons, but partly also because he wished to remain in Rome where he could more easily continue to thwart Pompey.

The next two years passed by without conspicuous events, but then new troubles arose. While Rome's attention had been turned in other directions a new enemy had grown to menacing proportions. The Romans had never loved the sea and had become a naval power only under the compulsion of the war with Carthage. Her African rival once destroyed, Rome had given little attention to her fleet. The policing of the seas, which was the duty of the dominant Mediterranean power, had been neglected during many years, and piracy had again become a formidable scourge. At last the senate could no longer shut its eyes to the necessity of action, but the commanders placed in charge failed miserably to accomplish anything. The seas remained unsafe and the pirates plundered far and near along the coasts. How long the Roman nobility might have tolerated this condition and the manifest incapacity of the ordinary authorities to deal with it, is matter for speculation merely. The pirates by a stroke of folly stirred the people to action. Grown too bold from long impunity, they ventured finally to intercept the grain ships on which the Roman mob depended for its dole of food. The misery of their subjects had not moved the populace of Rome particularly, but the prospect of famine for *themselves* was a very different thing. Indifference immediately gave place to anger. The mob was united in demanding swift and effective action, and since the lack of bread was in itself a clear demonstration of the incapacity of the senate's commanders, the people determined to appoint one of their own. The choice was easy, for Pompey was popular and bore the reputation of a general who had never failed. Every task assigned him had been successfully performed and his record was in no wise injured in the eyes of the rabble by the fact that so far fortune had always favoured him. The feeling of the people was far too strong not to find prompt expression, and one of the tribunes, Gabinius by name, availed himself of the newly restored powers of his office to bring a bill dealing with the situation before the assembly.

The Gabinian Law was sweeping in its provisions. Pompey was not named, but every one knew that he was meant. The purpose of the bill was to create, by popular action, a new great command. In general terms it provided that some man of consular rank should be entrusted with the sole charge of the war against the pirates. It clothed the man so chosen with wide and even extravagant powers for the intended campaign. He was authorized to raise a fleet and army for the war, and was given power to call upon the treasury for funds. Ships, men, and money were all placed at his disposal on a scale which far surpassed the actual requirements of the occasion. This may have been due to a desire to flatter the man who was certain to be chosen, or it may have been that the difficulty of the task had been vastly over-estimated. The most startling feature of the bill was not the resources it assigned to the commander but the jurisdiction which it gave him. His authority was to extend over the whole Mediterranean and he was invested with an *imperium* equal to that of the various governors over all Roman territory for fifty miles inland. This would give practical control of *all* the provinces of Rome since but little of her empire lay farther from the sea than fifty miles. To exercise his far-reaching *imperium* the commander was authorized to select a number of *legati*, or lieutenants, from the higher ranks of the senate. The term for which he was to hold his powers was fixed at three years.

The bill amounted to a practical dictatorship for Pompey ; yet the situation could be made to justify its main provisions. To crush the pirates a fleet was obviously necessary, and its exact size could hardly be determined in advance. An army was equally necessary, for if the pirates were permitted to retire to their strongholds, they could there await in safety the first favourable opportunity to renew their depredations. To destroy them they must be tracked down at once by land and sea, and for this purpose an army of uncertain size and the control of the coasts to an indefinite extent were required. The necessary operations might well last for a considerable time and three years were allowed by the bill. The Roman people meant to make an end, once for all, of the enemy who threatened their supply of food and to accomplish this they did not hesitate to set up a possible master for themselves. The senate and the nobles could not be expected to submit tamely to a bill which handed over all the power and resources of the state to a man whom they neither liked nor trusted. They resisted bitterly but in vain ; the clamour of the streets bore down all opposition. When a fellow tribune tried to stop Gabinius by interposing his veto, the precedent of Tiberius Gracchus was at once revived and the obstructive tribune gave way to avoid a formal removal from office. All opposition thus silenced, the bill was promptly passed and Pompey entered on a new command. What the senate would have refused to give, the people had enthusiastically granted, and the popular general must have felt that his policy in restoring to the assembly its power of independent action was amply justified by the result.

From the day the bill was passed in 67 B.C. till Pompey disbanded his army in 61, he was the Emperor of Rome in all but name. In a campaign far shorter than any one had dreamed of, he swept the pirates from the sea and brought about the surrender of their strongholds. By assembling overwhelming force, by showing his foes that if they fought to the bitter end they could expect no mercy, and then tendering reasonable terms as a reward for prompt surrender, the war was speedily ended, and Pompey found himself at the head of an army in Cilicia, the great pirate centre, with his task fulfilled. But a force that was overwhelming against the freebooters was equally so against the state that had commissioned him. Even in Cilicia, with his fleet and army at his beck and call, he had but to ask what he would and the government in Rome was powerless to refuse. This was so obvious that the Romans hastened to anticipate his wishes by an extension of his command for which the situation in the East afforded a good pretext.

In Asia Rome had been engaged for some years in a struggle with her old foe, Mithridates. This war had been, and at the moment still was, in the charge of Lucullus. At first that general had been brilliantly successful, and hitherto Pompey had seen his efforts to supersede him foiled. Now, however, the situation had changed ; the war, which had opened so successfully for Lucullus, had ended in a dismal failure and disgrace. His generalship had been completely adequate ; he was, perhaps, as good a soldier as Rome had, but one vital quality he lacked : he could not gain or hold the devotion of his men. In spite of the victories to which he led them, his soldiers hated him and his last campaigns had failed by reason of the mutiny and insubordination of his army. Under these circumstances the senate had decided on his recall[1] and had voted to entrust the final settlement of the East to new commanders of the ordinary stamp. But their very action in removing him had been a signal for a fresh crisis. The war, which had seemed practically ended, flamed out again and the men designated by the senate were obviously unequal to the new situation. It was necessary to make a change in the arrangements and but one change was possible. A new and serious war required a commander superior to the ordinary promagistrate, and such a one was

---

[1] Another factor in procuring the recall of Lucullus was the attitude of the Roman capitalists or knights. Lucullus had not originally been named as governor of the province of Asia, but he was later given full authority there for war purposes. In the exercise of his power he contrived to quarrel with the knights. The province was overwhelmed with debt and Lucullus undertook a drastic reduction of it. This infuriated the Roman capitalists who saw their extortionate profits thus curtailed and they neither forgot the measure nor forgave the author (Heitland, iii. 35–6). Ferrero has pictured Lucullus as an imperialist, but it appears to the present writer that Frank has conclusively disproved this. It was partly because he adhered to the older traditions of Roman policy that the knights desired his recall and Pompey's appointment. See Frank, *Roman Imperialism*, 307–14.

already actually upon the scene. Pompey, the ever victorious, was there at hand in the very region where the war would be fought out. His name and popularity would quiet the mutinous soldiers of Lucullus and the forces he had raised to fight the pirates would serve to reinforce their ranks. He had previously been known to desire the command, and, if it were now refused him, he might embark his legions and sail for Italy. Rome had at hand no army to oppose him and preferred to give with outward spontaneity what it was dangerous to refuse.

The Gabinian Law thus found a successor in the Manilian Law. This, we are told, was unexpectedly proposed by an obscure tribune of the people. The unexpectedness can only have lain in the man who gave his name to the measure, for Roman politicians can scarcely have failed to anticipate some such proposal. At any rate, the bill when laid before the people for their vote encountered little opposition. Whatever eloquence could do to make its passage easy was well done by two young men just rising into prominence, Caesar and Cicero both speaking in favour of it. Though oratory might be right and seemly in the enactment of a Roman law, in this case it was hardly necessary. No one dared to offer open opposition except those who knew themselves so definitely set down as enemies of Pompey that they had nothing to lose. If the great general should be provoked into invading Italy, none cared to offer themselves as marks for a proscription except such as felt that they were certain of inclusion. So men's tongues were tied by fear, and whatever they might say in private, in public they kept silent or approved. The powerful speech of Cicero may have done something to make compliance easier for some and may have rallied a few waverers, but can scarcely have influenced the inevitable result. That was determined not by flowing periods or balanced sentences but by the military situation of the state which left it helpless. The bill was passed and added to the powers Pompey already held under the Gabinian Law the sole charge of the war against Mithridates and the other Eastern foes of Rome. It vested in him the proconsular command of Cilicia, Bithynia, and Asia and authorized him to make war and conclude peace in the name of the republic as he might deem expedient. This bill added to the already irresistible power which he held the last fragments of military force which the state possessed, yet it procured a breathing space for the Roman politicians none the less, since, for an uncertain time to come, the new war would effectually tie his hands. For a year or two he could not interfere in Italy, and in that interval something might be done to arm the state against the day when new victories would leave him free to turn his attention to affairs in Rome.

Such a conception of the situation is fully borne out by the course of events in Rome following the passage of the Manilian Law. Of those who remained in the capital there were many who both feared and hated the absent proconsul and who fully meant to take advantage of the respite which their Eastern enemy was giving them. In the front rank of such men was to be found the rich and active Crassus, a prey for long to bitter jealousy of his former colleague. He was one of the few who had openly opposed the Manilian Law and he now set himself to work to save the state, and incidentally himself, from Pompey. This was a task which obviously involved considerable difficulties, yet one which did not seem impossible of achievement. At any rate, if Crassus failed, it cannot be attributed to any lack of effort.

The political affiliations of Crassus were of the most doubtful kind. A lieutenant of Sulla, he had fought for the aristocracy only to become a partner in Pompey's bargain with the democrats in 70 B.C. To thwart his colleague's Eastern ambitions he had joined the senate once again, leaving the democrats to rally around Pompey. The passage of the two great laws in favour of the latter convinced him that this was a mistake and he now sought to use the popular party for his own ends. Unable to eclipse his rival in a frank contest for the favour of the mob, he set to work by indirect means and by the use of other men. His vast

wealth made this course easy and promising. So rich a
man as Crassus could manage to pull many wires without
appearing in the open. His millions made him a strong
power in the financial world and among the Roman politicians there were many whom he could control. For many
years Crassus had spent money freely to secure influence
and had not spent in vain. It was his common practice,
we are told, to loan money freely to any one who had, or
seemed likely to acquire, the least importance. Nor was
the generous lender in a hurry for repayment. He was
content to bide his time until the moment came when he
could use his debtor. In this and other ways it gradually
came about that many of the senators could scarcely venture
to displease him greatly and that he could bring many of the
demagogues of the forum into line whenever he chose. If
to all these we add the numbers of the rabble whose votes
were so much property for sale, the influence which the
millionaire could exert was truly formidable. True, it was
not by any means omnipotent, but by clever management
and profuse expenditure he might accomplish much.

Accordingly in 65 B.C., the year after the passage of the
Manilian Law, with Pompey fully occupied in Asia, he succeeded in having himself elected censor for the year and in
securing the services of the ablest of the rising men of Rome,
no less a person than Gaius Julius Caesar. The later greatness of this man has served to cast a fictitious glamour over
his earlier career. By birth and marriage allied to the
popular party, although sprung from an old patrician family,
Caesar had narrowly escaped from Sulla's proscription by
the intercession of his aristocratic relatives and friends. He
had escaped, however, and as soon as quieter times permitted
he had entered politics upon the democratic side. His
private fortune was soon spent and he found himself a bankrupt demagogue. His splendid genius was his only asset,
but it was enough, for Crassus had the necessary means and
needed some one to carry out his schemes. A bargain was
thus easily concluded between the two, and for the next few

years the future conqueror of Gaul acted as the political manager of the great financier. For the year of Crassus's censorship his partner was one of the aediles and the two set busily to work.

Both men were gifted with too clear an insight not to discern wherein lay Pompey's power and to perceive the only means by which it could be met. Even if Crassus had been far more stupid than he was his own career would have enlightened him. He must have known that in 70 B.C. Pompey would never have selected him as his colleague in the consulship but for the army with which he had been ready to enforce his claims. If, when Pompey should return from Asia as the conqueror of Mithridates, Crassus was to hope for favourable terms, he must be able to appeal to a similar argument. His primary purpose, therefore, during the next few years was to obtain, by any means that offered, a military power to balance that which the final crushing of the king of Pontus would set free. But where and how and by what pretext could he obtain it ?

This question seemed comparatively easy to answer because of the circumstances of the moment. The recent shortage of grain in Rome had fastened the attention of the people upon the sources of supply. Some years before a worthless Alexandrian king had been murdered by the mob of his capital.[1] It was reported that he had left a will bequeathing Egypt to the Roman people. Whether the will was genuine or not no one had troubled to inquire, nor had the senate hitherto accepted or rejected the legacy in any formal manner. It now appeared to Crassus that this circumstance might furnish the oportunity he sought. The annexation of Egypt might be made popular by being represented as a means of securing to the mob an ample supply of grain and would furnish a pretext for raising an army. Crassus and Caesar, therefore, promptly brought the matter forward with some hopes of success. To help in the forma-

---

[1] The king was Ptolemy Alexander II. Bouché-Leclercq, *Histoire des Lagides*, ii. 118–21.

tion of their army by securing for themselves popularity in that part of the peninsula where the recruiting was the best, Crassus, as censor, proposed to extend citizenship to the inhabitants of the province of Cisalpine Gaul.  He was checked by his colleague in the censorship, but this can hardly have displeased the millionaire.  Gratitude in politics is apt to be of short duration and as matters stood the people of the Po valley, not having yet obtained the privilege they coveted, would continue to look to him as their champion for the future.

Though well conceived the Egyptian plan was none the less a failure.  The prompt victory of Pompey over the pirates had removed the immediate scarcity, and now that food was plentiful the mob were no longer interested in the source of supplies.  Moreover, Pompey was still the idol of the populace and an expedition to Egypt was too obvious a blow at him. An army in that country would hold a powerful position on his flank, a strategic fact which had doubtless commended the scheme all the more strongly to its authors.  Pompey could by this means be menaced without being named, and, under cover of anxiety about the people's food, an army could be placed precisely where it could threaten him if he attempted to return.  Unfortunately for Crassus the threat was just a little too obvious and the Roman mob, with food assured for the present, were not disposed to affront a man who was still their favourite.  The senatorial party, likewise, though with little confidence in Pompey, had no greater faith in his would-be rival.  If they needed a saviour they were not disposed to welcome Crassus in that role, however eager he might be to play it.  The dread, too, of increased responsibilities was strong, since the state already had as many provinces as it could govern with the existing machinery.  Caesar and Crassus, therefore, encountered opposition on all sides and were unable to get their enterprise so much as fairly launched.  Finding themselves unable to carry out their plan, they dropped it and turned their attention to new schemes.

If they could secure the election of friendly magistrates for the next year they might hope either to revive the Egyptian scheme or to devise and carry out some other plan, it mattered little what, so that it involved the raising of an army under their control. Accordingly, in 64 B. C. they made a desperate effort to carry the elections. Of the candidates for the consulship for the ensuing year they strenuously supported two, Catiline and Antonius by name. So energetic was their campaign in favour of these two that the aristocrats were frightened to the point of swallowing their pride. Catiline was a desperate and reckless adventurer ready for anything, while Antonius was a pliant tool of those behind him. If these two became consuls the nobles feared, and reasonably feared, the consequences. Of the candidates to whom in normal times they would have given their backing none had much hope of winning. They were thus forced to throw their whole support to. the least objectionable man who seemed to have a chance, and this man happened to be Cicero. The strong dread of Crassus and his allies thus forced the aristocrats of Rome to make a *new man* their champion and to support him for the highest office in the state, highest in dignity if no longer in real power. The result of the election with the issues thus confused was, on the face of it, ambiguous ; Catiline was defeated and Antonius and Cicero elected. The nobles had thus won half the battle, but in such a contest half a loaf was the equivalent of the whole. The plans of Crassus and of Caesar required action and one consul could prevent his colleague from doing anything at all. The programme he had been elected to put through having thus become impossible, Antonius went over to the winners and finally allowed himself to be bought off by Cicero, who ceded him the lucrative province of Macedonia in return for his support.[1] It happened, therefore,

---

[1] I agree with Holmes (*The Roman Republic*, i. 457–8) as against Hardy (*The Catilinarian Conspiracy*, 47–8) that the province was promised to Antonius early in the year, if not before Cicero took office, though the formal transfer came much later.

that for 63 B.C. Cicero was the sole consul, in fact if not in name, and the control of the chief magistracy thus rested entirely in the hands of the conservatives.

Caesar and Crassus had again been defeated in their plans, but they determined to make a final effort. Rullus, a tribune known to be their tool, brought forward an agrarian bill. The very name of such a measure might be popular with the mob and the bill was framed with considerable ingenuity. Its purpose, not of course avowed, was to place an army at the disposal of its real authors, who were keeping in the background. On the surface it proposed a mighty benefaction to the poor by directing that land should be purchased in Italy and assigned to them. To raise the money necessary the state was to sell its properties lying outside the peninsula. To direct the sale and purchase and assignment, an agrarian commission was to be elected and to enable its members to perform the duties delegated to them they were invested with the *imperium*. This would authorize them to sit as judges to determine what property was public and what private and to raise troops to carry out any decisions they might render. The significance of these provisions would seem clear. Crassus, and perhaps Caesar, were to be members of the commission. Acting in their judicial capacity they could declare the will of the late Ptolemy valid and Egypt the property of the Roman people. To obtain possession an army would be needed, and this the bill empowered them to raise and to command. Under cover of an agrarian bill the Egyptian enterprise could thus be resumed and finally carried out.

In spite of its apparent plausibility the scheme possessed one capital defect in that the clauses of the bill had to be framed in such general terms as to cause perturbation and alarm. No art could quite conceal the singular disproportion between the machinery which it was proposed to set up and the avowed ends it was to serve. Suspicion was inevitable that the intention of the bill was other than alleged. Besides, the Roman mob was no longer so land-hungry as in the past.

The longer they lived in Rome upon the public bounty under the corn-law, the less they cared for hard work on a farm. The largess of the state by relieving them of anxiety for their daily bread had taken away all serious desire for allotments of land. If they had sought for land at all, it would in most cases have been simply in the hope of selling it, and, even if the bill should pass and if it should be carried out in its professed spirit, it would be some years before they could hope to get anything. As a bribe to the mob, therefore, it was not particularly attractive. Yet the old tradition, which made the very name of agrarian bill suggest a measure for the people and against the rich, might have sufficed to carry it along, backed as it was by powerful friends and patrons, had it not met with resolute and vigorous opposition. Cicero, bent on discharging his obligations to the party that had raised him to power, employed all his eloquence to tear the bill to rags. He brought out in convincing fashion the discrepancy between the avowed purpose of the measure and the machinery which would be created by it. He showed the people that it could be of no real benefit to them, and last, but by no means least, he stripped away the specious disguise and exhibited it clearly in its true light as a direct blow at Pompey. The effect of Cicero's crushing exposure was decisive and the bill was allowed to drop.[1]

Crassus and Caesar had scored another failure and in discouragement they retired from the game. There was nothing further for them to do but to wait on Pompey and see what his course would be. But there were some in the democratic ranks who could not afford to wait. Of these Catiline was the chief. Seeing his last hopes foiled he now turned to conspiracy and violence. It is most unlikely that either Crassus or Caesar had a hand in this; to suppose that they were partners in the plot requires us to suppose that they were fools. In its essence the conspiracy of Catiline seems to have

---

[1] Perhaps the return of Pompey from the interior of Asia Minor to Syria in the winter of 64 had more to do with the dropping of the bill than Cicero's eloquence.

aimed simply at the seizure of the government by force. The
more atrocious parts of the project may reasonably be
regarded as simply the oratorical embellishments of Cicero.
It was plainly thus that his contemporaries viewed them ;
this is shown by the simple fact that Crassus was suspected
of complicity. Surely no man who really believed that
Catiline intended to burn down the city could imagine that
he had as partner, even in the background, the greatest
owner of tenements in Rome. Nor could any one believe
that the greatest capitalist and creditor of his day was risking
treason to abolish all debt. In short, no man who suspected
Crassus can possibly have taken Cicero's speeches without
a large amount of salt. If we assume that the aim of the
conspirators was rather to seize possession of power by force
than merely massacre and conflagration, the case presents
itself in a new light. Such an attempt was not without fair
chances of success. A year or two before Crassus and Caesar
might well have been objects of suspicion, but now— ? The
war in the East was ended and the hands of Pompey were
free. A tumult in Italy, if successful, would only furnish him
with a pretext to return at the head of his legions to restore
order. To keep Pompey from becoming the armed master
of Italy was the main object of Crassus. Can it be imagined
that now in sudden blindness he played with treason just
to bring about the very thing he dreaded ? His former
relations with Catiline, his plots and intrigues, more or less
known and suspected, would suffice to account for the
suspicion of contemporaries without the need of our believing
them well founded.[1]

In any case the energy of Cicero effectually crushed the

---

[1] The conspiracy of Catiline has enjoyed a fame beyond its just deserts
by reason of the speeches of Cicero. Those who suspected Crassus must
have taken some such view as that suggested in the text. The actual
intentions of the conspirators are not of much importance. Probably they
did intend to set some fires in Rome, very likely for the purpose of creating
confusion. Probably they did intend to murder some high officials, such
as Cicero, in order to disorganize the government. With so much for
foundation, Cicero's eloquent tongue and pen could readily do the rest.

conspiracy and Rome could wait in peace till Pompey chose
to come. That the latter was not well pleased with this turn
of affairs there is ample evidence to show. To Cicero it seems
never to have occurred that in suppressing the conspiracy
without Pompey's help he was deeply disobliging the great
general. Nor was this merely a matter of vanity on the
part of one who thought of himself as indispensable. If only
Catiline had developed a little more strength, as he might
easily have done had Cicero been less vigilant and energetic,
the senate must have called Pompey home with his army
as they had done in the days of Spartacus. His experience
in 70 B.C. cannot have failed to teach him how much the
presence of an army simplified Roman politics. Now, thanks
to Cicero's unwelcome success, ambition and patriotism,
which had seemed about to coincide, were thrust asunder
and he found himself obliged to choose between them. He
could not return with his army without a clear violation of
the law, for which he had neither pretext nor excuse. True,
one of the tribunes, Metellus Nepos, known to be Pompey's
man, made frantic efforts to provide him with a semblance
of justification,[1] but the device was too transparent to serve
the turn. Pompey could hardly appeal to arms to avenge
insults which the senate had not yet offered him. And even

[1] Hardy has advanced the view (in the *Journal of Roman Studies* and
later in a monograph on the conspiracy of Catiline) that Nepos was sent
to Rome to arrange an understanding with Crassus and Caesar and that this
developed into the Triumvirate. His chief reason for this is the inactivity
of Crassus and Caesar in 63, which seems to me sufficiently explained by
the return of Pompey to the coast of Asia in the winter of 64. The bill of
Rullus was probably brought forward before it was known in Rome that
Pompey was in Syria in touch with his fleet. When they learned this both
Crassus and Caesar recognized that further intrigues were too dangerous
and effaced themselves. Hardy also asserts that one tribune could accomplish nothing. But Nepos must have been sent to Rome before Pompey
knew that Catiline had failed, though he had probably heard that Rome
was disturbed by revolutionary agitation and rumours of conspiracies.
Such a situation might furnish an opportunity for his recall, and undoubtedly Nepos was to procure this if possible. One tribune could do
much to protect Pompey's interests by his veto, and had Cicero proved
weak Nepos could have proposed Pompey's recall with success. See
Holmes, *The Roman Republic*, i. 466–7.

if his men would have supported him, he shrank from open illegality. Hitherto, however much he had trampled on the spirit of the law, he had been able to keep within its letter. Now that he had to choose between his own ambition and the constitution of his country, he had sufficient conscience to take the better part.

For a year he lingered on in the East, hoping against hope that circumstances might yet play into his hands, and meanwhile answering the self-laudations of Cicero with a coldness which filled that brilliant consular with amazement and alarm. When nothing came of the delay he finally dismissed his army, as the law required, and returned to Rome a private citizen. If, in such a cause as he could have provided, his army would have followed him, a question the answer to which must be conjectural, he might have said that the empire of the world had been within his grasp and that he had ' made the great refusal '.

# IV. THE FIRST TRIUMVIRATE

FROM the position of dominance which he occupied in 62 B.C. Pompey fell swiftly. Cicero's words as to his headlong descent from the stars,[1] though used in another connexion, would have been appropriate at this time. The change in his position is so significant that it deserves some consideration. It revealed the complete helplessness of Pompey as soon as he had laid aside the sword and thus contained a lesson which could hardly be misunderstood. Remembering what had befallen him at this time, the proconsuls of the future would be far less willing to disarm. As his predominance in 62 pointed out clearly the path to power, so his humiliation in 60 indicated as clearly the essential condition of that power's continuance.

Returning to Rome in 61 B.C., Pompey dismissed his army in obedience to the law. Henceforth as a private citizen, eminent indeed, but only one among many, he must seek to carry out his policy. The nature of the position he had held and the character of the army he had led alike contributed to force a policy upon him. He could not retire entirely from politics and let things take their course, but was compelled to try to control that course in some particulars. As a politician, however, he encountered only humiliation and saw himself driven to employ means from which he shrank and to combine with men whom he loathed to gain the ends which circumstances imposed upon him. Under the sweeping provisions of the two great laws, especially the *lex Manilia*, he had carried out a general settlement of Eastern affairs ; to keep his army loyal he had made promises of future rewards to his soldiers. His men were no longer of the same class that had once filled the legions. In the past

[1] *Letters*, i. 117 ; *Att.* ii. 21.

they had, in the main, been farmers taken from the plough and while this was true the disbanding of an army was a comparatively simple matter and meant only that the men were mustered out and sent back to their homes. After the reforms of Marius, however, the legions had been filled with volunteers possessed of no property. To disband such an army meant to turn loose on society a horde of men without home or occupation and with nothing but their pay and what had fallen to their share from the spoils of victory. Such men quite naturally demanded some provision from the state whose battles they had fought, and looked to their general to see that it was duly made. The habits of the Roman mind, and perhaps the financial necessities of the state as well, combined to point to land allotments as the form which this provision should take rather than pensions, as modern usage would suggest. With armies of this type, each and every general was forced to hold out to his men the promise that, when their task was achieved and the victory was won, they should be rewarded by a grant of land. Retirement was no longer possible to one who had held a great command since, when he laid down the *imperium*, he must still persuade the state to redeem his pledges to his men. Thus after his army was disbanded Pompey found himself obliged to take an active part in politics. All through the East were princes and communities that had concluded peace with Rome trusting in his word, and that word he felt himself in honour bound to redeem by inducing the senate to give its formal sanction to his arrangements and so pledge the state to respect them in the future. In addition to this he must secure for his soldiers the land allotments which he had promised them. Both these demands, which Pompey was forced to make, seemed to him quite reasonable and such as ought to be granted without the slightest hesitation. To his angry disgust he soon discovered that neither would be seriously considered. To reach his ends he was obliged to resort to political rather than military methods and his ability as a politician was unequal to the task. This may have been no

great reflection upon him, since in the existing state of
Roman politics success was almost impossible. Even Caesar,
the most astute statesman and shrewdest manager of men
the age could show, failed equally when he undertook the
same task.[1] However that may be, the lesson of Pompey's
failure was quite unmistakable ; a Roman general imperatively needed a control of politics, and nothing but possession
of military force could give him that control. The whole
history of Rome from 62 to 54 B. C. served to make this fact
obvious to all.

Pompey began his political campaign in the natural and
obvious way : he came before the senate requesting the
ratification of his Eastern settlement, and he procured the
help of a tribune to introduce a bill making provision for his
veterans. Instead of ready acquiescence in his wishes, he
found himself face to face with a settled opposition and a
persistent obstruction which he was unable to overcome.
The conscript fathers viewed the matter in a very different
light and had no difficulty in finding plausible pretexts for
refusing, or at any rate not granting, his demands.

The opposition of the senate may have turned out to be
unwise, but it is quite intelligible, as a brief consideration
of the implications of Pompey's policy will show. In the
senate two sets of motives influenced the action of the members, neither of which alone might have been strong enough
to defeat him but which combined were sufficiently powerful for the purpose. The first of these was the jealousy and
dislike of Pompey, long kept in check by fear, but now
released from all restraint. Pompey had many private
enemies, foremost among whom were Crassus and Lucullus.[2]
His former colleague in the consulship had never made the
least concealment of his bitter animosity and naturally
seized this opportunity to humiliate his rival. Lucullus had
returned to Rome embittered by his failure in the East,
furious that another should have reaped the glory of his

---

[1] When consul Caesar was unable to carry Pompey's bills by legal means.
[2] Dio, xxxvii. 49 ; Appian, ii. 9.

victories, and especially angry at Pompey. Never an adept
in the art of courtesy and consideration for others, Pompey
had made no effort to spare the feelings of the unfortunate
man whom he was sent to supersede, but, on the contrary, had
seemed to seek for opportunities of affronting him. Lucullus
now saw a chance of which he eagerly availed himself to
pay the score. With such men as these were others who had
no personal grudge, but who regarded the predominance of
Pompey with genuine apprehension. He had risen to a
height which the constitution did not contemplate, and to
check him seemed to them a public duty. Hitherto he had
ignored the senate all too much in his career, and, as a lesson
to others, it was time to teach him his mistake. Now was
a good occasion to show proconsuls in the field that they
must finally answer to the senate and that they should conduct themselves accordingly. If Pompey were permitted to
settle the affairs of half the world as if that body were a
negligible factor in the government, it seemed to them that
a dangerous precedent would have been set and they were
anxious, on public grounds, to teach the general his place at
the first opportunity. Nor need they avow such motives
openly : there were other grounds for opposition that could
be put forward.

Quite aside from any jealousy of Pompey's past greatness,
or any desire to humiliate him in the present, there were
many plausible pretexts of which his opponents could make
use. It was true that he had received wide powers from the
people, but these were not in any sense unlimited. Had he
the right because of his exceptional command to lay before
the senate a large number of treaties and demand their immediate sanction by a single vote ? His enemies might urge
with much show of reason that the senate should examine
his acts one by one, if only to make sure that he had not
exceeded his powers. In so far as he had only done what the
Roman people had authorized well and good, but it was the
obvious duty of the senate to ascertain the fact before it
pledged the Roman state to observe his engagements for all

future time. This it could do only by a careful examination of his various arrangements, and for this purpose it was indispensable that they should be taken up separately and not acted upon in one indiscriminate mass. To Pompey this seemed to foreshadow very clearly that some of his agreements would be rejected, but the conscript fathers refused to yield to his objections.

Perhaps the opposition was the stronger because some of Pompey's arrangements affected seriously another department of public affairs, and one that had hitherto been almost a monopoly of the senate, namely the provincial administration. Pompey had added two new provinces to the empire, Bithynia-Pontus and Syria. To the annexation of Bithynia the senate had given its approval, but Syria was a new and perhaps unwelcome addition. It seemed not unreasonable, since it lay with the senate to provide governors for these new possessions, that it should be consulted in the matter and given an opportunity to discuss the question of whether it could meet the added burden. This was the more plausible because the increase in the number of provinces had far-reaching consequences. Sulla had left the senate a staff of magistrates just large enough to administer the territories which Rome then held. If any additions were made the senate would inevitably find itself short-handed. The situation could be met by only two expedients, to either of which there existed obvious objections. The term of two of the governors might be prolonged for a second year ; but this diminished their effective responsibility, since the prosecution of a governor who remained beyond the usual term in his province was no easy task, and there was, therefore, a real danger that, by leaving him in office for a second year, the senate would destroy all serious accountability for his acts. Nor could the other method, that of uniting two provinces under a single governor, be resorted to without grave risks, since this would really amount to the creation of a great command. The new annexations would thus entail formidable administrative problems throughout the Roman world, and many of the senators may have viewed the extension of the empire with genuine alarm. Some, no doubt, were swayed by blind prejudice and loyalty to inherited tradition, but such considerations as the above must have reinforced them powerfully. Whatever the motives of the conscript fathers, Pompey soon found that the majority were not disposed to accept without question the burdens he had placed upon their shoulders. When his Eastern settlement was brought before the senate and he demanded its ratification *en bloc*, Cato, a man of unbending principle and conviction if there were any such in Rome, took the lead in insisting that his measures should be considered one by one. If his arrangements were discussed separately, it was clear that the conscript fathers might accept some and reject or modify others, and Pompey felt that his honour was affected by the smallest alteration in his settlement.

While Pompey thus found himself unable to secure the ratification of his Eastern *acta*, he had no better success in his efforts to reward his veterans with land. In consultation with a tribune he had a bill prepared and brought forward for discussion. This measure encountered bitter opposition which could justify itself on general grounds without proclaiming enmity to Pompey as its source. Of all the public lands once held by Rome but one important tract had survived the various agrarian bills. This was situated in Campania and had hitherto been leased by the state, constituting the last considerable source of revenue still left in Italy itself ; aside from this Rome lived upon the income of her provinces across the seas. To redeem his promises to his men Pompey proposed to allot this Campanian domain, along with other lands, to his veterans. To this it was objected that it would be unsafe to leave the government entirely dependent on revenues which might be cut off by war or rebellion at any moment. The dislike of Pompey, covering itself with such excuses, flared up in a moment and proved to be so strong that even Cicero, good friend of Pompey as he thought himself, joined with the opposition.

The great orator himself describes his action in the matter and the general situation in these words :

The agrarian law is being vehemently pushed by the tribune Flavius, with the support of Pompey, but it has nothing popular about it except its supporter.  From this law I, with the full assent of a public meeting, proposed to omit all clauses which adversely affected private rights.  I proposed to except from its operation such public land as had been so in the consulship of P. Mucius and L. Calpurnius (the Campanian land).  I proposed to confirm the titles of those to whom Sulla had actually assigned lands.  I proposed to retain the men of Volaterrae and Arretium— whose lands Sulla had declared forfeited but had not allotted— in their holdings.  There was only one section in the bill that I did not propose to omit, namely, that land should be purchased with this money from abroad, the proceeds of the new revenues for the next five years.  But to this whole agrarian scheme the senate was opposed, suspecting that some novel power for Pompey was aimed at.  Pompey, indeed, had set his heart on getting the law passed.[1]

Yet Cicero imagined that Pompey would be satisfied with his proposals.[2]  That the general showed no immediate displeasure may be accounted for by the attitude of the senate. If that body was opposed to any sort of agrarian bill, Pompey might not think it wise to quarrel with an influential member who was willing to agree to something.  But Cicero's halfhearted and limited support soon proved to be of little use,

---

[1] *Letters*, i. 54-5 ; *Att.* i. 19.

[2] Strachan-Davidson thinks Cicero was simply trying to make Pompey's plan workable. (See his *Cicero*, 182.)  This seems hardly reasonable in view of Cicero's own language.  The bill must have been badly drawn indeed if it could only be made workable by the omission of all except one clause.  That the bill as drafted included the Campanian domain seems clear, and Caesar's later legislation seems to show that this was necessary for the purpose.  The essential difference between Pompey and Cicero may have lain in this, that while Cicero was ready to support a scheme for the purchase of land, Pompey desired an immediate distribution of some of the public land, accompanied by a plan for purchase to be carried out later.  He would thus be able to do something for his men at once instead of confining himself wholly to promises for the indefinite future.

and, even as amended by him, the agrarian bill was seen to have no chance of gaining the approval of the senate.

Since Pompey's consulship the sanction of the conscript fathers was no longer indispensable for the enactment of a law. The great general, unable to accomplish anything in the senate, turned to the people. He had vainly offered the optimates his alliance, but in the past he had several times obtained his wishes, over the head of the senate, by the action of the popular assembly and he determined to attempt it again. Unfortunately for him his influence over the people had been materially weakened during his absence. While he was in the East Crassus had been actively seeking to acquire the leadership of the democrats, and whatever crude party machinery existed was largely in his hands. All that his gold could buy, or Caesar's genius win, had been secured by the great financier, and Pompey could no longer count on the united support of the popular party. Crassus had not been active in thwarting his rival in the senate merely to oblige him in the forum, and when Pompey tried to override the senatorial obstruction through the action of the assembly, he found that the supporters of the senate joined to the followers of Crassus were too strong. The result of these conditions was that the general, victorious abroad, was powerless at home. Well might Dio say that he repented of having let his legions go too soon and having put himself at the mercy of his enemies.[1] He still controlled his veterans, and if he had been prepared to resort to force, he might have called on them to rally round him. But this would have been open treason and his conscience held him back. Thus he could do nothing but accept defeat and stand helplessly aside, humiliated and, as he felt, dishonoured. But it was not to be for long. It soon appeared that there was still a way out of his difficulties.

Ancient writers point to Caesar as the author of the startling combination that now took place, and this is wholly in line with all the probabilities. The enemies of Pompey

---

[1] Dio, xxxvii. 50.

seem never to have thought of the possibility of a combination between him and Crassus, since the two were open foes. Their feud had grown more bitter since 70 B.C. when they had held the consulship together. Yet the situation had some points of analogy with that which had existed when they had previously joined hands. Each was now at odds with the senate and each was helpless by himself. Pompey was furious at his humiliation and Crassus likewise found his plans thwarted by the conscript fathers. With singular shortsightedness the senate had chosen the moment of the breach with Pompey to open up a quarrel with the equestrian class. The friction in this case arose from two separate matters. A bill had been brought forward making the knights serving on juries in the courts liable to prosecution for accepting bribes. This measure the senate favoured in spite of Cicero. The other question was one concerning the farming of the taxes. The syndicate which had contracted for the taxes of Asia demanded that the terms of their bargain should be reduced by the senate. Cicero, though he was disgusted at the impudence of the demand, spoke strongly in its favour since he feared that otherwise the senate might alienate the powerful capitalist class. He himself tells us that it was Crassus who induced the knights to bring forward their demand.[1] The senate, however, led by Cato, rejected his counsels and Crassus thus added another to his already long list of failures and stood still further discredited in men's minds.

Thus neither Crassus nor Pompey had at the moment any reason to love the senate and neither could use that body to advance his aims. Each controlled a fragment of the popular party, but neither fragment by itself was large enough to enable its owner to accomplish anything. Yet if they should unite their forces the situation would be very different. Their followers combined could reasonably be expected to dominate the assembly and they could then enact whatever measures they might choose, if only they could get one of the magistrates

[1] *Letters*, i. 47–8, 52, 65 ; *Att.* i. 17, 18 ; ii. 1.

to bring forward their proposals. Against such motives for an agreement between them there was nothing but their mutual dislike. Caesar was not the man to let such feelings stand in his way and set himself to bring about a coalition.

When Pompey returned to Rome Caesar departed to Spain to serve his term there as propraetor. He had now returned and was a candidate for the consulship. In his canvass for this office he could count on the bitter opposition of the optimates, and he not unnaturally desired the united backing of the democrats. This he could only get by bringing Pompey and Crassus together as his supporters. To Crassus he was heavily in debt, while a combination of the followers of Pompey with the senate against him might be fatal. His task as a peacemaker was thus, in a sense, imposed upon him. Accordingly he set about his work, and with the ground prepared by the senate's failure to make a friend of Pompey and its simultaneous quarrel with Crassus and the knights, he speedily attained his object although it was one which previously had not occurred to any one as within the sphere of practical politics. Neither of the two turned a deaf ear to his persuasions and he was able to obtain the open support of both in his canvass for the consulship. In this way was brought about the first triumvirate, which was destined to dominate the politics of Rome for several years to come. In the eyes of contemporaries Caesar was a minor figure in the combination and was regarded as little more than the agent who carried out the orders of his partners. The former campaign manager of Crassus was not yet the conqueror of Gaul and his military genius was still unsuspected by his fellow-countrymen.

At first the triumvirate was less successful than its organizer may have hoped. The threat which such a combination involved frightened the senate into something closely akin to desperation. They probably did not yet know the full scope of the alliance, but they feared Caesar, especially when he had the backing of such partners.[1] His election

[1] Dio says expressly that the combination of the three was not known

they had little prospect of preventing, but they were determined that he should have a colleague from their own party. To gain this end they raised a large corruption fund and exerted all their efforts.[1] Under these circumstances the election resulted in the return of Caesar and a strong conservative by the name of M. Bibulus. This failure of the three to win more than a half victory was the equivalent of a defeat, since one consul had the legal power to stop every act of his colleague. Thus from the very start Caesar's consulship was predestined either to fail completely or to snatch success in plain defiance of the law.

Although he cannot have been blind to the difficulties in his path, Caesar began his consulship with a show of moderation. Before taking office he had made some overtures to Cicero with a view of securing his support.[2] These had failed and the optimates, whom he may have hoped to divide, were not only certain to be united against him, but they would have as their leader his fellow consul. He tried at first to meet this situation by a conciliatory attitude. He treated Bibulus with studied courtesy and sought to appease the hostility of the senate, but his efforts were without result. His promises to his partners included the securing of land for Pompey's veterans and this was the first task to which he set his hand. An agrarian bill was framed and laid before the senate for consideration. In proposing the bill Caesar invited the conscript fathers to co-operate with him in the matter and declared his willingness to make such alterations in his project as they might desire.[3] There was little to object to in the provisions of the bill, but the senators, perhaps because of a blind confidence in Bibulus and an equally blind detestation of Caesar, refused to yield an inch. Lacking reasonable criticisms they resorted to obstruction, and under Cato's leadership they showed themselves resolved to talk

till later. (Dio, xxxviii. 5.) Yet in the preceding book (xxxvii. 54) he makes both Pompey and Crassus support Caesar as a candidate. The two statements are easily reconcilable, I think, as above.

[1] Suetonius, *The Deified Julius*, 19.
[2] *Letters*, i. 69 ; *Att.* ii. 3.     [3] Dio, xxxviii. 2.

the bill to death. Caesar tried in vain to force a vote, and, to put a stop to endless discussion, he went the length of ordering the arrest of Cato in the hope that, if the chief obstructionist were once removed, some action would be possible. But the attempt to reach a decision in this way broke down before the attitude of the conscript fathers. When Cato was being led out under arrest so many of the senators rose to follow him that Caesar was obliged to abandon his purpose and release his prisoner.[1] It was now clear that nothing whatever could be done with the senate and Caesar turned to the assembly.

When the agrarian bill was brought before the people Bibulus promptly interposed his veto. Caesar tried in vain to argue the question and asked his colleague to point out the objectionable features of the measure. The only answer of the optimate consul was the declaration that there should be no innovations during that year. Caesar besought him to yield to the manifest wishes of the people and called upon the crowd to back his plea, declaring that Bibulus alone stood in the way of the bill. But Bibulus was not to be influenced by such appeals and merely replied that the bill should not be passed that year even if everybody favoured it.[2]

Caesar thus found himself brought to a full stop. He was unable to act through either the senate or the assembly unless he were prepared to violate the law. This, if his two partners would give him their support, he was in fact quite ready to attempt. To defy his opponents and to declare the bill carried in spite of legal technicalities would have been easy enough, but such a step could only be successful if backed by force. A *coup d'état* of this nature would be highly dangerous unless its authors were well assured that the defenders of the constitution would be powerless to offer serious resistance. It had been attempted in the past, but the results had hardly been encouraging.[3] If Caesar broke

---

[1] Dio, xxxviii. 3.  [2] Dio, xxxviii. 4.
[3] Saturninus and Glaucia had attempted much the same thing. They

E

the law the senate could direct Bibulus to restore order, and if his colleague could find the means to act, the results might be disastrous to Caesar. Even if the senate did not go so far as this it had the power to cancel as illegal any measure passed in violation of the constitutional requirements. To ignore the law and declare his bills enacted was neither safe non worth while unless Caesar was backed by such armed force that his opponents could not resist with anything but words and that the senate would not dare to annul his measures. The force essential to their purpose the triumvirs determined to provide under the guise of a law concerning Caesar's proconsular province.

By the Sempronian law of Gaius Gracchus the senate was obliged to name the provinces to be assigned to the consuls at the close of their term of office *before* their actual election by the people. The conscript fathers, foreseeing that Caesar would be chosen, had sought to provide a safeguard for the future by naming as the provinces for the consuls for 59 the charge of the roads and forests of Italy.[1] If this arrangement were allowed to stand, Caesar would be completely shelved as soon as his year of office had expired. Not only would he have no army under his command but his province would be one where it would be impossible for him to free himself from the load of debt that still hung over his head. He could hardly be expected to submit to this without a struggle, and it may safely be assumed that he had stipulated with his partners for their backing in an attempt to upset the senate's arrangements. The three now determined to carry out their understanding and to do it in such a way that success would furnish them with the means of putting through the remainder of their programme.

As soon, therefore, as the agrarian bill had been completely blocked by Bibulus, a new measure was brought forward. The nominal proposer was a tribune by the name of Vatinius,

---

lost their lives and failed to accomplish anything besides. Lepidus was a more recent case in point.

[1] Suetonius, *The Deified Julius*, 19.

who was a tool of the triumvirs. He laid before the assembly
a bill which conferred on Caesar the province of Cisalpine Gaul
for a term of five years dating from February 28, 59. This
would make Caesar's consulship and proconsulship run concurrently for nearly a year. The motive of this arrangement
is easy to guess in the light of what had gone before and
what was soon to follow.[1] Under cover of his governorship
of Gaul, Caesar would have the right to enlist troops and to
keep them in the vicinity of Rome until such time as he
might choose to set out for his province. While he remained
in Rome as consul his army at the gates of the city would
serve to overawe all opposition and would thus enable him
to put through whatever measures he and his partners might
have agreed upon, regardless of constitutional obstacles.
Moreover, his province had been so selected that, even after
his consulship should have expired, he could continue to
threaten Rome and so prevent the senate from attempting
to annul his legislation. Of all the provinces of the republic,
Cisalpine Gaul was nearest to the capital, and Caesar at the
head of a strong army in the valley of the Po would have
Rome at his mercy.

That such a law would meet with opposition was, of
course, to be expected. Even if the conscript fathers had
not seen the danger to themselves which it involved, there
were still ample reasons for bitter hostility. The measure
violated several of their cherished principles at once. They
were adverse to a long term for a provincial governor and
the bill gave Caesar a term of unprecedented length. In
addition to this it constituted a new encroachment of the
popular assembly on a field of administration which the
senate regarded as peculiarly their own. But the Roman
assembly cared little or nothing for considerations of this
kind. It had already been shown by the Gabinian law that
the people were quite ready to confer sweeping powers for
a term of years upon a general who possessed their confidence

---

[1] For a discussion of the Vatinian law the reader is referred to the
Appendix.

and favour. At the moment Caesar was popular with the rabble and the mob was reinforced by Pompey's veterans who were with him to a man. Under these circumstances argument was clearly useless and the only hope of the conservatives lay in obstruction. This they attempted, but they had a less favourable opportunity than in the case of the agrarian bill. Then they had been able to act under the leadership of Caesar's colleague in office, but as Vatinius was a tribune, Bibulus could no longer interfere. Some of the tribunes were, indeed, opposed to the bill, but they did not venture to employ their veto since this had to be interposed in person and the attitude of the mob was hardly reassuring. They found, however, another way in which they hoped to defeat the hated measure by announcing omens which, under the existing law, made any action by the assembly impossible, or, if it should be attempted, illegal. This had the advantage that it did not require their presence in the assembly, and three of the tribunes now resorted to this means of stopping Vatinius. But neither Vatinius nor his employers intended to be checked by omens and the bill was promptly voted by the people. That it was constitutionally null and void cannot be doubted, but that proved to be a matter of very minor consequence. It had been put upon the statute book, and until the senate cancelled it, Caesar had the right to recruit troops. With Pompey's veterans thronging the streets he was not likely to have any difficulty in finding men and it cannot have been long after February 28, when the bill was finally passed, before he had a considerable force camped near the city.

As soon as he was thus effectually armed, Caesar took up the agrarian bill again. The triumvirs had now definitely embarked upon the enterprise of setting up in Rome a military dictatorship and they had thoroughly made up their minds to put their measures through regardless of either law or constitution. To destroy any lingering hopes of a successful resistance on the part of the conservatives, and to make clear the impossibility of any serious attempt to defend the republic by deeds, Caesar called both Pompey and Crassus before a meeting of the people. The triumvirate was now for the first time openly avowed and Caesar's two partners proclaimed their firm support of the agrarian bill. This was not quite enough and Caesar put to Pompey the blunt question of what course he would take if force were resorted to against the bill. To this Pompey replied with the explicit declaration that if any one dared to draw the sword he would snatch up his shield.[1] The wrath of the conservatives at this speech was unbounded, since it destroyed their only hope of successful resistance to any violation of the constitution which Caesar might intend. Pompey was the one man in Italy who could raise an army on the spur of the moment. In spite of his support of Caesar's candidacy for the consulship they may have felt some hope that in the last resort they could obtain his help if Caesar went too far. Once before he had given his backing at the elections to a consul who had attempted to carry through a revolution ; but when the crisis came and Lepidus resorted to violence, Pompey abandoned his protégé and, rallying to the side of the senate, suppressed the rebellion. The conservatives may have thought that what had happened once might happen again, and this is the more likely if the real scope of the coalition of the three was yet unknown. The formal declaration of Pompey put an end to all such calculations, since by that act the one man who might have held Caesar in check despite his troops outside the city openly declared himself on Caesar's side.

In view of this new situation Bibulus called a meeting of the senators at his own house. After due discussion it was resolved to make no attempt to meet a violation of the law by force but to resist by every legal means that could be found.[2] In pursuance of this decision Bibulus, supported

[1] Dio, xxxviii. 5 ; Plutarch, *Caesar*, 14, and *Pompey*, 47. The public avowal of the triumvirate may very well have taken place before the passage of the Vatinian law. It has been placed at this point in the narrative quite arbitrarily. The significance would be the same whenever the incident occurred.                    [2] Appian, ii. 11.

by three tribunes, appeared upon the scene when Caesar
tried to put the bill to a vote in the assembly, but Caesar
was no longer to be stopped or hindered by the constitution.
The would-be obstructors of his legislation were driven from
the forum and so roughly handled that they were glad to
escape with their lives. After this the agrarian bill was
passed and solemnly declared a law.

The violence and illegality of these proceedings are self-
evident. Bibulus and the tribunes had at least succeeded
in stripping off every pretence of constitutional action and
making Caesar's contempt of law both obvious and flagrant.
No doubt the optimates—and many men who were not
adherents of the senate—shuddered and were filled with
rage and consternation. But what were they to do? The
question of whether a bill purporting to be a law had really
been enacted in a valid way was for the senate to determine.
Accordingly Bibulus convened the conscript fathers the next
day and laid the matter before them. This was logical
enough, but in the existing circumstances it was futile in
the extreme. If the senate desired to annul the law, it must
obviously be prepared to deal with Caesar and his soldiers.
Theoretically this was easy. The senate should declare
martial law and Bibulus should restore order. Unfortunately
he had no troops to cope with those of his colleague, and,
while that was so, the senate had too much discretion to
attempt to act. No doubt the conscript fathers sympathized
deeply with Bibulus and raged at heart over his wrongs, but
when he called for action not a voice was raised and not
a motion offered.[1] Whether the agrarian bill was really
a law or not—and it was clearly not—both it and the
Vatinian law were on the Roman statute book and the senate
dared not make a move to take them off.

After this defeat Bibulus shut himself up in his house for
the remainder of the year and refused to discharge any of
the duties of his office. One thing, however, he could do
even in retirement. He could invalidate whatever his lawless

[1] Dio, xxxviii. 6; Suetonius, 20.

colleague undertook to do in the way of legislation  By the
Roman law, when one of the consuls was engaged in observ-
ing the heavens for omens no legal meeting of the assembly
could be held.  Bibulus availed himself of this device and
from his house he issued edicts declaring that he was occupied
with this theological astronomy.  Caesar, of course, paid no
attention to the edicts, but the stubborn optimate nevertheless gained his real object by providing the senate with
a pretext for declaring all Caesar's laws null and void if in
the future that step should become possible.

With the opposition driven from public life, Caesar's
course was quieter and smoother, though not more legal,
than before.  Since moderation and conciliation were now
obviously useless, he at once proposed a second agrarian bill
which provided for the allotment of the Campanian and other
land still held by the state which the first bill had not
touched.  The conservatives might rage but they were too
completely cowed to offer any opposition.  Cicero put the
situation in a sentence when, on hearing of the new proposal,
he represented Pompey as meeting all criticism with the
brief retort, ' I shall coerce you by means of Caesar's army.' [1]
This, as Cicero was well aware, closed all discussion.  For
the moment Caesar was a dictator and he proceeded to put
through the entire programme of the three.  Not only was
the second agrarian bill passed rapidly, but all Pompey's
Eastern *acta* were ratified, while Crassus and his equestrian
friends were gratified by a generous reduction of the terms
of their bargain for the taxes of Asia.

Caesar had attained his objects and those of his partners,
but only by means of violence and sedition.  The republic
had been overturned and in its place a military despotism had
been set up in Rome.  This triumph of the three rested on
force and on that alone—the force of Caesar's soldiers and
his mobs.  Such a revolution could not but inspire the
bitterest anger and dismay in all who felt a real attachment
to the supremacy of law.  To the intensity of these feelings

[1] *Letters*, i. 106 ; *Att.*, ii. 16.

the letters of Cicero to Atticus throughout this year bear
eloquent testimony. Nothing but terror held the opposition
quiet. So far the three had been content with driving their
opponents from the forum, but would they stop with that ?
Already in April, before the law dealing with the Campanian
land had been announced, Cicero avowed his fears lest
Pompey, ' finding himself belaboured by the tongues of all,
and seeing these proceedings easy to upset, should begin
striking out '.[1] For himself he declares that he has so completely lost all energy that he prefers to submit to the existing
tyranny rather than fight. In May he is apprehensive that
trouble is brewing worse than has yet happened. He writes
that Pompey ' is getting up a disturbance. We (the conservatives) have everything to fear. He is preparing a
despotism and no mistake '.[2] In June or July he says
bitterly, ' We are bound hard and fast on every side, and
are no longer making any difficulty as to being slaves, but
fearing death and exile as though greater evils, though they
are in fact much smaller ones . . . you see the citizens allowed
to express their sentiments, but debarred from carrying
them out with any vigour. And to omit details, the upshot
is there is now no hope, I don't say of private persons, but
even of the magistrates being ever free again. Nevertheless,
in spite of this policy of repression, conversation, at least in
society and at dinner tables, is freer than it was. Indignation is beginning to get the better of fear, though that does
not prevent a universal feeling of despair '.[3] In July he
wrote to his friend :

About politics I will write briefly : for I am now afraid lest
the very paper should betray me. Accordingly, in future, if I
have anything more to write to you, I shall clothe it in covert
language. For the present the state is dying of a novel disorder ;
for although everybody disapproves of what has been done, com-

---

[1] *Letters*, i. 102 ; *Att.*, ii. 14. The words which Shuckburgh translates
' begin striking out ' are *ruere incipiat*. Winstedt's version ' may run
amuck ' seems to me better. The proceedings must be the Vatinian and
agrarian laws.

[2] *Letters*, i. 108 ; *Att.*, ii. 17.        [3] *Letters*, i. 109–10 ; *Att.*, ii. 18.

plains, and is indignant about it, and though there is absolutely no difference of opinion on the subject, and people now speak openly and groan aloud, yet no remedy is applied : for we do not think resistance possible without a general slaughter, nor see what the end of concession is to be except ruin.[1]

Although the triumvirs had accomplished their immediate aims and opposition was confined to dinner tables and letters, one of the all-powerful three was decidedly unhappy. Pompey was glad, no doubt, to gain the things on which he had set his heart, but he shrank from paying the price, perhaps because he found the cost much greater than he had expected. When he joined the triumvirate he may not have foreseen the lengths to which it would be necessary to go, and may quite well have thought that the three could easily frighten the conscript fathers into a more reasonable mood. At any rate he found the bitter resentment of his opponents hard to face and all the more so, probably, because his conscience was ill at ease. At first he sought to evade the responsibility and to throw the blame on others, and Cicero has given a vivid picture of him while attempting this. Hitherto, the orator wrote, Pompey has fenced with these questions.

' He approved Caesar's laws, but Caesar must be responsible for his proceedings in carrying them ' ; ' he himself was satisfied with the agrarian law ' ; ' whether it could be vetoed by a tribune or no was nothing to do with him ' ; ' he thought the time had come for the business of the Alexandrine king to be settled ' ; ' it was no business of his to inquire whether Bibulus had been watching the sky on that occasion or no ' ; ' what was going to happen if Bibulus came down to the forum at that time he could not have guessed.'[2]

If Pompey was troubled in conscience, Caesar must have felt the need of binding him all the more closely to himself. At this time Caesar would certainly have been ruined had Pompey turned against him, since, in this case, he must have shared the fate of Lepidus. He was not likely, therefore,

---

[1] *Letters*, i. 115 ; *Att.*, ii. 20.          [2] *Letters*, i. 106 ; *Att.*, ii. 16.

to leave any means untried to keep the waverer firm. With this object in view Caesar arranged a marriage between his daughter Julia and Pompey. The news of this marriage, coming to Cicero in May, filled the orator with dire misgivings since it foreshadowed the continuance of that unholy alliance which had subverted the republic.[1]

By this arrangement Caesar strengthened his hold upon the all-important Pompey, but it did not make the three partners any the more popular. As the summer advanced the opposition grew—not stronger—but more general. A reason for this is easy to conjecture. Rome had more than once before seen laws rushed through the assembly with more or less illegality and violence. Many Romans had at the start regarded Caesar merely as another Gracchus or Saturninus. As the year wore on it became more and more apparent that while these leaders had passed some particular law, or laws, in disregard of technicalities, Caesar had done nothing less than destroy the constitution of the republic. As this became clearer it would be only natural that many who had supported him at first should fall away. By July even the knights so far forgot the matter of the Eastern taxes as to join in demonstrations against the masters of the city. The three at once dropped ominous hints that both the knights and the populace had better mend their manners.[2] Even the mob was turning against Caesar. In July Cicero declared to Atticus that nothing was now ' so popular as the dislike of the popular party '.[3] In another letter he says that the three ' feel that they do not possess the cordial goodwill of any section '.[4] In a third he repeats that ' all on that side, whether promoters or mere hangers-on, are falling out of fashion, though no one opposes them : there never was a greater unanimity of feeling or talk everywhere '.[5]

---

[1] *Letters*, i. 108 ; *Att.*, ii. 17.

[2] *Letters*, i. 112–13 ; *Att.*, ii. 19. The knights were threatened with the loss of their special seats at the theatre and the populace with some restriction on the distribution of corn.

[3] *Letters*, i. 115 ; *Att.*, ii. 20.      [4] *Letters*, i. 117 ; *Att.*, ii. 21.

[5] *Letters*, i. 120 ; *Att.*, ii. 23.

Still no one dared to move and Cicero concludes that although 'everybody entertains the greatest detestation for those who are the masters of everything' yet 'there is no hope of a change '.[1]

As the feeling against the triumvirate grew, the edicts of Bibulus, drawn up in bitter and scathing language, were immensely popular. Pompey was roused to fury by them,[2] and this filled Cicero with genuine alarm. ' I fear,' he wrote, ' they have been exasperated by the hisses of the crowd, the talk of the respectable classes, and the murmurs of Italy.' The orator admitted that at first the despotism had been popular with the multitude, but now he declared that ' they have become so universally hated, that I tremble to think what will be the end of it '.[3] For the information of his friend Cicero describes at some length the unhappy position in which Pompey found himself. ' Accordingly,' he wrote,

that friend of ours, unaccustomed to being unpopular, always used to an atmosphere of praise and revelling in glory, now disfigured in body and broken in spirit, does not know which way to turn ; sees that to go on is dangerous, to return a betrayal of vacillation ; has the loyalists his enemies, the disloyal themselves not his friends. Yet see how softhearted I am. I could not refrain from tears when, on the 25th of July, I saw him making a speech on the edicts of Bibulus. The man who in old times had been used to bear himself in that place with the utmost confidence and dignity, surrounded by the warmest affection of the people, amidst universal favour—how humble, how cast down he was then ! How ill-content with himself, to say nothing of how unpleasing to his audience ! Oh, what a spectacle ! No one could have liked it but Crassus—no one else in the world ! Not I, for considering his headlong descent from the stars, he seemed to me to have lost his footing rather than to have been deliberately following a path.[4]

But the plight of Pompey inspired Cicero with fear as well as sorrow. ' I fear ', he wrote frankly, ' lest one so impulsive and so quick to strike, and so unaccustomed to personal

---

[1] *Letters*, i. 119–20 ; *Att.*, ii. 22.   [2] *Letters*, i. 114 ; *Att.*, ii. 19.
[3] *Letters*, i. 116 ; *Att.*, ii. 21.   [4] *Letters*, i. 116–17 ; *Att.*, ii. 21.

abuse, may, in his passionate resentment, obey the dictates of indignation and anger '.[1]

Caesar must have felt that Pompey was wavering. Cicero wrote to Atticus to tell him that the general ' is exceedingly dissatisfied with his position, and desires to be restored to the place from which he has fallen ; that he confides his annoyance to me, and is without disguise seeking for a remedy '.[2] The orator did not think one could be found, and he was right, but Caesar can hardly have been blind to such feelings on the part of his indispensable ally or have viewed them without alarm. If the rule of the triumvirate was losing what popular support it had once had, and if the most important member of the combination desired, even vaguely, to break away, it was essential to take precautions. Pompey's leanings toward a reconciliation with the conservatives must be checked at once and Caesar must place himself in a position where he could dispense entirely with the favour of the mob. It seems likely that this double motive lay behind the dubious incident which followed. Suddenly an informer by the name of Vettius was produced to testify that he had been employed by the conservatives to murder Pompey. On examination his story broke down hopelessly, however, and he was shortly afterwards murdered in prison. With his death the charge was allowed to drop. Whether Pompey was frightened or not it is impossible to say, but the incident furnished a pretext to have the assembly vote Caesar the protection of a guard.[3] With troops within the city itself the last step had been taken in the consolidation of the despotism.

It remained for the masters of Rome to take precautions against a possible reaction when Caesar's term expired. To guard against this they must secure friendly magistrates for the next year who, backed in case of need by Caesar's army in Gaul, could hold the senate and its partisans in check. Bibulus succeeded in postponing the elections, but

---

[1] *Letters*, i. 117 ; *Att.*, ii. 21.   [2] *Letters*, i. 120 ; *Att.*, ii. 23.
[3] Appian, ii. 12.

they were finally held in October and two consuls were declared returned on whom the three could count. As an added safeguard it was resolved to remove the men most capable of leading the opposition. These men were Cato and Cicero. The first was sent off to Cyprus on a special mission the acceptance of which would debar him in the future from questioning the validity of Caesar's laws. Cicero proved more difficult to deal with. Caesar tried to induce him to accept some position which would close his mouth in a similar fashion, but was met by a refusal. The three at length made up their minds that, if the orator would not go quietly, he—and others—should be taught a lesson. They decided to banish him from Rome, and for this purpose they had conveniently at hand both a pretext and an instrument. The pretext was the execution of the Catilinarian conspirators, which in the view of the popular party was illegal, and the instrument was a tribune who was a bitter personal enemy of Cicero. No sooner were the new tribunes installed in office in December than Clodius, acting as he boasted at the suggestion and with the approval of the three,[1] brought in a bill of which the purport was to banish Cicero because as consul he had put Roman citizens to death without a trial. Before the bill was carried Caesar had laid down the consulship, but his army was still camped outside the city, and Clodius called a meeting of the people without the walls of Rome in order that Caesar might attend. He, of course, spoke out in condemnation of the execution of the conspirators, though he professed sympathy for Cicero personally. The legal scruple on Caesar's part is certainly a touch of irony, but with his army there at hand resistance was quite clearly hopeless and Cicero bowed before the storm and, brokenhearted, left his native country for the East.

With matters in Rome thus arranged, Caesar was free to depart for his province, where his presence was urgently required. That province had, however, undergone a considerable extension, and one of vast importance, since the

---

[1] Cicero, *Respecting the Answers of the Soothsayers*, 22.

Vatinian law was passed.  The measure of Vatinius had given
Caesar Cisalpine Gaul and Illyricum for the period of five
years, but after its passage the sudden death of Metellus
Celer, the proconsul of Transalpine Gaul, had left that
province vacant and Caesar had induced, or compelled, the
senate to assign it to him.  This measure, urged by Pompey,
had been accepted by the conscript fathers because they
feared that if they should refuse, Caesar would seize the
province by a second Vatinian law.[1]  If this were done he
would receive the added district for a term of years, but if
it came to him by the action of the senate it would be held
for one year only, though the appointment might be renewed
from time to time.  It was, therefore, obviously to the
interest of the senate, if Caesar could not be prevented from
getting the province, to forestall popular action by conferring it themselves.

Though the motives of the senate are easy enough to
understand, those of Pompey are somewhat less obvious.
In later years Cicero reproached him for having armed
Caesar against himself.  It seems quite evident that the
governorship of Transalpine Gaul had been no part of the
original bargain between the three.  Had it been so it is
difficult to see why both Gauls had not been assigned at once
by the law of Vatinius.  There can have been no thought of
placating the optimates by a show of moderation, and the
most probable explanation is that the Vatinian law gave
Caesar all that had been agreed upon at that time.  Had the
original intention been allowed to stand unaltered, Caesar
could never have begun the conquest of Gaul at all.  It was
his possession of the Transalpine province that made his
military achievements possible.  It seems quite evident that
the conquest of Gaul was not a thing that Pompey intended
in the least.  Perhaps, if he had foreseen its possibility, he
would not have consented to the addition of the new province
to his father-in-law's command.  If conquests were to be

---

[1] Suetonius, 22.  The part played by Pompey is clear from Cicero's
later reproaches. See *Letters*, ii. 281 ; *Att.*, viii. 3.

made, Pompey was very much of the opinion that he, and not another, was the one to make them. In agreeing to the extension of Caesar's power he may have had no further motive than to prevent the sending of an adherent of the senate to that province. A war in Gaul was possible, if not imminent, which might call for a large army, and the three would naturally wish to keep that army in safe hands. If the situation should grow serious it is quite possible that Pompey expected to take over the command. It may be confidently affirmed that if he fostered Caesar's greatness to the point where it was a danger to himself, he did so quite unintentionally.

If the conquest of Gaul was no part of the programme of the triumvirate, it is by no means certain that it was intended by Caesar. It is quite possible that it was not until he was actually in his province that he fully realized the opportunity. It is very likely that he meant to go to war with some of the independent tribes, since, even if he were not anxious for martial glory, a war offered the best chance of paying off his debts. There is no evidence, however, that he went to Gaul with any settled plans of conquest.

Whatever the original purpose of Caesar may have been, he was no sooner in his province than war broke out, and that without any act of his. The migration of the Helvetians was obviously a movement which a Roman governor was bound to stop, and from this as a beginning the rest followed easily. Within the next few years the proconsul of the Gauls found himself launched upon a career of conquest which his partners had never intended. They had, however, little choice but to accept his policy whatever it might be. Crassus was probably pleased to see Pompey's prestige as the only great general of Rome diminished by the rising reputation of Caesar. On his side Pompey could not venture to act without the support of either Crassus or the senate. Against Caesar the millionaire would give him no assistance, and the events of Caesar's consulship had left Pompey at open war with the optimates. He could, therefore, do nothing to stop

Caesar even if he wished, and it is not likely that for some time he felt any great apprehension or jealousy of the man who was to overthrow him. He may have feared that he might yet have to depend on Caesar's army to protect him from his foes, and in such an event a certain amount of glory and success would give Caesar a stronger hold upon his soldiers.

The real danger to Caesar lay not in the possibility that his two partners would try to call a halt but in their inability to work together after he had left Rome. It is a mistake of modern historians to view the triumvirate as a sort of coalition government. The facts seem clearly to reveal it as a temporary combination for limited and definite ends. After those ends had been achieved the combination ceased to have a programme except in a purely negative sense. The means by which Caesar had put through their measures made it essential to his partners to prevent the return of the conservatives to power lest all the Julian laws by which they profited should be annulled. Beyond that, Pompey and Crassus had no interests in common and they at once resumed their temporarily suspended feud. Under these circumstances Rome began to drift rapidly toward veritable anarchy since the forces of disorder were no longer under any strong control. Crassus and Pompey would not permit the senate to resort to any energetic measures, and while they were at odds with one another they were unable to replace that body in any effective way.

The immediate question which precipitated the troubles was the recall of Cicero. Pompey seems to have consented to the orator's exile with reluctance and he now demanded that the banished consular should be permitted to return. Perhaps Pompey hoped to pave the way to some reconciliation with the senate, perhaps his conscience reproached him for his desertion of a friend and he wished to make amends. Crassus had no desire to humour his colleague, whom he had never ceased to hate, and he had not the slightest love for Cicero. Though he did not care to take a place in the front

ranks of the opposition to his partner he was quite prepared
to use his influence in secret. The leadership of the resistance
to Cicero's recall thus fell to Clodius, who entered on this
task as a labour of love. The reckless tribune had already
quarrelled with Pompey on other matters, but the proposal
in regard to Cicero roused him to actual fury. He had the
mob of Rome well organized and he turned his rabble loose
on Pompey. In doing this he ran little risk as long as the
great general and the senate remained apart. Caesar's army
was no longer at the gates of Rome and there was no force at
hand to keep the peace. It is true that troops could readily
be raised, but this required a commission from the state. As
a mere private citizen Pompey could not recruit soldiers, nor
could the consuls without the sanction of the senate. As the
consuls for the year were tools of the triumvirs the conscript
fathers were unlikely to decree a revival of the military
despotism of the year before solely in order to accommodate
a man whom they detested as much as they did Pompey at
this moment. While they were in this frame of mind Pompey
did not dare permit them to arm anybody else for fear that
they might use the forces so obtained against him. If, therefore, Clodius abstained from a direct attack upon the senators
he would have little to fear.[1] He saw this clearly and with
his mob succeeded in driving Pompey to the shelter of his
house. Yet both he and Crassus dreaded any reconciliation
between their victim and the senate and Pompey's efforts to
secure the recall of Cicero might lead to a coalition. To
prevent this Clodius launched an attack upon the validity of
Caesar's laws regardless of the fact that the legality of his

---

[1] Heitland (*The Roman Republic*, iii. 172) thinks that Pompey could
easily have put an end to the anarchy if he had wished. He blames him
for not acting and calls him solemn and irresolute. It is not easy to see just
what Pompey could do. He could not raise troops without the sanction
of the senate unless he were prepared to violate the law. But his attitude
during Caesar's consulship had clearly shown that he had his scruples
about breaking the law in person. Moreover, if he had dared a breach of
the law would he have been successful? According to Cicero all Italy was
against him at the time. Certainly the mob and the conservatives were.
Action might well, therefore, seem both dangerous and illegal.

own tribuneship was bound up with them.[1] Of course he had no intention of permitting them to be annulled, but, by raising the question, he drove a wedge between Pompey and the nobles. The senators could not uphold the Julian legislation without repudiating all their principles, while Pompey could not allow it to be attacked without risking all he had gained by the triumvirate. By bringing up the issue Clodius could thus keep Pompey isolated and continue to harrass him at his pleasure.

Pompey could find no way to meet this situation except to call in the help of a counter-rioter. One of the tribunes for the next year, Milo by name, was selected for this task, and quickly raised a gang of gladiators and cut-throats to fight the mobs of Clodius. He succeeded in getting the upper hand so far that in August of 57 B.C. Cicero's recall was finally voted by the assembly, and the orator returned in triumph to his country. The rioting did not end with this, however. Clodius out of office proved quite as turbulent as in, and he and Milo between them made the streets of Rome a veritable pandemonium. The senate had co-operated with Pompey to bring back Cicero, but the nobles had by no means forgiven him his share in recent events. Cicero might hate Clodius, but the conservatives had probably little wish to see him crushed and none at all to accomplish this by making Pompey virtually dictator. Moreover the question of the Julian laws must have been a formidable barrier between them. In vain Cicero, who felt himself bound by ties of gratitude to the general who had procured his return, tried to bring about an understanding between his patron and the senate. The time had not yet come for such a project to succeed, and the failure of the attempt could only prolong the existing anarchy.

A shortage in the grain supply occurred at this time to add fuel to the flames. Pompey hoped to make use of this to

---

[1] Cicero, *For his House*, 15. See also Pocock in the *Classical Quarterly*, xviii. 59–65. I cannot agree with his interpretation of Cicero, but his suggestion as to the motives of Clodius during this stormy year seems to me illuminating. I am inclined, however, to make Crassus the man behind Clodius rather than Caesar.

obtain new glory and, if possible, an army. The senate, urged by Cicero, and probably fearing that the mob would turn upon themselves, sanctioned a bill giving the charge of the grain supply to Pompey. This, however, fell short of what the general desired. Cicero plainly intimates as much in a letter to Atticus. ' A second law ', he wrote, ' is drawn up by Messius (one of the tribunes), granting him power over all money, and adding a fleet and army, and an *imperium* in the provinces superior to that of their governors. After that our consular law seems moderate indeed : that of Messius is quite intolerable. Pompey professes to prefer the former ; his friends the latter.' [1] The vital difference in the two bills probably lay in the fact that one provided for an army and the other did not. On this occasion Pompey's wishes were not gratified and he obtained only what he said he wanted, namely the consular bill which gave him authority and honour, indeed, but left him without an army and therefore at the mercy of the mob of Clodius, except for such protection as Milo could afford him. Nominally pleased but really disappointed, he turned at once to a new scheme for accomplishing his purpose. The king of Egypt had been dethroned and the question of his restoration was now before the senate. Pompey was anxious that the conscript fathers should commission him to replace the fallen monarch in power, and hoped in this way to get an army. But the senate had no wish to give him one, and found in religion a convenient pretext to avoid it. A passage in the Sibylline books was found and was interpreted to fit the case. Cicero put it plainly when he wrote : ' The senate supports the trumped-up religious scruple, not from any respect to religion, but from ill-feeling towards him, and disgust at the king's outrageous bribery.' [2]

While the Alexandrian business was still under discussion the disorder steadily increased. Crassus had no desire to see his old rival gain any new success and Clodius was eager to humiliate him. The shortage of grain furnished the mob leader with a good ground of attack, as Pompey had not yet been able to relieve the situation. He availed himself of this while taking further advantage of the great general's half-concealed ambitions in the Egyptian matter. One meeting of the people as described by Cicero will be sufficient for the present purpose.

Pompey spoke, or rather wished to speak. For as soon as he got up Clodius's ruffians raised a shout, and throughout his whole speech he was interrupted, not only by hostile cries, but by personal abuse and insulting remarks. However, when he had finished his speech—for he showed great courage in these circumstances, he was not cowed, he said all he had to say, and at times had by his commanding presence even secured silence for his words—well, when he had finished, up got Clodius. Our party received him with such a shout—for they had determined to pay him out—that he lost all presence of mind, power of speech, or control over his countenance. This went on up to two o'clock—Pompey having finished his speech at noon—and every kind of abuse, and finally epigrams of the most outspoken indecency were uttered against Clodius and Clodia. Mad and livid with rage Clodius, in the very midst of the shouting, kept putting questions to his claque : ' Who was it that was starving the commons to death ? ' His ruffians answered, ' Pompey '. ' Who wanted to be sent to Alexandria ? ' They answered, ' Pompey '. ' Whom did they wish to go ? ' They answered, ' Crassus '. . . . About three o'clock, as though at a given signal, the Clodians began spitting at our men. There was an outburst of rage. They began a movement for forcing us from our ground. Our men charged : his ruffians turned tail. Clodius was pushed off the rostra : and then we too made our escape for fear of mischief in the riot.[1]

Amid such scenes as this Pompey might well feel that he had fallen into the depths once more. He told Cicero that Clodius and his other enemies were being backed by Crassus and that plots were being formed against his life. To protect himself he called in his friends from the country as an offset to the Roman mob.[2] The triumvirate seemed to have gone completely to pieces. Caesar was away in Gaul while at

---

[1] *Letters,* i. 213–14 ; *Q. Fr.,* ii. 3.      [2] *Letters,* i. 215 ; *Q. Fr.,* ii. 3.

home Pompey and Crassus had abandoned all pretence of
friendship or co-operation and Clodius, the irresponsible mob
leader, held the streets, checked only by the rival gangs of
Milo. Under these circumstances a revival of the senate's
power seemed not only possible but probable. Already the
conservatives had secured the control of the chief magistracy
of the republic, since the two consuls for 56 B.C. were both of
their party [1] and largely under the influence of Cato.[2] The
conscript fathers could thus dominate the executive branch
of the government and they had looked on well content while
the consul Marcellinus signalized his year of office by supporting Cicero against Clodius and by thwarting Pompey's
unavowed ambition to be dispatched to Alexandria. As the
year went by their hopes rose higher and they dreamed that
the senate's supremacy might be entirely restored. They
began to talk of putting an end to Caesar's career of conquest
in Gaul and of acting on the suggestion of Clodius by annulling
his laws. Domitius Ahenobarbus, who was now a candidate
for the consulship, declared openly that he would deprive
Caesar of his command,[3] and Cicero, probably dragged on by
his party, announced that he would raise the question of the
Campanian lands in the senate. The optimates were soon to
find that they had made a tactical mistake. Their threats
served to drive the three together again and the fear of a conservative revival led straight to a renewal of the triumvirate.

However great their personal hostility, neither Pompey
nor Crassus had any wish to see the senate again in control.
The millionaire's imagination had been fired by Caesar's
victories and he was ardently desirous of military glory for
himself. Great as was his influence among the needy nobles
in the senate, he must have realized that this body would
never give him an army of its own free will. Pompey on his

---

[1] The determination of the triumvirs that neither of the consuls should
preside at the election for the next year when Crassus and Pompey were to
be candidates is evidence of the party standing of the two consuls. See
also the references in the next note.

[2] Plutarch, *Cato Minor*, 39. That the consuls acted in harmony is shown
by Cicero. *Letters*, i. 220 ; *Q. Fr.*, ii. 6.                    [3] Suetonius, 24.

side saw the provision for his veterans, that had caused him so much trouble, threatened by the nobles. The senate had indeed given him the charge of the grain supply, but they had given less than he wished, though all for which he dared openly to ask, and they had refused him the Egyptian command. It was plain that they neither liked nor trusted him and that, if he were again to command an army, he must look elsewhere. Both men were prepared to realize that they had allowed their personal dislike to carry them too far, and both were ready, if their personal ambitions were gratified, to patch up their coalition once more. Caesar, on his side, was no less anxious to renew the combination. The senate's animosity he must have realized very fully. If it gained control of the government in Rome, he could cherish few illusions as to what he might expect. Already they had shown their hand as a result of their overconfidence. The question of the consular provinces for 54 B.C. was then before the house. The senate could not, indeed, revoke the Vatinian law or interfere with its provisions. But it will be remembered that under this law Caesar was given the governorship of Cisalpine Gaul and Illyricum only. His most important province, Transalpine Gaul, from which as a base he was actually carrying on his great campaign, he held only from year to year by the vote of the senate. The conscript fathers could legally dispose of this province with entire freedom, and, if they chose, could supersede Caesar there at the close of 55 B.C. and could thus bring his military career to an abrupt close. Unless he were prepared to begin a civil war there and then, which was not by any means the case, it was vitally important to him that his command in Transalpine Gaul should not be interfered with. This he could hope for only if his former partners would come to his assistance, and if they were to do so, he must be prepared to pay them whatever they demanded for their help. Thus for the second time the necessities of his position forced him to play the part of peacemaker and to employ all his talents to reconcile Pompey and Crassus with each other. In this he was entirely successful. It was arranged that his two partners should visit him at Luca, a small town near the frontier of his province, and here the triumvirate was renewed and its programme for the immediate future settled.

The terms of the agreement were not at once made public, and when they were the triumvirate was found to be a very different thing from what it had been at the start. In the first combination Caesar had reaped the greater part of the profits. Now his partners claimed their share. It was too much to expect that they would consent to leave all the armed strength of the coalition to one of its members, even if they had had no military ambitions of their own. They determined that the military forces of the coalition should be increased and that each of the three partners should have his share. Accordingly it was resolved that Pompey and Crassus should both hold the consulship again, and that at the expiration of their year of office both should receive important proconsular provinces. What these should be was likewise decided in advance. Pompey was assigned the two Spains with an army, and Crassus was to receive Syria with another army. These commands were to be held for the term of five years, and to balance these concessions Caesar's term in Gaul was to be extended for the same length of time. For giving his consent to these arrangements, which armed his partners for a possible future struggle with himself, Caesar has been blamed by some modern critics. Yet that the conditions which he granted to his colleagues would turn out to be dangerous to himself was something which could not be foreseen. It was certain that the two would never join their forces against him, and, hence, as long as they both lived, he might feel himself secure. Just how secure one can appreciate by trying to imagine what would have been the course of events when he and Pompey came to the final struggle for supremacy if the East had been occupied by Crassus with a strong army under his command. It is obvious that in such circumstances, if Pompey had dared to draw the sword at all, he must have surrendered almost at once to one or the other of the two. With Caesar rushing at him from the north, he could not, as he did, elude his adversary by retreating to Greece. If he had ventured on the attempt, the forces of Crassus would have come upon him before his hastily raised army had been hammered into shape. While both his partners lived, therefore, Caesar was reasonably safe, and even the death of one of them might not prove disastrous if his army remained powerful and could be kept in friendly hands. The one event which could make the terms agreed upon at Luca involve a serious element of risk was the very thing that speedily befell. This was not merely the death of Crassus in the East, but his death in the midst of such an overwhelming disaster that his army was destroyed as a striking force.

We may conclude, therefore, that Caesar made no great mistake as things stood, or as their future development could be reasonably forecast. The immediate effect of the renewal of the combination left little to be desired by the three. As soon as it was known that they had come to terms, the opposition, lately so confident, collapsed. The men who had been attacking them made haste to sue for peace. Cicero, who had declared his intention of bringing before the senate the question of the Campanian lands, made haste to drop the subject and set to work composing what he himself described as his recantation. All men in silence waited to see what the three would do, for no one knew exactly on what terms they had renewed their league. The uncertainty was not of long duration, for Pompey and Crassus soon announced themselves as candidates for the consulship. The only man who tried to stand against them was prevented by mob violence from entering his candidacy, and the two were chosen without the slightest open contest. All that remained was to propose and enact the laws that gave effect to their arrangements for the provinces, and the compact of Luca had been carried out in all essential particulars. The attempt at a senatorial reaction had failed and the command of the army and the Roman world had been divided among the triumvirs.

# V. CAESAR

THE renewed triumvirate which seemed all-powerful in 55 B. C. was not destined to endure for any length of time. The close personal ties which bound two of its members together were loosened when in 54 Julia, the daughter of Caesar and the wife of Pompey, died suddenly. In the next year another blow of fate destroyed it entirely.

By the bargain concluded at Luca Crassus had received Syria for the term of five years. The millionaire, a capable soldier in his youth, had long been seeking an opportunity for military glory. His chance had now come and he seized it with eagerness. As governor of Syria he would have sole charge of Rome's relations with the rising power of Parthia. In the East he dreamed that he might rival the achievements of Caesar in Gaul and return to Rome with all the glory of a splendid conquest. A war with Parthia he found it easy to contrive, but the campaign, on which he embarked light-heartedly enough, proved far more difficult than he had anticipated. The Parthians were a new people with whom the Romans had but recently come in contact, and Crassus knew them no better than his fellow-countrymen. He failed to realize in advance of actual experience the nature of Parthian warfare, and he paid for his misunderstanding with his life. The strength of his adversaries lay in their light cavalry, and pitched battles formed no part of their strategy ; their plan was to retreat before the foe and draw him ever farther from his base of supplies until a favourable opportunity offered to cut off his communications and surround his army in a hostile country. Crassus fell into this trap, and as a consequence his army was destroyed and he himself treacherously slain, while attempting to negotiate with his foes.

The defeat and death of Crassus put an end to the triumvirate and left Caesar and Pompey face to face. The question of supremacy was one which could no longer be evaded or disguised. While the masters of the world were three in number one of the three could yield to the wishes of his two partners without too great humiliation ; whoever yielded now must openly take the second place himself and concede the leadership to the other. With the death of Crassus either Pompey or Caesar must be admittedly supreme, and the practical destruction of the army of Crassus removed a potent check on Pompey which might have prevented him from resorting to arms. It is unlikely that Pompey would have challenged both Caesar and Crassus, but against Caesar alone he dared to make a stand.

Besides the dissolution of the triumvirate, other forces were also tending in the direction of a struggle for supremacy. Pompey would hardly have ventured to oppose even Caesar alone without the support of the senate and its party. Such a combination, which at one time would have seemed almost impossible, was now fast becoming more or less inevitable. The chief cause for this was the growing fear of Caesar. His wonderful conquest of Gaul had not only given him a splendid military reputation but a powerful and devoted army as well. During his term as consul he had shown clearly his contempt for the constitution of the republic, and to many the most vital problem of the day seemed that of saving the state from his dictatorship. To accomplish this it was clear that Pompey must lead the opposing party. Indeed without him resistance was so hopeless that it might well be called impossible. There seemed but two alternatives open : either to submit to Caesar and accept his supremacy without a struggle, or to seek an alliance with Pompey and to make him the leader of those who sought to defend the republic against the unscrupulous proconsul of the Gauls. Neither alternative was pleasant to the Roman aristocracy, but there was little hesitation as to which was the less bad. The nobles neither loved nor trusted Pompey and they cherished many deep resentments against him, but these

feelings were much weaker than the fear and hatred with
which they regarded Caesar. As the menace from Caesar
seemed to them to grow more and more ominous, the
senatorial party was driven to seek an alliance with his rival.

It was the mob of Rome that gave the final impulse to
the reconciliation. From the close of 55 B. C., when Pompey
and Crassus laid down the consulship, the city had been
left to all intents and purposes without a government. The
triumvirs, having gotten what they wanted for themselves,
were satisfied to let matters drift, but so long as their combination existed it was strong enough to prevent the senate
from taking any vigorous or efficient action. Meanwhile
the three were occupied with their own interests : Caesar
was absent in Gaul, Crassus departed for Syria even before
his year as consul had expired, Pompey remained in Italy,
it is true, but made no move to interfere in politics. As
proconsul of the Spains he should have gone at once to his
province, but instead he stayed in Italy recruiting troops
for Spain and governing that country by his legates. This
was no doubt within the letter of the law, but it was clearly
a violation of its spirit. There was no fixed rule as to when
a governor should set out for his province, but it had certainly
never been intended that a proconsul of Spain should remain
in Italy for longer than was necessary to make the needful
preparations for taking over his command. Pompey, however, chose to linger near Rome and to keep at hand a considerable body of his newly recruited troops. Perhaps he
foresaw that the growing disorder would finally force the
senate to call on him for help and wished to be ready when
the time came. He was coming to fear the greatness of his
partner, and he had long been inclined toward an alliance
with the conservatives.[1] Hitherto his advances had been

---

[1] Pompey had shown himself very ill at ease during Caesar's consulship,
and his conduct afterwards in bringing Cicero back from exile and in other
matters at that time seems to show an attempt on his part to come to
terms with the senate. The conscript fathers, however, could not be induced to give him what he wanted and he turned again to Caesar and
renewed the triumvirate at Luca.

repulsed, but, if the nobles had at length learned their mistake, he was not likely to reject their overtures. In the meantime he adopted a policy of ' watchful waiting '.

With the government paralysed Rome was soon plunged in utter anarchy. The two triumvirs had hardly laid down the consulship when the turbulence broke out. The whole of 54 B. C. was a time of such disorder that it was found impossible to hold the regular consular elections. The next year opened without consuls, and when at last they could be chosen in a moment of temporary quiet, they were unable to relieve the situation. Clodius and Milo were both candidates for office and each was backed by a riotous mob. Their personal hatred of each other envenomed their political hostility and their perpetual clashes turned the Roman streets into a pandemonium. Pompey was the one man in Italy who had physical force behind him and he could—or would—do nothing without some show of legal right. This the senate alone could give him, but that body was not yet ready for such a step. In such a state of things elections were again impossible and the year 52 B. C. opened without magistrates in office. At the beginning of the year a climax was suddenly reached in the disorders. Clodius and Milo met by accident outside the city and Milo seized the unexpected opportunity to murder his opponent. The news of this event precipitated a final riot in Rome, where the followers of Clodius rose in fury on learning of the death of their favourite and burned his body and the senate house together. The situation was now felt to be quite unendurable. Fear of the mob, combined with the dread of Caesar, swept away the scruples of the conscript fathers and they decreed that Pompey should be named as sole consul to restore order. Even the rigid Cato yielded to the obvious necessity of the case and frankly owned that the constitution must bend if it were not to break entirely. Pompey's policy of watchful waiting had thus been justified by the result and he entered the city, dictator in all but name, and this at the invitation of his former foes.

With the troops at his disposal Pompey had little trouble in restoring order and quieting the mob. His sole consulship, however, went far beyond the terms agreed upon at Luca, but, though from the moment of his election Pompey began to draw near to the conservatives, he was far from ready for a definite break with Caesar. To placate his partner and probably to fulfil his pledges,[1] Pompey used all his influence to pass a law proposed by the ten tribunes allowing Caesar to stand for the consulship without coming to Rome in person. This concession satisfied Caesar and Pompey was left free to deal as he might choose with other matters. As soon as he had restored order he held the elections in due form and set to work with vigour to punish the most flagrant of the recent offenders. The juries were remodelled and the courts now met under the protection of his soldiers. Milo, in spite of his former services, was promptly brought to trial and banished for the murder of Clodius. Many others shared his fate and stringent laws were passed against violence and corruption at elections. These laws applied not only to the future but were made retroactive as well, and every public man in Rome was thus brought potentially within their scope. Means were thus found to expel from Italy the most turbulent of the Roman politicians and incidentally those most obnoxious to the senate, with which body Pompey's alliance grew constantly more close. As if to make his change of policy more evident, Pompey contracted a new marriage and this time chose his wife from an old aristocratic family identified with the conservative party. Soon after this he made his new father-in-law, Caecilius Metellus, his colleague in the consulship. This took from his position its unprecedented character but at the same time ranged him definitely upon the side of the senate.

The fears which the conservatives had long felt of Caesar's future action had been increased by recent events. The law

[1] It is not improbable that such a measure had been definitely agreed upon at Luca.

of the ten tribunes revealed his plans with an unmistakable
clearness. It was now obvious that Caesar planned to
become consul again without leaving his province or giving
up his army. But though his design was now known, this
very law created a legal tangle of such a sort that there
seemed no way in which he could be stopped. In order to
understand what followed it will be necessary to examine
this curious legal situation at some length.

As the law stood, Caesar's command in Gaul would
terminate in 50 B. C.,[1] but it would be impossible to supersede
him before January 1, 48. The legal complications which
brought this about were not accidental but were rather the
result of a deliberately contrived plan. Caesar meant to
be elected consul for the second time in the course of 49,
and he was fully determined not to give up his provinces
and army till he was ready to assume the consulship. He
had carefully worked out his arrangements for this purpose
and seemed certain of success. As proconsul of Gaul he had
a perfect right to remain in his province till his successor
arrived to take over the government, and, under the existing
legal system, it would be impossible for the senate to send
a successor before the beginning of 48, when Caesar would
be ready to leave, if he had not already left, for Rome.

The reasons for this may be briefly stated. Under the
Vatinian law Caesar's command would have expired March
1, 54 B. C., but in 55 his term had been prolonged by a law
proposed by Pompey and Crassus, the two consuls for that
year. This second term was for five years, like the first, and

---

[1] The date usually given by English historians is March 1, 49. The question as to the time when Caesar's proconsular command expired has given
rise to much discussion. A number of different dates have been suggested
and at present most German scholars seem inclined to favour 50. The
matter is discussed in the article on the *Lex Pompeia-Licinia* in the Appendix, where references are given to the various views on the subject.
For the purpose of this chapter the difference between the two years is
not very important. Whether Caesar's term ended in 50 or extended to
March 1, 49, it is certain that he meant to stay beyond it and that Pompey
was determined to prevent this. The events that followed must be interpreted in much the same fashion whichever date may be selected.

the new *quinquennium* was to be counted from the date of the passage of the law, that is from some time early in 55. The law, however, contained a peculiar clause which forbade any discussion of a successor to Caesar before March 1, 50.[1] Now since the Sempronian law required that the senate should select the consular provinces before the election of the consuls who were to receive them, this clause would make it impossible for the senate to assign the Gauls to the consuls for 50. The first consuls to whom Caesar's provinces could be assigned would be those for 49, but they would not be able to take over their commands till the end of the year, owing to their duties in Rome. The only way to supersede Caesar before 48 was, therefore, to make the Gauls praetorian rather than consular provinces. Against this Caesar had another weapon ready to his hand. The Sempronian law had deprived the tribunes of the power to veto the assignment of the consular provinces, but that right still held good in the case of the praetorian. If the senate should attempt to send out a propraetor to supersede Caesar, any one of the ten tribunes could interpose a veto, and Caesar intended to have at least one tribune always ready to protect his interests. With this legal tangle to protect him, Caesar could feel certain that if his candidacy *in absentia* were admitted, he could retain his provinces till the time arrived for him to go to Rome as consul, and that he would not be obliged to lay down one office before he was ready to take up the other.

In this situation what Caesar could do, and meant to do, was clear enough. Quitting Gaul at the last moment to assume the consulship in Rome, he would be able, during his year of office, to provide himself with a new proconsular command for any term he chose, and for this purpose he could take his pick among the provinces. No one could imagine for a moment that he would allow any legal or constitutional forms to stand in his way. The events of 59 were

---

[1] This may be considered as practically certain from the following passages : Cicero, *Letters*, ii. 78 ; *Fam.*, viii. 8 ; and Caesar (or better, Hirtius), *Gallic War*, viii. 53.

amply sufficient to dispel any such illusions. In all probability Cicero simply reflected the general opinion when he wrote to Atticus : ' Imagine him consul a second time after our experience of his former consulship ! " Why, comparatively weak as he was then," you say, " he was more powerful than the whole state." What, then, do you think will be the case now ? ' [1] If Caesar once became a candidate, it seemed impossible to prevent his election,[2] and once in office there was no hope of restraining him. That such a prospect should have made the blood of many senators run cold may easily be understood. Pompey alone could help them, and he was ready to do so since he had begun to share their apprehensions. It is quite unlikely that at this time he had any thought of war, but he had made up his mind that Caesar's plan of passing directly from one office to the other must be thwarted, and, on this point, at least, he was ready to join hands with the conservatives. In the correspondence of Cicero there are various passages that reveal Pompey's attitude during the next two years. While Cicero was absent in Cilicia his friend, Caelius Rufus, wrote to him the news in Rome. From these letters it is clear that in the course of 51 Pompey had resolved that Caesar must give up his army before he became consul.[3] Later, by the end of 50, the letters of Cicero himself to Atticus show that Pompey had come to fear the second consulship of Caesar, regardless of his army, declaring openly that it would mean the overthrow of the constitution.[4] It is possible that the change was due to the increasing influence of the conservatives, with whom Pompey's alliance grew constantly more close.

It is probable that the events of Caesar's first consulship had left a deep impression on the mind of Pompey. Caesar

---

[1] *Letters*, ii. 232 ; *Att.*, vii. 9. The words were written in December, 50, but the sentiment expressed must have been felt much earlier.

[2] The whole conduct of the conservatives makes this clear. Cicero never seems to have doubted Caesar's election if he stood for the office.

[3] *Letters*, ii. 51, 177, 196 ; *Fam.*, viii. 9, 11, 14.

[4] *Letters*, ii. 230 ; *Att.*, vii. 8. See also to the same effect *Letters*, ii. 232 *Att.*, vii. 9.

had then governed Rome as a dictator in defiance of the constitution. True, he had owed his power largely to Pompey and had used it largely for Pompey's benefit ; this did not modify Pompey's determination that Caesar should not be dictator of Rome again. In 59 Caesar had overawed all opposition, because he had an army to support by force his lawless acts, and Pompey was resolved that he should not do this a second time. If Caesar became consul while he still kept his province he might bring his troops to Rome under the pretence of a triumph—as Pompey had done in 70 B. C.— and restore the essential conditions of his dictatorship in 59. The only safeguard was to force him to surrender the command of his army before he became consul. This did not remove all danger, but it was the least that Pompey would consider. All this did not mean that Pompey clearly foresaw a war with Caesar. It was by no means certain that some compromise could not be agreed upon by which Caesar would give up his army while Pompey would concede him a second consulship. Perhaps in 52 Pompey would have consented to even more favourable terms to Caesar. At any rate neither Pompey nor the Roman world in general recognized as a fact that Caesar would fight rather than accept any terms that Pompey would grant. The civil war was yet hidden in the future.[1]

While Pompey was effecting his reconciliation with the conservatives Caesar's hands were tied by the last desperate revolt of the Gauls under Vercingetorix. This gave Pompey ample leisure to make his arrangements without serious interference. The first necessity was to break down the legal safeguards by which Caesar had defended his position. To accomplish this Pompey, during his consulship in 52, proposed a new law regulating the provincial administration. By this it was provided that there should henceforth be an interval of five years between the holding of a magistracy in Rome and the governorship of a province. Thus a consul or

---

[1] As late as December, 50, Pompey thought, or pretended to think, that Caesar would submit rather than fight. Cicero, *Letters*, ii. 230 ; *Att.*, vii. 8.

F

a praetor at the end of his year of office would become a
private citizen for five years and would then be assigned
a province to govern as a proconsul or propraetor. For the
first few years after the passing of this law there would be
a shortage of governors, and this Pompey proposed to meet
by the assignment of governorships to such of the ex-magistrates as had not hitherto held a province. This law of
Pompey's repealed the Sempronian law which had hitherto
been in force and which protected Caesar so effectually. By
the new system the senate could appoint a successor to
Caesar as soon as his legal term expired.

Under the existing conditions in Rome, with Pompey
master of the city, the new law concerning the provinces was
passed without the least difficulty. The purpose was not
openly avowed, of course, but the law was justified as a
means of checking the furious competition for the offices
which had been recently convulsing Rome.[1] In spite of such
disguise the real object could hardly be doubted, especially
when Pompey introduced and carried another law, one clause
of which required that a personal canvass should be made by
all candidates for office. This directly repealed the special
privilege just given Caesar and he naturally protested. Pompey, perhaps not yet sure of the conservatives, gave way and
added a provision exempting Caesar, but, as he made this
change in his bill after it had been voted by the people, its
legal force was somewhat doubtful.[2]

Caesar's position was thus completely changed. He could
no longer count with certainty on going directly from the
proconsulship to the consulship, but might find himself
during some months a private citizen. The danger of this
was clear enough. Under the Roman law a man could not
be prosecuted in the courts while he retained the *imperium*,
but the moment that he laid it down he could be called on to

---

[1] Dio says that the law had been proposed by the senate in the preceding
year with this object. Dio, xl. 46.

[2] Suetonius, *The Deified Julius*, 28. Marcellus in 51 argued that Caesar's
privilege had been cancelled, but Cicero seems to regard it as still in force.
See *Letters*, ii. 228 ; *Att.*, vii. 7 ; and also *Letters*, iii. 121 ; *Fam.*, vi. 6.

answer for his acts. Now some of Caesar's enemies were firmly resolved to bring him to trial as soon as he became a private citizen. For this his career, whether in Rome or Gaul, would furnish ample grounds. His trial would take place before courts controlled by Pompey, and, even if he should be acquitted, the mere fact of prosecution would debar him from becoming a candidate for office until the trial was finished. That Caesar feared this we have contemporary evidence. During the year that Cicero was absent in Cilicia Caelius Rufus wrote to him that ' Caesar is fully persuaded that he cannot be safe if he quits his army '.[1] Asinius Pollio, one of Caesar's officers, has left on record the story that after the battle of Pharsalia, as Caesar gazed upon the field of his great victory, he exclaimed, ' They would have it so. After so many great deeds, I, Gaius Caesar, would have been condemned if I had not sought the help of my army.' [2] It may

---

[1] *Letters*, ii. 196–7 ; *Fam.*, viii. 14.

[2] The exclamation of Caesar is quoted from Pollio by both Plutarch and Suetonius. (Plutarch, *Caesar*, 46 ; Suetonius, *The Deified Julius*, 30.) There is also evidence that threats of prosecution were openly made against Caesar. It should be noted that the law of Pompey against corruption at elections was made retroactive and all persons who had been candidates for office in Rome since 70 B. C. were liable under it. This looks very much as if the conservatives feared that they could not get evidence from Gaul in time to use against Caesar and devised the provisions of this law so that they could prosecute him on a charge for which the evidence was available in Rome. Did Pompey intend to make such a use of the law ? Some have held that he had no clear understanding of the law but had merely passed what his conservative friends asked for without seeing the real significance of the clauses in question. Meyer (*Caesars Monarchie*, 243 note 1) thinks that this theory credits Pompey with a degree of naïveté that is incredible. This seems reasonable, but there is one objection. Cicero in his letters ignores this danger to Caesar. From this we can hardly help inferring that the orator did not take it very seriously. If Pompey had any intention of using the law against Caesar, it is highly probable that Cicero would have known it. The great general was no adept at concealment, and the description of Caelius Rufus had much truth when he wrote that Pompey ' is accustomed to think one thing and say another, and yet is not clever enough to conceal his real aims '. (*Letters*, ii. 16 ; *Fam.*, viii. 1.) Perhaps the explanation is that Pompey had no intention of using the law against Caesar himself, but did mean to employ it to get rid of a number of politicians, some of them Caesar's partisans. It would obviously be much easier to persuade Cicero of the sincerity of such an

be considered certain that Caesar was fully convinced that
for him to become a private citizen would not only mean the
end of his career, but that he would be in great danger unless
protected from his enemies by an official position. Moreover,
it was much more than his personal fortunes that was involved. Even if Caesar had been ready to sacrifice his own
career and run the risk of being made a victim of the fierce
resentment of the Roman nobles, he had the interests of his
army to consider. His veterans would certainly expect such
an allotment of lands as Pompey's soldiers had received, and
Pompey's experience had made it clear that if Caesar should
lay down the sword and retire to private life, his men would
remain unrewarded for their years of service. The senate
hated Caesar far more intensely than they had Pompey when
he returned from the war against Mithridates, and, if Pompey
had been unable to get anything from the conscript fathers,
Caesar could hardly expect more generous treatment. In
addition to his personal ambition and apprehensions, the
pressure of his army and his obligations to his soldiers would
compel Caesar to fight for his position if necessary. Hence,
in all the negotiations that followed, Caesar clung desperately
to this one point : he must succeed to the consulship without
becoming, even for a short time, a private citizen. But this
was just the one thing that his opponents would not yield.
Because of this, the later attempts at compromise were futile
and amounted to little more than playing for position, each
party trying to cast upon the other the odium of appearing
as the aggressor.

While providing himself with a legal weapon against Caesar,
Pompey was not likely to leave his own position weakened
by any doubts or questions which a little legislation could
remove. By entering the city he had, according to the

attitude than it would Caesar. Whatever the solution of the difficulty, it
seems clear that Cicero was very little concerned about any risk that
Caesar might run from a prosecution. Even if Caesar could have been
convinced as to Pompey's intentions, he might reasonably doubt whether
Pompey could control the conservatives once the menace of the Gallic
legions was removed by Caesar's laying down the command of his army.

Roman law, forfeited his proconsular *imperium*. He had no intention of giving up his provinces and he was shrewd enough to wish to avoid any legal difficulties in the future. He, therefore, took the precaution of having his Spanish command extended for some years, which would prolong his powers for some time beyond those of Caesar. The future thus secured, Pompey was ready to lay down the consulship and to resume his former practice of governing Spain from the country towns around Rome and in other parts of Italy. He doubtless felt confident that, when the time came, he could force Caesar either to renounce the second consulship altogether, or to take it on conditions which would deprive his tenure of the office of its dangers. If Pompey kept an army ready at hand in Italy while Caesar was obliged to surrender the legions of Gaul, it might be possible to hold him within such limits as Pompey should see fit to impose.[1]

By the beginning of 51 B. C. Pompey had completed his arrangements, and Caesar also was free to act, but neither had any desire to force an immediate crisis. Whatever feelings might actuate reckless and violent partisans, the Roman world at large shrank back from civil war. Whoever struck the first blow would have to bear a heavy responsibility, and, if he seemed to act on slight or frivolous pretexts, he would find public opinion strongly in favour of his adversary. It was true that public opinion had lost much of its former weight, but it was still a force that neither of the rivals cared to disregard. As a consequence they temporized and sought to put each other in the wrong. Caesar could not have marched on Rome as he did if Italian opinion had been decidedly against him, as might have been the case if he had

---

[1] On the eve of the civil war Pompey threatened to go to Spain if Caesar became consul. However, by that time Pompey had committed himself much further than at the beginning of 51 and he was trying to frighten the conservatives into supporting him more vigorously than some of them wished to do. The letters of Cicero show that he had then come to object to the second consulship of Caesar on any terms. The earlier plan of Pompey may have been, as suggested above, to let Caesar have the second consulship and to remain in Italy at the head of an army. See Cicero, *Letters*, ii. 232 ; *Att.*, vii. 9.

struck in 51. Pompey, on his side, not only needed to gain public sympathy as completely as possible, but he was still too ill at ease among his new allies to be in haste.

The difficulties of Pompey in dealing with the conservatives are made sufficiently clear in Cicero's letters. It is probable that while the revolt of Vercingetorix rendered Caesar powerless to strike, the whole conservative party had supported Pompey in breaking down the legal defences of the common enemy, but not all of them were ready to go the length of civil war. When an armed struggle seemed imminent many hesitated and would gladly have drawn back. At the last moment there was a considerable section of the party which wished to come to terms rather than fight. Some, no doubt, feared Caesar's army, others distrusted Pompey, feeling that his success in a war, far from saving the republic, would merely make him its master in place of Caesar. This was Cicero's conviction and it was plainly shared by many in the senate. This division among his supporters must have occasioned Pompey much anxiety, and at times he may have doubted how far he could trust the wavering conservatives. But in fact the senate had little choice and the decision lay with Pompey ; if he had sufficient confidence in his own strength to force a crisis, the conscript fathers could do nothing except follow him, however reluctant they might be, or however much they might condemn his policy. Cicero expressed these sentiments more than once to Atticus. The orator shrank from civil war and would have preferred any other solution. He distrusted Pompey and feared his victory almost as much as his defeat. In the critical December of 50 B.C. when the negotiations reached the breaking-point he wrote frankly, .

> The political situation gives me greater terror every day. For the loyalists are not, as people think, united. . . . What we want is peace. From a victory, among many evil results, one, at any rate, will be the rise of a tyrant.[1] ' Fight ', say you, ' rather than be a slave.' To what end ? To be proscribed, if beaten : to be

[1] *Letters*, ii. 224–5 ; *Att.*, vii. 5.

a slave after all, if victorious ? ' What do you mean to do, then ? '
say you. Just what animals do, who when scattered follow the
flocks of their own kind. As an ox follows a herd, so shall I
follow the loyalists or whoever are said to be loyalists, even if they
take a disastrous course.[1]

After the war had begun he declared bitterly, ' There is now
no question of the constitution. It is a contest of rival
kings.' [2] Yet whatever he might feel, however much he
might prefer to do ' anything rather than fight ', as he himself declared, he knew that he was powerless and that his
eloquence could no longer alter the course of events. He saw
this clearly and expressed it candidly when he told his
friend : ' What is to happen when the consul says : *Your
vote, Marcus Tullius ?* I shall answer in a word : " I vote
with Gnaeus Pompeius." Nevertheless, in private, I shall
exhort Pompey to keep the peace.' [3]

Under such conditions Pompey did not dare, even if he
wished, to launch a direct attack on Caesar. His policy was
to thwart Caesar's plans by strictly legal means, and, if
Caesar refused to accept the check, to throw on him the
odium of a resort to arms. On his side Caesar was determined not to be outmanœuvered in this fashion. In spite of
Pompey's new legislation, intended chiefly, if not entirely,
to accomplish his defeat, he meant to defend himself with
every legal weapon at his disposal, seeking to thrust the
responsibility for provoking war upon his adversary.

As soon as he had disposed of Vercingetorix, Caesar began
the diplomatic game. Early in 51 B.C. he made his first
demands upon the senate. Probably he had little hope of a
complete success, but he may have aimed at forcing Pompey
to come out in the open and abandon his ambiguous attitude.
Hitherto Pompey had disclaimed any hostility to Caesar,
and the latter may have thought it possible by a bold move
to break up the alliance between Pompey and the conserva-

---

[1] *Letters*, ii. 228 ; *Att.*, vii. 7.
[2] *Letters*, ii. 374, and also to the same effect 219 and 293 ; *Att.*, x. 7, and
vii. 3, and viii. 11.
[3] *Letters*, ii. 219–20, and also 226 and 229 ; *Att.*, vii. 3, 6, and 7.

tives before it became firmly cemented. Whatever his expectations were, Caesar put forward the demand that the potential menace to his position in the recent laws of Pompey should be removed by an extension of his *imperium* in Gaul until the end of 49. If this were granted, Pompey's recent legislation would lose all force against Caesar, but would still accomplish what Pompey had claimed was its sole object. Caesar justified his demand by arguing that the law of the ten tribunes had extended his *imperium* by implication.[1] On the face of it this law had merely given Caesar the right to become a candidate for the consulship in his absence. But he could urge with some show of reason that this privilege assumed that when the election was held he would still be the proconsul of Gaul. Reasonable or unreasonable, this request brought no result.

If Caesar wished to draw Pompey into the open, the conservatives were no less eager to accomplish the same result. One of the consuls, Marcellus, who was an ardent partisan of the senate, proposed to supersede Caesar in his provinces at once before his legal term had expired. But this was going much too fast for Pompey, and the matter was allowed to drop. The conservatives were still uncertain of their leader's attitude, and Cicero was asked to try to discover his intentions. The orator was then on his way to take up the governorship of Cilicia under Pompey's new law. He had an interview with Pompey in the south of Italy and wrote back the cheering information that Pompey was an admirable citizen, prepared to meet any emergency. Doubtless his correspondent, Caelius Rufus, could read between the lines when Cicero added, ' For he takes the same view, as we ever do, as to who are good and bad citizens.' [2]

Encouraged by this and other similar reports, the nobles

---

[1] Cicero recognized the justice of Caesar's claim when he wrote to Atticus, ' Do I approve of votes being taken for a man who is retaining an army beyond the legal day ? For my part, I say *no* ; nor in his absence either. But when the former was granted him, so was the latter'. *Letters*, ii. 228 ; *Att.*, vii. 7.

[2] *Letters*, ii. 33 ; *Fam.*, ii. 8.

renewed the proposal to supersede Caesar, but in a much more moderate form. In September the senate voted that the question of a successor to Caesar should be brought before that body on the first of March of the following year. Caesar's tribunes offered no objection to this, but when his opponents sought to go farther than a mere discussion and to prevent the use of the tribunes' veto in the future, they promptly interposed. The chief result of the debate was the declaration which was drawn from Pompey. He spoke in favour of the discussion of the question of a successor to Caesar and when asked what he would do if the resolutions of the senate were vetoed by the tribunes, he replied that it made no difference whether Caesar refused to obey the senate, or secured some one to prevent the senate from passing a decree. This certainly amounted to a threat, though he still refused to treat the suggestion of war seriously, and when asked as to his course if Caesar should determine to keep his army and to be consul both, he answered only with the query, ' What if my son should choose to strike me with his stick ? ' [1]

By his declaration as to his attitude in case one of Caesar's tribunes tried to use his veto, Pompey had joined hands with the conservatives in an unmistakable manner, but still with a half-hearted effort to leave open a retreat. Enough had now been said to render such a retreat improbable, and, though Pompey perhaps did not yet wish to face the fact, Caesar must henceforth have reckoned him an open enemy. His union with the conservatives had, moreover, been skilfully executed ; he had allied himself with them, yet without giving Caesar a decent pretext to draw the sword. Though the proconsul of Gaul was well aware of the real meaning of his rival's course, all that the public saw was that the senate was resolved to do its duty by taking under its consideration a grave public question and that Pompey, like a patriotic citizen, would protect its freedom of discussion. The conclusion to which the debate would lead was not yet known,

[1] These details are from a letter of Caelius Rufus to Cicero, then absent in Cilicia. *Letters*, ii. 76-8 ; *Fam.*, viii. 8.

and Caesar could not venture to begin a civil war on the ground that he might in the future be adversely affected by decrees which the senate had not yet passed, and, so far as the public probably could see, might never pass. The temper of the senate had not yet been openly shown and was in fact uncertain. Caesar might very well distrust it, and, though he could not fight on the issue of its probable future action, he would very naturally seek to arm himself against it.

In the election for 50 B.C. two opponents of Caesar had been returned as consuls, but in the elections for the tribunes he had been successful. This difference in the results in the two cases may readily be understood if it is borne in mind in what manner the voting was conducted. The votes in the Roman assembly were not counted by individuals but by groups. In the choice of the consuls the group by which the vote was taken was the century ; this was based on property in such a way that the wealthy class enjoyed an influence out of proportion to their number. In the tribunician elections, on the other hand, the voting was by tribes, and in the division of the people into tribes property was not considered.[1] On this occasion the result was modified when the conservatives contrived to set aside the election of one of the tribunes and to replace him by one of their supporters in the person of C. Scribonius Curio. In doing this they had played directly into Caesar's hands. Probably they expected Curio to block any action of the other tribunes in favour of Caesar, and they had not considered what might happen if he should turn against them. Pompey in the senate had recently uttered a warning against any action by a tribune known as Caesar's partisan. That astute leader, therefore, determined to avail himself of the services of an enemy. Such action would leave Pompey helpless to follow up his threat, for it would be absurd to hold Caesar responsible for what his adversaries did. Thus Curio was in a position to be of much greater use to Caesar than an avowed supporter could have been. The reckless life of the new tribune had

[1] Cicero plainly regards the lower classes as favourable to Caesar.

left him overwhelmed with debt, while Caesar had the plunder
of Gaul at his disposal. A bargain was soon struck and
Curio, for an enormous bribe, agreed to play Caesar's game,
but to refrain as long as possible from coming out openly
upon his side. By this unexpected move Caesar was able
to block Pompey's plans, and all the better because of Pompey's own law concerning the provinces. By that measure
Pompey had repealed the Sempronian law to enable the
senate to send out a successor to Caesar as soon as his term
expired. In doing this, he overlooked the fact that he had
also repealed the limitation which the Sempronian law had
placed upon the tribunes' veto which debarred the tribunes
from all interference with the assignment of the consular
provinces by the senate. This clause had been repealed
along with the rest of the law, and Curio was thus armed
with the power to stop *any* provincial appointments, whether
consular or praetorian, a point which Pompey was soon
destined to discover and regret.

Curio began his tribuneship by making various bids for
popularity. He still posed as an enemy of Caesar but began
more and more to assume the tone of an independent patriot
and to harass Pompey with specious proposals which the
latter could not very well refuse and yet was wholly unwilling to accept. The discussion of the provinces which had
been set for March failed to reach any conclusion. Curio and
one of the consuls whose neutrality Caesar had secured with
gold were probably in part responsible for this. When other
means seemed likely to fail, Curio proposed, as a solution of
all difficulties, the simultaneous retirement of both Caesar
and Pompey. When this suggestion was brought forward
Pompey was ill in southern Italy. He wrote at once to the
senate saying that he was ready to lay down his command
in Spain whenever those who had bestowed it on him might
request. This sounded well but Curio found it much too
vague. On his side Pompey made an offer of compromise,
and intimated that he would consent that Caesar should
remain in Gaul until November 13. This, from Caesar's

point of view, was valueless, and Curio resolutely opposed
it while pressing his own demand of a joint resignation.
Cicero's correspondent in Rome, Caelius Rufus, summed up
the situation in these words :

> Pompey as yet seems to have thrown all his weight on the side
> of the senate's wish that Caesar should leave his province on the
> 13th of November.  Curio is resolved to submit to anything
> rather than allow this : he has given up all his other proposals.[1]
> Our people, whom you know so well, do not venture to push
> matters to extremes.  The situation turns entirely on this :  Pom-
> pey, professing not to be attacking Caesar, but to be making an
> arrangement which he considers fair to him, says that Curio is
> deliberately seeking pretexts for strife.  However, he is strongly
> against, and evidently alarmed at, the idea of Caesar becoming
> consul-designate before handing over his army and province. . . .
> Mark my words—if they push their suppression of Curio to
> extremes, Caesar will interpose in favour of the vetoing tribune ;
> if, as it seems they will do, they shrink from this, Caesar will stay
> in his province as long as he chooses.[2]

On the main question the senate came to no conclusion,
since it would not put pressure on Curio to compel him to
withdraw his veto of any decrees concerning the provinces.
They did, however, pass one decree, that Pompey and Caesar
should each contribute one legion for a campaign against
Parthia.  To meet this demand Pompey withdrew a legion
which he had loaned to Caesar and Caesar had to furnish one
of his own.  Both thus came from Caesar's army and the
proposal had the effect of weakening his forces.

In August the elections for the ensuing year were held ;
Caesar's candidate for the consulship was defeated, but
among the tribunes he secured the return of two of his supporters, namely Cassius and Mark Antony.  The existing
deadlock seemed likely, therefore, to be indefinitely prolonged.  This very fact rendered the extreme conservatives
more desperate, and, at the same time, some baseless rumours
gave them greater boldness.  When the legions for the Par-

[1] Perhaps the various bills he had brought in as bids for popularity.
[2] *Letters*, ii. 176–7 ; *Fam.*, viii. 11.

thian war arrived, a report began to circulate that all was
not well with Caesar's army ; it was said that the men were
weary of his never-ending wars and that they would fight
for him no more. These rumours, credited by many, led the
conservatives to force the issue. Accordingly in December
the question of his successor was again brought up. The
consul, Marcellus, demanded that Caesar be declared an out-
law if he failed to surrender his army and province on a fixed
day. The senate voted the decree while Curio sat silent in
his place. Proceeding farther, the consul made the proposal
that Pompey should give up his command in Spain. As thus
put, it seemed a direct affront to Pompey and the senate
promptly rejected it. Then, and not till then, did Curio
arise. He, did not attempt to use his veto, but demanded
a vote upon the motion that both men should lay down their
extraordinary powers. Perhaps the senators were frightened
when they realized that the decree, as it had just been voted,
was an open declaration of war ; probably most of them
were eager to grasp at what appeared a chance of compromise. Whatever the motive, in spite of seeming inconsistency, the senate now by a vote of 370 to 22 accepted
Curio's resolution. Thus by the venal tribune's clever move
Pompey was practically defeated and placed in an embarrassing position. If he refused to comply, he, and not Caesar,
was in revolt against the senate. If he agreed, he would
disarm himself before his enemy. The play for position had
ended in a victory for his rival, and, if the latter could make
use of his advantage, public opinion might be ranged upon
his side. From the dilemma in which Pompey found himself
only the sword could extricate him, and so at last he nerved
himself for the resort to war. The magistrates in office were
his friends, as against Caesar at least, and they prepared to
try to find some fragment of legal justification for their chief.
Marcellus a few days later made a strong effort to induce the
senate to declare Caesar a public enemy, and, failing in this,
he left Rome and went to join Pompey, then in Naples,
calling on him to take up arms and save the state.

Pompey promptly accepted the invitation and proceeded to Luceria to assume command of the two legions destined for the war with Parthia and temporarily stationed there. As proconsul of Spain he had no legal authority over them, and the senate had passed no formal decree assigning them to him.  His rights in the case rested wholly on the consuls' declaration of martial law and summons to himself to act. He thus cast in his lot with the extremist element in the senate which was bent on war, and this at the very moment when his violence and haste would stand out in the most striking contrast to the moderate and conciliatory bearing of his opponent.  For Caesar was quick to take advantage of the skilful move of Curio.  The latter left Rome as soon as his term of office expired on the 10th of December and hastened to Caesar's headquarters in Cisalpine Gaul.  From here he hurried back bearing a letter from Caesar to the senate.  In this Caesar recounted his services and professed himself quite willing to lay down his command if Pompey would but do the same.  In brief he declared himself prepared to render due obedience to the vote of the senate.  What would have happened had his offer been accepted we can only guess.  Probably Pompey was too deeply committed to draw back, and Caesar was well aware of it before he wrote his letter.  Certainly nothing less than such an attitude on his part could have enabled him to reap the full advantage of Curio's victory in the senate.

There are clear indications that Pompey's hasty violence produced a reaction in the public mind.  In that critical December after Pompey had taken arms, Cicero wrote to Atticus :

The political situation gives me greater terror every day.  For the loyalists are not, as people think, united.  How many Roman knights, how many senators, have I seen prepared to inveigh against the whole policy, and especially the progress through Italy now being made by Pompey.[1]

In another letter he declares that he knows of no class that

_Letters_, ii. 224 ;  _Att._, vii. 5.

can be called loyalists and expresses doubts as to the knights.[1]
In yet another he affirms that he has met scarcely any one
who does not think it better to yield to Caesar's demands
than to fight.[2] After Caesar's last offers were rejected, Cicero
speaks of his party's most insane decision,[3] and after the
war had begun, when he notes the revulsion of feeling in
Caesar's favour, he exclaims, ' What grave mistakes and vices
on our side are accountable for this I cannot think of without
sorrow '.[4] These feelings cannot have been wholly lost upon
even the most reckless partisans of war, and they were all
the more determined to drag the senate after them and so to
gain some better legal standing for their leader.

Pompey was now fully committed to the side of war. In
that same December Cicero reported a long conversation
with him to Atticus, declaring that Pompey had no wish for
peace, having become convinced that if Caesar became consul, even after giving up his army, it would mean the overthrow of the constitution.[5] All that remained, therefore,
was for Pompey to force the senate to declare itself upon
his side.

The last stormy sessions of the conscript fathers need not
be recounted at length. Timid senators still shrank back,
Caesar's tribunes interposed and forced the reading of his
letter mentioned above against the wishes of the consuls.
On the senate it seems to have produced little effect.
Although conciliatory in tone it ended with a threat which
may have angered the hesitating members. In any case, in
view of Pompey's attitude, the proposal of a joint resignation could lead to no result, since the senate had no means
of forcing Pompey to accept. Caesar seems to have instructed
his friends to make still other offers to the senate in case
those in his letter were rejected. Of his provinces he consented to give up all except Cisalpine Gaul and Illyricum,
and of his army all except two legions. In return he

---

[1] *Letters*, ii. 227–8 ; *Att.*, vii. 7.     [2] *Letters*, ii. 225 ; *Att.*, vii. 6.
[3] *Letters*, ii. 241 ; *Att.*, vii. 10.     [4] *Letters*, ii. 304 ; *Att.*, viii. 13.
[5] *Letters*, ii. 230 ; *Att.*, vii. 8.

demanded only that he be permitted to retain these until he
should have been elected consul. Pompey seems to have
been more or less inclined to accept these offers, but the
consuls rejected them.[1] All efforts at compromise having
failed, nothing was left the senate but to take a final decision.
Pompey threatened, urged, and encouraged, the wavering
were intimidated, and so, at last, the final vote was passed ;
Caesar's proposals were rejected and war was declared against
him. Caesar's tribunes vetoed the decree, and, the senate
having declared martial law, they left the house and fled to
join their master in the disguise of slaves.[2]

So finally, after long negotiations and intrigues, the
inevitable war had come, but the manner of its coming was
a blow to Pompey and his cause. His attempts to drive
Caesar into open illegality had failed, and, as a result, the
champions of the constitution began the struggle against
its enemy by breaking it themselves.[3] Their disregard of
the veto of Caesar's tribunes was, perhaps, justified by the
passage of the ' last decree ', but even so it gave a popular
pretext to their opponent of which he made prompt use.
More significant was the paradoxical position in which, as
a result of Caesar's tactics, they found themselves. The
conscript fathers had by a very large majority passed a vote
directed against both rival generals. After this they had,
almost at once, declared war on the one who offered to
obey and entrusted the command of all their forces to the
one who refused to comply with their decision. The defenders

---

[1] Appian, ii. 32 ; Cicero, Letters, iii. 121 ; Fam., vi. 6, may refer to these
offers.

[2] They appeared thus before his army, but it was probably only a
theatrical device. Cicero does not suggest that they had been in danger
(Letters, ii. 234 ; Fam., xvi. 11), nor does Caesar in his own account allege
real violence.

[3] Meyer (Caesars Monarchie, 274–5) contends that the action of the
consuls in appointing Pompey to command was legal. This may have been
the case, but it was nevertheless unconstitutional, just as a sudden wholesale creation of peers would be in England. To take the steps they did
without the authority of the senate for their action was directly counter to
the professed principles of the optimate party.

of the senate had themselves defied it and were now attacking Caesar as a traitor for offering to submit to its authority. Such must have been the way in which the events in Rome would strike many Italians who were not closely in touch with the inside realities of things, and that they should be given such an appearance was a victory for Caesar at the very beginning of the war, not yet a victory in the field but soon to be translated into one.

In January of 49 B.C., when the sword was actually drawn, neither party to the struggle was well prepared for war. While negotiations were in progress it was impossible for either side to take any step which would have been too obvious a menace to the other. When hostilities began the bulk of Caesar's forces were upon the farther side of the Alps,[1] and Pompey's army in Italy had yet to be recruited. Though both leaders were unready, there were shrewd observers in Rome, Cicero's friend Caelius Rufus among them,[2] who reckoned Caesar's army as the stronger of the two. Pompey, however, seems to have entered on the contest full of hope and confidence. A short time before the outbreak of the war Cicero had a long conversation with him and was much encouraged by Pompey's calm assurance of success and contempt for Caesar's power.[3] Later, when events had disillusioned him, the orator spoke bitterly of his leader's blindness and folly. That Pompey misjudged the whole situation is obvious enough, but it is possible to understand his blunder. In the first place he had reason to believe that Caesar's army was not entirely loyal to its chief. Such rumours had been spread in Rome by the officer

---

[1] Ferrero (*Greatness and Decline of Rome*, ii. 181) thinks that the presence of only one legion in Cisalpine Gaul shows that Caesar did not look upon war as possible. Yet to have brought his army across the Alps without a reasonable excuse would have been a direct provocation to Pompey and would have thrown the responsibility for the war on himself. If it was worth while to carry on negotiations at all it would have been folly to throw away all possible advantage from them.

[2] See his letter to Cicero, illuminated by his conduct during the war. *Letters*, ii. 197 ; *Fam.*, viii. 14.

[3] *Letters*, ii. 230–1 ; *Att.*, vii. 8.

who brought the two legions into Italy for the Parthian war, and, in addition to such reports, the ablest of all Caesar's lieutenants, Labienus, was now in communication with the senate and was soon to desert to Pompey's side. Even if Caesar's army did support him, it was in the Transalpine province and the newly conquered parts of Gaul. A revolt of the recently subdued territories might be expected if Caesar withdrew his troops, and such a rising might imperil his whole army and must terribly handicap him. If he dared to fight and if his soldiers followed him, it would require time to bring them across the Alps and this would give Pompey an opportunity to make the necessary preparations. It seems probable that Pompey took it for granted that Caesar would be unable to assume the offensive, but would be obliged to wait in Gaul for the attack of his enemies. If he did this, Pompey could hope to crush him between the Spanish army and the army to be raised in Italy.[1] The possibility of a sudden dash on Rome seems to have occurred to Pompey, but, if Caesar seized the city in this way, it would be a trap unless he held the towns between Rome and his province. If Italy rallied to Pompey and Caesar occupied Rome with a small force, he could be cut off from his army and crushed with ease. Pompey was supremely sure that the Italians were with him heart and soul ; for this the demonstrations which took place when he was ill in Naples were in part to blame.[2] In his confidence he lost sight of the disastrous effect of his diplomatic defeat and the illegal violence of his party's recent acts. But his antagonist was fully alive to the turn in public opinion which

[1] On the strategic situation, see Meyer, *Caesars Monarchie*, 289–90, and Kromayer in Hartmann and Kromayer, *Römische Geschichte*, 141–2. Kromayer thinks that Caesar was beaten in the diplomatic negotiations, but this seems to the present writer clearly an error. His discussion of the general military situation is admirable though brief. That Pompey considered the possibility of the capture of Rome is certain from Cicero, *Letters*, ii. 231 ; *Att.*, vii. 8. It is also clear that Cicero conceived Pompey's plan as indicated above, namely, to let Caesar occupy Rome and there cut him off. See *Letters*, ii. 232 ; *Att.*, vii. 9.

[2] Plutarch, *Pompey*, 57.

these things had provoked. Having succeeded in putting his opponent in the wrong, Caesar was not the man to lose the fruits of a hard-earned success for lack of daring or initiative. Without waiting for the bulk of his army he gathered up such forces as he had at hand and boldly crossed the Rubicon, a little river which formed the southern boundary of Cisalpine Gaul.

Had Italy been strongly upon Pompey's side the crossing of the Rubicon would have been followed by an immediate check, or ultimate disaster. But public sentiment had veered toward Caesar. Town after town threw open its gates to him without resistance, nowhere did any one attempt to make a stand, and Pompey's recruiting officers fled from his advancing cohorts. As he came swiftly on, Caesar caught the bewildered recruits gathered for Pompey's army and enrolled them in his own. Without serious opposition he pushed on into the heart of Italy.

The successful offensive of Caesar fell like a thunderbolt upon the senate and the nobles. Their army was still to make and the recruits did not pour in as they had expected. Cicero had been dispatched to Capua to assist the levy, and there, in the very district where Caesar had settled the veterans of Pompey, he confides to Atticus that ' the settlers do not make a very eager response '.[1] On the side of the conservatives there was only utter confusion and bitter disillusionment with Pompey. Cicero wrote to his friend :

How utterly incapable our general is you yourself observe, in having had no intelligence of the state of affairs even in Picenum : and how devoid of any plan of campaign, the facts are witness. . . . Every one agrees that he is in a state of abject alarm and agitation.[2]

But in the midst of the chaos among his enemies Caesar relentlessly advanced, and they were powerless to arrest his progress.

Pompey soon saw that it was useless to try to save the

[1] *Letters*, ii. 251 ; *Att.*, vii. 14.  [2] *Letters*, ii. 247 ; *Att.*, vii. 13a.

capital and decided to abandon it. This order, unexpected
by his supporters, moved them to fury at what they thought
his cowardice, but he knew his own weakness far too well
to risk a battle. Besides his raw recruits he had at hand
only the two legions so recently obtained from Caesar that
he dared not trust their loyalty. He hurriedly retreated to
the south, and the nobles had no choice but to follow him.
The senate and the magistrates left the city, forgetting in
their frantic haste a large amount of money in the public
treasury, and sought refuge in the camp of Pompey. Caesar
was thus left free to occupy Rome whenever he might choose.
The retreat of Pompey filled Cicero with the utmost indignation. ' As to our leader Gnaeus,' he exclaimed, ' what an
inconceivably miserable spectacle ! What a complete breakdown ! No courage, no plan, no forces, no energy ! I will
pass over his most discreditable flight from the city, his
abject speeches in the towns, his ignorance not only of his
opponent's, but even of his own resources—but what do you
think of this ? ' [1] and he proceeds to tell Atticus of the
forgotten money left in Rome. A little later he writes more
calmly but with almost as much bitterness :

As to my remark . . . that I preferred defeat with Pompey to
victory with those others, it is quite true : I do prefer it—but
it is with Pompey as he was then, or as I thought him. But with
a Pompey who flies before he knows from whom he is flying, or
whither, who has betrayed our party, who has abandoned his
country, and is about to abandon Italy—if I did prefer it, I have
got my wish : I am defeated.[2]

But though to Cicero, and doubtless to many others,
the abandonment of Rome seemed the end of all things, the
contest was by no means really settled by it. Pompey was
still in arms in Italy, though with but the one desire of
escaping across the sea as soon as possible. He had the raw
recruits from whom in time an army might be made, but he
was too experienced a soldier to dream that they were

[1] *Letters*, ii. 263 ; *Att.*, vii. 21.　　[2] *Letters*, ii. 288　*Att.*, viii. 7.

capable of meeting Caesar's veterans at once. His plan was
to seek safety in the East till he could put his levies into
shape. He precipitately retreated towards Brundisium, the
chief port of southern Italy, from which he could transport
his forces into Greece. Caesar, on his part, was bent on
cutting off his flight and ending the whole war in one short
campaign. It thus became a race between the two with
Brundisium as its goal, but rapid as were Caesar's move-
ments, when he reached the port he found his rival there
ahead of him and safe behind the walls.

Caesar's first campaign had been at once a brilliant
success and a failure. He had driven Pompey out of Italy,
but had been unable to end the war, and he must now face
a long and doubtful struggle. His position, far from being
secure, was really critical. Public opinion, won over to his
side by his success in the negotiations, had begun to turn
against him. The flight of Pompey, carrying with him the
magistrates and the leading senators, seemed to place the
whole machinery of legal government in his hands. Whoever
might have been the aggressor at the start, Pompey now
seemed the champion of the law. Appian expressly states
that after Pompey sailed from Brundisium public opinion
turned in his favour.[1] Cicero had noted the change in feeling
even earlier, as soon indeed as Pompey fled from Rome. On
January 19 he had written to Atticus :

There is an extraordinary outcry—I don't know what people
are saying with you, but pray let me know—at the city being
without magistrates or senate. In fact, there is a wonderfully
strong feeling at Pompey's being in flight. Indeed, the point of
view is quite changed : people are now for making no concessions
to Caesar.[2]

The change in sentiment was, no doubt, fostered by the
expectations men had entertained as to Caesar's policy.
Most seem to have anticipated a proscription like that of
Sulla. In December of 50 Cicero had said of him that he
would not be ' more merciful than Cinna in the massacre of

---

[1] Appian, ii. 40.      [2] *Letters*, ii. 242-3 ; *Att.*, vii. 11.

the nobility, nor less rapacious than Sulla in confiscating the property of the rich '.[1] After the war broke out Atticus expressed his fears of Caesar's probable cruelty and Cicero agreed with him that Caesar would ' spare no form of brutality '.[2] Later, when Caesar's course seemed to belie these apprehensions, Cicero grew sufficiently hopeful to doubt ' whether he will copy Phalaris or Pisistratus '.[3] Nevertheless, he found it very difficult to feel much confidence, and when Atticus expressed hopes of Caesar's moderation he retorted : ' How can he help behaving ruthlessly ? Character, previous career, the very nature of his present undertaking, his associates, the strength of the loyalists, or even their firmness, all forbid it.' [4] A personal interview with Caesar brought little encouragement, since the charm and courtesy of the leader were neutralized by the sight of his partisans and followers. Of them Cicero wrote to Atticus in deep disgust : ' For the rest, good heavens ! What a crew ! what an *inferno* ! to use your word . . . What a gang of bankrupts and desperadoes ! ' [5]

Yet Cicero discerned clearly that a policy of moderation and mercy might be to Caesar's advantage. He confessed this to his friend when he wrote :

By heaven, if he puts no one to death, nor despoils any one of anything, he will be most adored by those who had feared him most. The burgesses of the country towns, and the country people also, talk a great deal to me. They don't care a farthing for anything but their lands, their poor villas, their paltry pence. And now observe the reaction : the man in whom they once trusted they now dread : the man they dreaded they worship.[6]

This feeling was strengthened by the threats which Pompey's party were making against all who did not join them. Apart from any considerations of personal temperament, Caesar might think it well worth while to calm the frightened public and to make the contrast between himself and his opponents

[1] *Letters*, ii. 228 ; *Att.*, vii. 7.   [2] *Letters*, ii. 243 ; *Att.*, vii. 12.
[3] *Letters*, ii. 262 ; *Att.*, vii. 20.   [4] *Letters*, ii. 316 ; *Att.*, ix. 2a.
[5] *Letters*, ii. 353–4 ; *Att.*, ix. 18.   [6] *Letters*, ii. 304 ; *Att.*, viii. 13.

stand out as sharply as possible. In March Cicero had written
that ' Pompey has set his heart to a surprising degree on
imitating Sulla's reign. I am not speaking without book,
I assure you. He never made less of a secret of anything '.
From such a policy Cicero shrinks in horror, but fears the
same from Caesar.[1]

Though Caesar displayed great magnanimity from the
start, it was but slowly that even his supporters came to put
faith in his continuing this policy. In April Curio told
Cicero that ' Caesar was not by taste or nature averse from
bloodshed, but thought clemency would win him popularity :
if, however, he once lost the affection of the people, he would
be cruel '.[2] Only two days after this conversation with
Curio, Cicero received a letter from Caelius Rufus, who had
joined Caesar at the outbreak of the civil war, in which the
deserter told the hesitating consular frankly, ' If you think
that Caesar will maintain the same policy in letting his
adversaries go and offering terms, you are mistaken. His
thoughts, and even his words, forbode nothing but severity
and cruelty '.[3] Such expressions might be intended to
frighten Cicero and prevent his joining Pompey in the East,
but they may very well have meant that Caesar perceived the
drift of public sentiment toward his rival and was irritated
by it. Certainly he did not change his policy of clemency
and moderation, although he may have uttered threats.

The task that faced Caesar in Italy was one of serious
difficulty. He was compelled to improvise a government of
some sort and to do this with such materials as Pompey
had left behind. With most of the senate and the magistrates gone this problem was very far from simple, since,
to serve the ends for which it was designed, it was essential
for Caesar to give his government as much as possible the
appearance of legality. A senate, or some body which could
pass as such, was necessary for his purpose. He set to work
at once to gather at Rome as many of the senators as possible.

---

[1] *Letters*, ii. 325-6 ; *Att.*, ix. 7.  [2] *Letters*, ii. 365 ; *Att.*, x. 4.
[3] *Letters*, ii. 367 ; *Fam.*, viii. 16.

There were some few of the conscript fathers who were his partisans, and there were more who, either disgusted with Pompey or convinced that his cause was lost, now came over to his side. Yet among them all there was a woful lack of names that commanded popular respect. It would have been a real gain to his cause if he could have persuaded Cicero to join him. The orator, sent by Pompey to Capua, had remained there a prey to indecision and bitter misgivings until Caesar's advance had cut him off from Brundisium. On his way to Rome, after Pompey's flight to Greece, Caesar endeavoured to induce him to attend the meeting of the senate which he intended to call. But though at a personal interview Caesar pressed the orator with the greatest urgency, Cicero refused to lend the sanction of his name to what he regarded as a mockery of the senate.[1] So Caesar had to do the best he could without him. That best was only to establish a sort of provisional government at Rome under one of the praetors, while he himself prepared to fight the contest to a finish in the field.

As matters stood, Caesar was between the armies of his foe. Pompey had a large, though untrained, force in Greece and another strong army in Spain. Caesar might thus be attacked upon both sides at once. Unable to follow Pompey because of the lack of ships, he resolved to deal with Spain, confident that the lack of training on the part of Pompey's men would render him powerless to take the offensive for some time to come.

In Spain Caesar was successful in one swift campaign. Indeed no success, unless it were rapid, would have been of much avail, since his aim was simply to crush Pompey's forces there *before* his army in the East was ready for action. As it was, the generals of Pompey were defeated, and their forces were re-enlisted under Caesar or disbanded. The western army of his rival ceased to exist, and the ground was cleared for the final duel between the two.

[1] For an account of the interview, see *Letters*, ii. 353 ; *Att.*, ix. 18 ; and also *Letters*, ii. 358 ; *Att.*, x. 1.

The military events of the campaign that ended at Pharsalia need not be followed in detail. Several times Caesar seemed in imminent danger of complete disaster, but each time fortune, or Pompey, intervened to save him. His crowning mercy came when Pompey, unable to withstand the clamours of his officers and of the senate that encumbered him, yielded his better judgement to their overconfidence, and, leaving an impregnable position in his camp, offered battle in the open plain of Pharsalia. There the superiority of Caesar's men could make itself felt and the splendid veterans of the Gallic war crushed the newly improvised army of his foes. For the first time in his life Pompey fled from the field of battle defeated, and the Roman world lay at Caesar's feet. It is true there still remained much fighting to be done. Pompey, seeking refuge in Egypt, was murdered there, but his followers, rallying in Africa, prolonged the struggle. Defeated here, they made a last stand in Spain, where they were finally crushed at Munda. That they were able to rally at all after Pompey's overthrow was due in large part to the fact that Caesar found himself involved in a petty war in Egypt at the critical moment and could not follow up his victory with sufficient energy.[1] Though the Egyptian episode thus served to prolong the war, it could not affect its final outcome. Still the very fact that the struggle had been so protracted enhanced its bitterness and greatly increased Caesar's difficulties when he undertook the task of reconstruction.

The work of reorganizing the Roman state which fell to Caesar after the victory over Pompey he was forced to undertake in the midst of his campaigns in Africa and Spain. This may, in part, serve as an explanation of its imperfect character, for Caesar's government bore to the end very much the appearance of a temporary expedient. This the wars in which he found himself involved would serve at once to explain and justify. It was only after Munda that he began

---

[1] This seems clear from the course of the events. It was also Cicero's opinion. See *Letters*, iii. 55 ; *Fam.*, xv. 15.

to indicate his permanent intentions, and then the time allowed him by his enemies was too short and the steps that he had taken at the time of his death too few to make it possible to determine what he would ultimately have done. Yet the main lines of his policy are unmistakable, and the questions in dispute are largely matters of name, of title, and of outward forms.

When, after Pharsalia, a very large section of the Pompeian party laid down its arms and submitted to the conqueror, he could at last proceed to organize a government upon a better basis than had been possible before. Had the war ended with Pompey's defeat, public opinion would probably have run strongly in Caesar's favour, but when it dragged on and flared up again in Africa, the tide turned against him. Those of the vanquished party who had yielded to the victor now drew back, fearing that they had made their peace too soon and alarmed lest the party they had deserted in its adversity might even yet prevail. When Caesar ended the African war by the battle of Thapsus, he stained his triumph, in the eyes of the old nobility, by the execution of some of his most bitter foes. When he returned to Rome in 46 B.C., he found the state of public feeling far less favourable than it had been immediately after Pharsalia, and this, as will appear quite shortly, materially complicated the task of establishing a stable government.

The history of Rome, since the military reforms of Marius, had made it clear to all that only a government which held the sword could hope to stand. The career of Sulla demonstrated the power of the soldier and the career of Pompey had served to demonstrate as clearly the dependence of a victorious general upon the civil power. When the conqueror of Mithridates had disbanded his troops without assuring himself of some means of controlling the republican machine, he had stepped at once from the height of glory into the valley of humiliation. His descent had been too sudden and dramatic, and its underlying causes too plainly visible for Caesar not to read the lesson of his fall. Thwarted

and powerless, Pompey had seen himself obliged to enter the
first triumvirate. Both he and his two partners in that combination had seen the need of grasping again the sword
which he had laid aside, and thus the proconsulship of Caesar
had been brought about. Events had led the three to divide
the command of the army among themselves, and this
division had resulted in the civil war just ended. The outcome of that final struggle had left Caesar as a military
autocrat in Rome. The whole course of events combined
to show that he could not safely lay aside, or share with
others, the command of the army. But it was no less obvious
that he must have some kind of civil government to assist
him in his work. No great community has ever yet been
permanently ruled þy martial law, and Caesar cannot have
imagined that such a government was adequate for the
whole civilized world. But the traditions of the past made
the republic the only form of civil government of which men
had any clear conception. Cicero had written to his friend
that ' when laws, jurors, law courts, and senate are abolished '
there could be no security.[1] Though the orator wrote thus
in a moment of excitement, there can be little doubt that
such feelings were general. Caesar's task was to restore
enough of the old constitutional forms to pacify public
opinion while retaining adequate authority in his own hands.
It was thus essentially the same problem that Augustus had
later to meet, but circumstances made its solution far more
difficult for Caesar than for his adopted son.

The very policy which Caesar had pursued contributed to
complicate the situation. When he first advanced on Rome
many looked for a reign of terror after the model of Sulla.
Caesar, however, had chosen otherwise and had surprised the
world by his moderation and clemency. That this was partly
due to the natural disposition of the man need not be doubted,
but it was also in some degree a matter of policy. One motive
for the adoption of that policy may have been his clear perception of his future needs. If Pompey were vanquished,

[1] *Letters*, ii. 326 ; *Att.*, ix. 7.

Caesar would be forced to govern, and he can have had but little confidence in the greater part of his own party. It is unnecessary to take literally all Cicero's bitter words respecting Caesar's followers, yet the suspicion can hardly be avoided that they were as a class hardly the sort of men to administer an empire. Many of them were reckless bankrupts or men with dubious pasts. It would seem that Cicero had some basis in fact for his words when he wrote to Atticus : ' Of what sort, again, will he find his confederates or subordinates, whichever you please to call them, if those are to rule provinces, of whom not one could manage his own estate two months ?   I need not enumerate all the points, which no one sees more clearly than yourself. Still, put them before your eyes : you will at once understand that this despotism can scarcely last six months.' [1]   In the bitterness of his feelings, Cicero may have painted his picture in unduly sombre colours, but it is true that some of Caesar's partisans *did* turn out badly when he sought to use them in his government. Curio had been eminently serviceable as a tribune, but when he was entrusted with a military command he lost his life and his army by his rashness. Q. Cassius, another useful tribune, when appointed governor of Farther Spain, succeeded by his misconduct in stirring up trouble, and finally lost his life after laying the foundation for a formidable rebellion against his master. Whenever Caesar's back was turned there was disorder in Rome fomented by his own partisans. From all of which it seems sufficiently clear that there was much rotten material in his party and a decided lack of men of the right sort, since, although he is accounted a shrewd judge of men, Caesar promoted so many of the unworthy to positions where they were able to do harm. In spite of all their faults and vices, the republican nobility still had almost a monopoly of official experience and still possessed a very powerful hold upon the imagination of mankind. Without them it was a difficult, if not an impossible, task to govern the Roman world. A perception of this

[1] *Letters*, ii. 382 ; *Att.*, x. 8.

fact may have had something to do with Caesar's adoption
of a policy of clemency. He spared no pains to win over the
aristocracy which had supported Pompey in the civil war,
and he conferred important offices upon his pardoned foes.
It is significant to note that at the time of his death so many
of those who had fought against him were holding high office
in his government, or had been selected by him to hold such
office in the near future. The number of such men is evidence
that the dictator was, for some reason, deeply anxious to use
his former enemies to rule his empire.[1]

But Caesar's policy of clemency was not without its draw-
backs. One of these his murder revealed with startling clearness. Another, and one less frequently perceived, was that
as a result of it the senate contained a majority belonging to
the opposition. Caesar might trust individual nobles to the
extent of giving them high offices ; it was another matter to
trust the conscript fathers as a body. They were, to a large
extent, his vanquished and pardoned enemies who continued
to nurse their bitterness in secret.

But this body, sullenly hostile to the dictator at heart,
was a necessary wheel in the republican machine. No restoration of the old constitution was possible without the co-
operation of the senate, and this was just what Caesar was
unable to secure. Thus when he undertook to construct
a civil government he found a senate which he dared not
trust, yet with which he could not entirely dispense. It was
impossible to give the conscript fathers a serious share in the
control of affairs without the danger that they would use
the power thus conceded to make his position untenable, in

[1] Heitland suggests some of these considerations. In connexion with
Caesar's cordial treatment of Cicero after Pharsalia he says : ' To win the
adhesion of a man so distinguished and of so high a character in civil life
was just what Caesar wanted. None knew better than he that most of his
chief associates were men of dubious character and damaged reputation.
They might serve his purpose in the war, but men of a more respectable
type would be needed in the work of peace' (*The Roman Republic*, iii. 323).
Perhaps the *Anticato* was due to a desire on Caesar's part to check the spread
of a cult for the stern republican which might make it more difficult to use
the nobles in his government.

other words without the risk of finding himself in the situation of Pompey when he consented to disarm ; and yet, if Caesar did not take the senate into partnership, he could not gain the support of public sentiment.

An obvious way to meet this difficulty would have been to reorganize the senate in such a fashion as to make it a safe partner in the state. But this was not an easy thing to do. If the Pompeian party was spared, its members could hardly be excluded from the senate, since without them that body would have lost all moral weight in Roman eyes. If they remained, they formed a majority secretly hostile to Caesar. If he sought to overcome this majority by a wholesale creation of new peers—to borrow English terminology—he would bring the senate into popular contempt and so render it useless for his purpose. He tried the experiment of appointing new senators till this danger became manifest.[1] Only one way remained and that was to bring about a gradual transformation of the senate through the magistracies. Under the pretext of the increased needs of the imperial administration the number of the magistrates could be augmented and new men thus ennobled and introduced among the conscript fathers. The provinces, whose number Sulla had fixed at ten, had been increased by Pompey to twelve, and Caesar's conquest of Gaul would now add several more. Taking advantage of this the dictator raised the number of the praetors to sixteen and of the quaestors to forty. This would create a considerable number of new senators each year and would gradually alter the political complexion of the senate and the character of the aristocracy at the same time. But this only embittered the nobility the more. Caesar had destroyed their political importance and he now menaced their social pre-eminence as well. Distinctions and honours seemed worthless if they must be shared with a crowd of upstarts, and the haughty and exclusive aristocracy of Rome felt that Caesar had spared them in war only to humiliate and degrade their order at his

---

[1] The new senators whom Caesar appointed were the jest of Rome.

leisure, and in this feeling may be found one motive for his murder.

The resentment of the nobles only made Caesar's dictatorship the more necessary to him and he sought to justify it, in the eyes of the general public at least, by new wars and conquests. Perhaps, like Napoleon, his head was turned by military glory and success so that he came to love war for itself. But, like Napoleon, he may also have seen in war a plausible excuse for his autocracy and in victory the means to blind his subjects to the loss of their freedom. Whatever may have been his motive, he had scarcely ended the war at home before he began to plan a new campaign for the conquest of Parthia. No doubt the wish to rival Alexander the Great had something to do with this design, but another motive must surely have been the hope that such a war would serve to solve, or at least to help in solving, the difficulties at home. While Rome was at war his military dictatorship would not be so open to attack, and if he could return from the East with the added laurels of a conqueror of Parthia, all opposition might be overcome and the way smoothed for a permanent settlement.

In the midst of war Caesar's position as a temporary autocrat admitted of excuse. He had taken this position at the start as a matter of obvious necessity. Later it was consolidated and extended. When he first occupied the city with his forces he had been named dictator. He held the office for only eleven days, but it was voted to him again after Pharsalia. The second grant of the dictatorship was for ten years, and after Munda it was given to him for life. Along with the dictatorship other powers were conferred upon him which made him absolute master of the Roman state, and reduced all other factors of the government to utter insignificance. Not only was Caesar dictator for life with all the authority which that title implied, but he possessed as well the powers of the tribune and the censor. The first were given him, like the dictatorship, for life, the second for three years with the title of *praefectus morum*. As *pontifex maximus* he was the head of the Roman religion, and lastly he was one of the two consuls for each year. Yet even this it seemed was not enough, and the power was voted to him to name most of the annual magistrates. Still further, since he was intending to set out upon a Parthian campaign, he was allowed to designate the consuls and half the praetors for several years in advance. Thus the entire government was centred in his hands. The assembly was powerless to intervene, whether by means of its legislative or electoral functions. The senate was quite helpless, since by his censorial power he could control its membership, as consul could determine what matters should come before it for discussion, and by his tribunician power could prevent it from passing any decree of which he disapproved. The magistrates were his nominees and that same tribunician power in his hands made any attempt at independent action on their part impossible. With such a concentration of powers in his hands he could have used the famous phrase ' l'état c'est moi ' in sober seriousness.

Did Caesar intend the position thus briefly summarized to be a permanent one ? In substance yes, but whether precisely in this form it is impossible to say. If his life had been spared he might, on his return from the Orient, have exchanged his *title* of dictator for some other *name*. But that he meant to keep the substance of his power in *some form* his contemporaries were convinced, and it can scarcely be doubted that in this they were correct. It was in this sense that they interpreted his oft-repeated saying that he would never imitate Sulla. At first they seem to have taken this to signify that he would not resort to a proscription. Gradually, however, they came to construe it to mean that he would never abdicate. As this conviction grew and deepened and as Caesar's measures seemed to menace the very existence of the old nobility the way was paved for the tragedy that followed. Romans might submit to be governed by the sword in an emergency, but they were not yet ready to accept it as a permanent régime. They had regarded Caesar as a second Sulla without the stain of blood. They had assumed that as soon as peace was restored he would use his power to establish a settled government. They did not see that they themselves had rendered this impossible, and, when Caesar gave no sign of fulfilling their anticipations, they angrily attributed it to his insatiable and criminal ambition. Such a hope and such a disappointment we see clearly enough in Cicero, and events soon showed that his feelings were shared by many others. When the victory of Munda had put the seal on Caesar's mastery, the orator had striven to approach him with advice. He had written for the autocrat a long treatise on the subject of his future policy, but on learning from those who composed Caesar's court that it was quite unacceptable he had laid his stillborn work away and in his public attitude revealed his growing bitterness and disillusionment. Even Caesar, though surrounded by flatterers, could not fail to see the growth of hostile sentiment. On learning that Cicero had been kept waiting in his antechamber for an audience, he had exclaimed : ' Can I doubt that I am exceedingly disliked, when Marcus Cicero has to sit waiting and cannot see me at his own convenience ? And yet if there is a good-natured man in the world it is he ; still I feel no doubt that he heartily dislikes me.' [1]

Though these words show that he was by no means blind to his danger, he took no precautions. Perhaps he overestimated the intelligence and insight of his enemies. He had so long been face to face with the realities and problems of empire that he may have failed to appreciate that much that was clear to him was hidden by a haze of custom and tradition from the eyes of others. He must have known that his death could not really serve his foes, and very probably he did not fully grasp the fact that this was not so clear to them. Disdaining to protect his person, he spent the last months of his life busy with work and plans for future conquest and heedless of the conspiracy which was taking shape around him.

[1] *Letters*, iv. 6 ; *Att.*, xiv. 1.

G

The personal motives that influenced the murderers of Caesar matter little, but the public considerations by which they justified their act to themselves and others are of significance. They hoped by killing Caesar to restore the republic, and there were certain appearances which gave a colour of plausibility to such a hope. The republic had not been in any sense abolished. Magistrates, people, senate all existed, but while the dictator stood above them clothed with such powers as he then held, they were powerless to move except at his command. Yet they were there and Caesar seemed the only obstacle to their working. If he were gone, the magistrates, senate, and people would once more be free to act independently. Events soon showed that such a view, though plausible, failed utterly to take account of some of the most serious factors in the case. It took the outside show of constitutional forms for the realities. It assumed that the dictator, who was an obvious obstacle to the senate's independence and control, was the *only* obstacle, forgetting that for many years past the conscript fathers had been quite unable to dominate the state. All this the conspirators overlooked, and thus it was that, when they struck, their blow was aimed at Caesar alone and no plans whatever were made as to what was to follow. The murderers seem to have been quite confident that with Caesar removed the constitution would automatically resume its normal operation. When this result failed to follow Caesar's death, their surprise and bewilderment were at once ludicrous and tragic.

Of the moral aspect of the deed no Roman could feel any doubt, if once he were convinced that Caesar was a tyrant. Rome had taken over the ethical thinking of the Greeks without serious question or criticism. In that morality they found it laid down as an axiom that the slaying of a tyrant was not only the right but the positive duty of the citizen. By tyrant the Greeks had designated any ruler, no matter what his character, who had seized power illegally and who ruled against the constitution of the state. In the eyes of his opponents, Caesar could not fail to be regarded as a tyrant under this definition, and in so far as they regarded him as such, they felt no question that his murder was a righteous act. Its expediency they might and did see subsequent reason to doubt, but never its morality. The fact that Caesar was dealing boldly, and yet wisely and successfully, with many of the pressing problems of the moment could not avail to excuse in their eyes his failure to find a constitutional settlement which they would accept. His projects for the conquest of Parthia only filled them with keener alarm and made them feel the need of haste. If Caesar hoped by Eastern victories to win acceptance of his rule at home, this prospect only inspired his defeated foes with added fear. If he were allowed to depart for the East all chance of striking such a blow was lost till his campaign was finished. When he returned, the lapse of time and his new glory might have made all hope of shaking off his despotism an idle dream. They resolved, therefore, to act before the opportunity was gone and while they still could delude themselves with the hope that their action would be fruitful of results.

Moved by such considerations, in addition to their personal motives, the plot against the dictator was formed, and for these same reasons, many in the senate welcomed the deed, although they had no part in the actual conspiracy. Caesar's refusal to protect himself by a strong military guard made success comparatively easy and on the Ides of March the conqueror of Pompey was murdered in the senate and a new chapter of Roman history was opened.

## VI. THE DESTRUCTION OF THE REPUBLICANS

THE murder of Caesar fell like a thunderbolt on Rome, leaving men dazed and bewildered. The conspirators seem to have expected that the death of the tyrant would be hailed with acclamations and rejoicings by the liberated people, but instead of this the only greeting was an ominous silence. The senators, terrified by the tragedy, had fled from the senate-house and the populace outside had scattered to their homes, so that the triumphant murderers found themselves in the midst of a sudden solitude.

The silence filled the conspirators with surprise and consternation. They had no plan of action, never having dreamed that action would be necessary. Faced by an unexpected situation they withdrew to the Capitol and sent out hasty messages to their friends and those upon whose sympathy they felt that they could count. If the constitution was to resume its regular working, the first step was to reassemble the senate, and the proper person to call it together was the surviving consul, Mark Antony. It was, therefore, necessary to communicate with him at once. He had been one of Caesar's trusted lieutenants and the conspirators had deliberated long and earnestly whether they should murder him at the same time as Caesar. Ultimately it was decided to spare him, apparently on moral grounds. Caesar's life was forfeit because he was a tyrant, but it did not appear clearly that Antony was one. So one of the conspirators had detained Antony at the door of the senate-house while the murder was committed. From that tragic scene he fled precipitately to his own house for safety. Once there and reassured for the moment, he, like the assassins in the Capitol, spent the night in hurried consultation and uncertainty. Before he took any step he wished to know precisely who the men were who had done the deed and what forces were behind them. When envoys of the conspirators approached him the next day they found him willing to convoke the senate, but unwilling to trust himself in the power of the assassins. The usual meeting-place of the conscript fathers was near the Capitol, much too near in Antony's opinion, and he accordingly convened them in the Temple of Tellus, which was near his own house. Here the conspirators did not venture to attend, but their friends turned out in force, Cicero among them.

The attitude of the great orator is so instructive that it may be well to interrupt the narrative for a moment to consider it. He had no part in the conspiracy, but he heartily welcomed and cordially approved the deed, as might have been expected from his past. When the civil war broke out his sympathies were with Pompey and the senate, but circumstances, or his own hesitation, prevented him from joining his leader very promptly. However, he had finally followed his party to the East where the battle of Pharsalia seemed to him the end of the war.[1] Returning to Italy, he was readily pardoned by Caesar, but from this time on he took no active part in public affairs, occupying himself instead with literary work. As the hope of any sort of republican restoration at the hands of Caesar faded and the dictatorship seemed more and more a permanent fact of Roman life, Cicero grew steadily more bitter and despondent. After the Ides of March his only feeling was a savage exultation at the tyrant's death, and he made eager haste to range himself among the friends and supporters of the murderers. Henceforth all his efforts were concentrated on the one aim of restoring the republic. That republic he identified completely with the senate, and this fact furnishes a clue to much that followed. Now that Caesar was dead, the Roman world was confronted with the question of who should govern in his place. Not many years before, a proud

[1] See his letter to Cassius, *Letters*, iii. 55 ; *Fam.*, xv. 15.

aristocracy had ruled Rome and had used the senate as
their instrument of government.   The first triumvirate had
thrust them out of power for a time.   When Caesar and
Pompey had begun to drift apart the nobles had sought to
take advantage of the rivalry between the two and had made
Pompey their leader.   Caesar's victory and dictatorship
had effectually barred the way against any recovery of
power by the aristocracy, whom he had beaten and pardoned
but whom he could not trust.   This situation led to the
tragedy of the Ides of March, and now the vanquished
nobility prepared to make a desperate effort to regain their
lost control.   The senatew as now—as always—their instrument, and the republic was the name by which they designated
their supremacy.   Those who opposed them in the struggle
were not consciously aiming at some other form of government, but were simply fighting to prevent the authority
of the state from passing into the hands of their recently
defeated enemies, for, in spite of Caesar's recent reforms,
the old Pompeian party was still dominant in the senate.
In this struggle Cicero was heart and soul with the conscript
fathers, and in this he was simply following the convictions
of his whole life.   In modern times some critics have seen
in his attitude toward the aristocracy only the servility of
a parvenu seeking at any cost to gain admittance to the
ranks of an old and proud nobility.   There is, however,
another and more creditable explanation.   The senate must
have seemed the only practical alternative to a military
despotism.   In the days of C. Gracchus men might dream
that a democracy was possible in Rome, but the course of
events since then had been sufficient to dispel the illusion.
One after another the popular leaders had failed ignominiously
in the attempt to govern.   How was it possible for Cicero,
or any one with any vision of reality, to imagine that the
rabble of the Roman streets could rule the world ?   It was
not a question of ruling well :   who could believe that the
rival mobs of Clodius and Milo were capable of governing
at all ?   The army and the senate might govern, but the

Roman people had demonstrated their utter incapacity. If Cicero could not bring himself to accept a military despotism, he had no choice but to support the senate. That the conscript fathers were by no means perfect he was well aware from personal experience, but in spite of all he clung to them as the only possible instrument of government under which the things he prized most highly could exist. Freedom, government by discussion and by law—in his view these could only be secured under the senate's rule. Caesar had represented nothing but violence and arbitrary force, and these he deeply hated. Now that the tyrant was dead, the only hope of freedom lay with the senate, and the cause of the senate was bound up with that of the conspirators. It was as their ardent friend and champion that he attended the session of the senate on that memorable 17th of March.

The conscript fathers, when they assembled in the Temple of Tellus, found themselves confronted with formidable difficulties. The logical course was to declare Caesar a tyrant if they approved the murder, as the majority actually did. Such a step would have freed the conspirators from all blame, but it would also have annulled all Caesar's acts by declaring that his government had been illegal, and the consequences of such a declaration were likely to be serious in the extreme. Caesar had been so long in power that vast numbers of people were affected by his acts. Within the Temple of Tellus itself were many senators who held their seats by virtue of his appointment, or through some office that he had conferred, and many others had received promotion from him. If he were declared a tyrant, many senators would have to quit the house and many more would have to step down to a lower rank. To this they were naturally averse, and this was only a beginning of the consequences. If Caesar had been a tyrant, the elections under him had not been valid and neither Rome nor the provinces possessed legal magistrates or governors.[1] In fact the whole

---

[1] Appian attributes to Antony a speech setting forth these considerations. Antony is represented as saying : ' Those who are asking for a

machinery of the state would be utterly disorganized. The
senate might, of course, pass a decree authorizing the existing provincial governors to continue to exercise their
functions for the time being, but in Rome itself new elections
must be held at once.   The attitude of the people was
uncertain, and no party could feel sure of how elections
under present circumstances would result.   The men then
holding office might easily fail to be returned and all those
to whom Caesar had promised the various magistracies
during his absence in the East would run a risk of losing
them.   There was thus a powerful group of senators who
were unwilling to see Caesar declared a tyrant, and even the
friends of the conspirators might well doubt the wisdom of
such a course.   If there were reasons for hesitation in the
senate-house itself, the situation out-of-doors was even more
ominous.   How the murder would be received by Caesar's
soldiers was sufficiently doubtful in any case, but, if the news
came coupled with a declaration which annulled their title
to the lands they held from him, an explosion was a certainty.
The dead dictator had disbanded many thousands of his
veterans and had assigned them lands in various parts of the
peninsula, and many others were even then in Rome awaiting
their rewards.   The only troops in the city were his, and
while the senate deliberated, many of his soldiers and disbanded veterans thronged around the place of meeting with

vote on the character of Caesar must first know that if he was a magistrate
and if he was an elected ruler of the State all his acts and decrees will
remain in full force ; but if it is decided that he usurped the government
by violence, his body should be cast out unburied and his acts annulled.
These acts, to speak briefly, embrace the whole earth and sea, and most of
them will stand whether we like them or not, as I shall presently show.
Those things which alone belong to us to consider, because they concern
us alone, I will suggest to you first. . . . Almost all of us have held office
under Caesar ; or do so still, having been chosen thereto by him ; or will
do so soon, having been designated in advance by him ; for, as you know,
he had disposed of the city offices, the yearly magistracies, and the command
of provinces and armies for five years.   If you are willing to resign these
offices (for this is entirely in your power), I will put that question to you
first and then I will take up the remaining ones.'   Appian, ii. 128.   The
translation is that of Horace White in the *Loeb Library*.

pressing demands that Caesar's promises should be redeemed. Under these conditions the conscript fathers could not shut their eyes to the danger of ill-considered action, however logical.

Since the senate dared not repudiate Caesar's acts, it was impossible to brand him as a tyrant. Yet if this were not done, then obviously his death was murder and logically the conscript fathers were bound to punish the assassins. In this dilemma Cicero came forward to propose a compromise. He advised that Caesar should not be declared a tyrant and that his acts and promises should be alike confirmed. This would reassure the veterans and would provide the state with a legal government. To protect the conspirators he urged the senate to pass an act of amnesty and in this way silence all question in regard to the dictator's death. That tragic event was to be treated as some great natural calamity, in face of which the long-divided parties of Rome might join hands in a reconciliation. All animosities were to be laid aside and the past covered by a general oblivion. The senate would accept all Caesar's laws without inquiring how they had been passed, the partisans of Caesar would accept the fact of his death without question of how, or through whom, it had come about.[1] The conscript fathers welcomed the proposal as the only possible way out of their difficulty.

After much discussion, therefore, the amnesty was voted and the acts of Caesar ratified. As to the disposition of his body, the senate voted for a public funeral. This last was no part of Cicero's policy, though he may not at the time have seen its full danger. Atticus warned him that all was over if the public funeral was allowed,[2] but the warning was probably too late to alter the result. In all likelihood the motive of the senate was simply to carry out consistently the view they wished to have taken of the murder. If Caesar had been a consul, it seemed only natural that he should be buried as such. If no inquiry was to be made into the past,

[1] Dio, xliv. 32.   [2] *Letters*, iv. 29 ; *Att.*, xiv. 14.

on what grounds could the customary honours be refused ? And would such a refusal strike his soldiers as consistent with the ratification of his acts ? Whether for these or other reasons, the senate sanctioned a public funeral and permitted the surviving consul to speak in honour of his colleague.

Thus Antony obtained a chance to test the feeling of the populace. The speech which he delivered has not been preserved, and even its exact nature is a matter of some doubt. Probably it consisted chiefly of the reading of the various decrees of the senate and the people in the dead man's honour, with comments on them by Antony himself. Caesar's will was also read and produced a deep impression, partly because of several legacies to the Roman people, but perhaps as much because of a clause in which one of the leading conspirators, Decimus Brutus, was named among his heirs. Without an open declaration of war upon the senate,[1] Antony contrived to provoke an outburst of popular fury. The people, stirred to a frenzy of rage and grief, burned Caesar's body in the forum, and then swept through the city seeking to wreak vengeance on the murderers. To save themselves the ' demi-gods ', as Cicero called the conspirators, were forced to flee from Rome, while the senate, terrified by the disorder, looked on helplessly. With the republicans thus scattered and intimidated, Antony was left free to shape his course as he might choose.

What Antony's ultimate choice would be could hardly be a matter of much doubt. His private interests forced him to seek to rally the partisans of the dead dictator, if possible, and so put himself at the head of a strong Caesarian party. He was a lieutenant of Caesar and had risen solely by the favour of his master. To the old nobility he had long been odious, and if their party, vanquished on the battlefield,

---

[1] This seems clear from the uncertainty of the senate as to Antony's attitude for some time after the funeral oration. Varying accounts have come down to us as to the character of the oration itself. I have followed that of Appian, ii. 143–7.

should regain power by the dagger, he could hope for nothing better than to be permitted to retire into private life.  That the aristocracy would really forgive his past, or suffer him to continue in high office, was more than he could reasonably expect.  Whatever he obtained from the conscript fathers he must gain by working on their fears, or by taking advantage of their difficulties.  This he could do more easily at the head of a strong party than in any other way.  Nor was Antony's position in this respect unique.  Caesar had gathered about him a large number of officers and politicians who could hope for no advancement—some, perhaps, hardly even for safety —in a Rome dominated by the senate.  Antony, by virtue of his consulship, was the natural leader of such men, and if he made a move, he might expect them to rally around him.

If there were leaders in abundance for a Caesarian party in opposition to the senate and its claims to rule the state, the rank and file of such a party was equally ready to the hand.  The decree of the senate ratifying Caesar's acts had by no means quieted the apprehensions of his veterans. Setting aside all considerations of passion and of sentiment, though these were very powerful forces, there were obvious reasons for distrust.  The senate had promised much, but how far would it be safe to trust such promises ?  Could the Roman nobles be expected to reward men for defeating them ?  If they did so, they would condemn themselves, for if Caesar's soldiers were meritorious servants of the state for having vanquished Pompey, what must the latter's partisans have been ?  No matter what the real intentions of the senate, it would have been little short of a psychological miracle if Caesar's men had put much faith in their promises.  Cicero saw this clearly when he wrote to Atticus, ' I return to the case of the veterans. . . . Do you suppose these men feel any confidence in retaining their grants so long as our party have any footing in the state ? '[1]  In a later letter he declared that the Caesarians kept repeating that the acts of Caesar would be set aside the moment that the senate ceased to be afraid.[2]

[1] *Letters*, iv. 18 ;  *Att.*, xiv. 10.      [2] *Letters*, iv. 47 ;  *Att.*, xiv. 22.

The materials for a Caesarian party were thus obviously in existence, and its power was likely to be out of all proportion to its numbers.  At the moment of the dictator's tragic death the military forces throughout the Roman world were entirely Caesarian.  The legions under arms had all been recruited by him, and his disbanded veterans, all seasoned soldiers, were the best available material from which new legions could be quickly formed.  Nowhere could the senate look for the support of regular troops, and though the republicans had many partisans, they would be mostly raw recruits who could not face his veterans immediately.  The power of the army had not been broken by Caesar's death, and that army was not prepared to acquiesce in the restoration of the aristocracy to full control.  The real issue after the Ides of March was not whether the senate should take over the government, but whether the Caesarian soldiery would find a single leader around whom they could unite. Would Antony succeed to Caesar's place, or would the army of the dictator divide its allegiance among several rival chiefs ?  If this last should happen, would these chiefs join hands against the senate as a common foe, or would they fight among themselves ?  If they fought among themselves, would the struggle be sufficiently prolonged to give the senate time to organize new armies upon which it could rely ? These questions were the true ones that confronted the Roman world, and the constitutional issues that were raised only served to mask and to disguise them.  In its essence the new struggle was simply the old battle between Caesar and Pompey fought over again under new leaders.

Antony had quickly seen the situation as it was.  Although the vision of others might be as keen, he alone was in a position to act. . His aims were dictated by the circumstances in which he found himself, but at the start he showed some hesitation and uncertainty.  This may, at first, have been real enough, since even after his own purposes were clearly formed, it might seem wise to make sure of the army before he declared irreconcilable war upon the senate and its supporters. It was possible that Caesar's veterans, although they feared the restoration of the senate, would be unwilling to accept Antony as their leader. If he could not obtain an adequate support from them, it might be advantageous to come to terms with the conspirators. Antony's vacillating conduct at the beginning seems to indicate that he had no desire to burn the bridges behind him until he had made certain that the road in front was open. As a consequence he mingled bids for the leadership of the Caesarians with concessions to the other side. He soon ceased to hesitate, however, for his success was all that he could wish and the game seemed wholly in his hands if he possessed the courage to play it boldly.

The decree of the senate ratifying all Caesar's acts and even his intentions proved of immense assistance to Antony. Caesar's papers had fallen into his hands after the Ides of March, and he availed himself without scruple of the opportunity thus presented. Under the authority of the senatorial decree he could do whatever he chose, alleging as his warrant that such had been the intention of the dead dictator as was shown by some note or memorandum that he had left behind. The resulting situation was paradoxical and filled the republicans with anger and dismay. In name Caesar remained the master of the state, and the conscript fathers were so far removed from any effective power that the conspirators, whom they wished to protect, dared not show themselves in Rome. ' Good God,' Cicero exclaimed in his exasperation and disillusionment, ' the tyranny survives though the tyrant is dead ! We rejoice at his assassination, yet support his acts ! ' [1] ' Can it be true ? ' he wrote bitterly in another letter to Atticus, ' Is this all that our noble Brutus has accomplished—that he should have to live at Lanuvium, and Trebonius should have to slink to his province by by-roads ? That all the acts, memoranda, words, promises, and projects of Caesar should have more validity than if he were still alive ? ' [2] ' Yes in truth,' he summed the matter up

---

[1] *Letters*, iv. 15 ; *Att.*, xiv. 9.        [2] *Letters*, iv. 16 ; *Att.*, xiv. 10.

dejectedly, ' we have been freed by heroic champions with the result that we are not free after all ! ' [1]

Instead of improving, the situation grew rapidly worse as Antony became bolder.  Before long he began to find the genuine memoranda of Caesar ill adapted to his purposes, and he met the difficulty by more or less extensive forgeries. If Cicero had bitterly resented his subjection to Caesar's notebooks, he felt it still more keenly when he found himself the slave of Antony's fabrications.  In view of this new posture of affairs he wrote to one of the conspirators :

We seem not to have been freed from a tyranny—only from a tyrant : for though the tyrant has been killed, we obey his every nod.  And not only so, but measures which he himself, had he been alive, would not have taken, we allow to pass on the plea that they were meditated by him.  And to this indeed I see no limit : decrees are fastened up ; immunities are granted ; immense sums of money are squandered ; exiles are being recalled ; forged decrees of the senate are being entered in the aerarium (treasury).  Surely then nothing has been accomplished except to dispel the indignation at our slavery and the resentment against an unprincipled man : the Republic still lies involved in the confusions into which he brought it. . . . Up to the present it has avenged its injuries by the death of the tyrant through your hands : nothing more.  Which of its dignities has it recovered ? Is it that it now obeys the man in his grave whom it could not endure in his lifetime ?  Do we support the rough drafts of a man, whose laws we ought to have torn down from the walls ? [2]

From all of which Cicero drew the obvious moral that much remained to be done.

Such laments, though well founded, were of very little use.  Antony had taken advantage of the disorders in the city following the funeral to obtain a bodyguard, and, with his soldiers around him, was in secure control.  The conspirators were helpless and could only nurse their rage and wait impatiently for Antony's consulship to end.  With the new year other men must come to the front, and the consuls whom Caesar had designated for 43 B. C. were unfriendly

---

[1] *Letters*, iv. 29 ; *Att.*, xiv. 14.     [2] *Letters*, iv. 36–7 ; *Fam.*, xii. 1.

to Antony.  As soon as they took office the republicans might hope to find some chance for action.  But this possibility was quite as clear to Antony as to his enemies, and he undertook to guard against the danger.  The best protection would be a province and an army held for a term of years, a great command, in short, such as had saved Caesar from being called to answer for his acts when consul.  By the arrangements of the dead dictator Antony was to receive Macedonia as his proconsular command, but this appeared unsatisfactory under the changed conditions.  If Antony were to go across the seas, the senate would have an opportunity to raise an army in Italy with which to attack him.  The example of his master had not been wasted on Antony, who determined to establish himself in the valley of the Po at the head of a strong army.  To do this he proposed to transfer the legions assembled in Macedonia for the Parthian war to Cisalpine Gaul and to take immediate possession of that province.  Not only would this strengthen him, but it would weaken his opponents.  The province which he meant to seize had been assigned by Caesar to Decimus Brutus, in whose hands it would be dangerous to leave it, as Cisalpine Gaul was one of the best recruiting grounds in Italy.  Established in the Po valley within an easy march of Rome and with a strong army under his command, Antony could dominate the situation.  The only difficulty in the way of these arrangements was that they were directly contrary to those of Caesar.  In this matter, however, Antony could not afford to be consistent, and he resolved to modify Caesar's arrangements.  The constitutional sovereignty of the Roman people had not been in any way abridged, and in the eyes of the law, the acts of the assembly were still the final authority.  Accordingly Antony brought before the assembly a bill transferring the Macedonian army to Cisalpine Gaul and giving him the government of that province for six years.  With his bodyguard about him he could easily pass any bill he chose, and this one was enacted with great promptness.  The republicans looked on in helpless despair, for this arrangement meant the indefinite prolongation of Antony's dictatorship. While his supremacy had seemed only a temporary accident they had found it almost unendurable, and now it seemed likely to continue for years to come. Rather than submit to that they were ready to do anything, but at first there seemed nothing that they could do. Just when the situation looked blackest a sudden hope dawned in an unexpected quarter, and the Caesarian party, hitherto a unit, began suddenly to split to pieces.

The attempt of Antony to rally the whole body of veterans under his leadership had for a time seemed likely to succeed, but now a rival appeared upon the scene in the person of Caesar's adopted son. With the death of the dictator the male line of his family became extinct, and his nearest relative was his sister's grandson, Gaius Octavius by name. In the last days of his life Caesar had shown marked favour to this youth, and by his will adopted him and made him heir to his personal fortune. His political position Caesar could not of course bequeath, though had he lived it is probable that he would have found a way to designate his grandnephew as the successor to the throne. The Ides of March destroyed any such prospect, and Octavius could only claim to inherit Caesar's name and private property. Even this legacy seemed so dangerous that the family of Octavius urged him to refuse it, but the young man, then about nineteen years of age, rejected their advice without the slightest hesitation. The news of the assassination reached him at Apollonia, where he had been sent to complete his education. The legions intended for the Parthian war were encamped near the town, and this proximity had enabled Octavius to make friends with many of the officers who were destined to be of eminent service to him in the future. They now came forward with offers of protection ; but Octavius, rightly divining that he had little need of it at the moment, hastened to Rome to claim his perilous inheritance.

The appearance on the scene of an adopted son of Caesar

was not a pleasing development to Antony, although at first he attached small importance to it, not dreaming that Octavius, whom he regarded as a mere boy, was a person to be considered seriously, but he was soon forced to modify this estimate, since the insistence of Octavius upon his rights was something that could not be entirely ignored. When Caesar died there existed a great deal of confusion between his private fortune and the money of the state which happened to be in his hands at the time. The problem of distinguishing between the two might have been difficult at best, but, as matters stood, neither party to the case was in a mood to be impartial. Antony, now as always, found himself in want of funds, while Octavius, already angered by many public slights, was in no humour to submit quietly to being cheated of what he regarded as his rights. Octavius was soon claiming large sums which Antony could not, or would not, pay, and the two became open enemies. Causes of quarrel rapidly multiplied when once hostilities had been begun. Although Octavius had been adopted by the will of Caesar, certain legal formalities must be completed before the adoption was valid in point of law. These Antony was able to thwart, and though Octavius assumed the name of the dictator and began to style himself C. Julius Caesar Octavianus, his right to this designation was open to dispute. The matter proved unimportant, since the name was popularly used, and the name of Caesar, if borne with any shadow of right, was a power with the veterans.

In open conflict with Antony, Octavian, as he should now be called, watched with alarm the consul's juggling with the provinces. If Antony succeeded in carrying out his plans, the youthful Caesar could not hope to play a part in Roman affairs. As it was clear that the senate could not check his rival, Octavian resolved to appeal to the veterans for support. For such a step he had already received much encouragement ; on his way to Rome the veterans had flocked around him eagerly, and he doubtless knew that many among them, disliking Antony, would welcome the appearance of some other leader. The consul was a dashing soldier, not without political insight and ability, but he was reckless, self-indulgent, and dissolute, and hence there was an undercurrent of opposition to him among the Caesarians. While Antony was still in Rome his enemies did not dare to make a move, but when, after the passage of his provincial law, he left the city to take command of the Macedonian legions, an opportunity presented itself. Octavian at once hastened to Campania, where many of Caesar's veterans were settled, and called on them to join him. Liberal financial inducements were added to the magic of his name, and the appeal met with an enthusiastic response. Although he had no legal right whatever to recruit soldiers, he was soon at the head of a considerable force, and, while gathering troops in Campania, he also made effective use of his friends in the Macedonian army. Antony had been authorized to bring over four legions from Greece to Italy, and to his dismay half this force on their arrival, refusing to obey his orders, went over to Octavian. This desertion was a very unexpected blow to Antony. The boy whom he had despised was splitting up the army on which he had confidently counted, but he could not stop to deal with this unforeseen development. Decimus Brutus had established himself in the Cisalpine province, and, so far from having any intention of surrendering it, he was now busily engaged in strengthening himself there. Antony determined to dispossess him at once, and to neglect the young Caesar for the moment. He, therefore, gathered up his sadly diminished forces and hastened to the valley of the Po.

With Antony's departure for the north Octavian was left to pursue his course unchecked, but he was well aware that he had received a respite, not a pardon, and that, when Antony had disposed of Decimus, his turn would come. In truth his position was extremely precarious. He was at the head of an army without a commission from the state and was therefore, in the eyes of the law, a rebel and a traitor. If he must fight Antony, he was anxious to gain some legal

standing, and the senate and its party alone could give it
to him.  Besides this, his forces were not strong enough to
enable him to face his rival single-handed.  It was obviously
necessary to come to terms with the conservatives, for the
time being at any rate, and he eagerly offered the senate the
protection of his sword.  On their side the conscript fathers,
led by Cicero, were anxious to avail themselves of his services.
The policy of Cicero in forming a combination with Octavian
has been subject to much censure, then and since.  Nevertheless it seems to admit of a very simple justification.  In
times of crisis one cannot choose his friends with too great
nicety ;  had Cicero rejected the aid of the young Caesar,
he would only have ruined the senate's cause a few months
earlier.  It is unnecessary to assume that he was duped or
deceived in the matter.  When he first met Octavian it was
with quite enough suspicion, and, if he finally cast his doubts
aside, it was only under compulsion.  Once convinced that
it was necessary to trust Octavian, it was only common
sense to try to persuade himself and others to trust fully ;
to accept Octavian's services and then to alienate him by
perpetual distrust would have been a stupid blunder.  The
one chance of retaining his loyalty was to treat him with
apparent confidence, and, if no precautions could be taken
against his possible treachery, nothing was to be gained by
brooding on it.  As to an alliance with Octavian the senate
had practically no choice.  It was necessary to check Antony
and save Decimus Brutus, and the only way open of accomplishing this was to make use of the young Caesar for the
purpose.  Decimus was making desperate efforts to raise
an army in Gaul, but his forces were not yet in a condition
to face the troops of Antony unaided.  In the East, Marcus
Junius Brutus and Cassius were likewise hard at work
recruiting armies, but they were much too far away to give
any effective help.  If Decimus was to be rescued the means
must be found in Italy, and, without Octavian, they were
not to be had.  Both the new consuls, Hirtius and Pansa,
designated by Caesar to hold the office during 43 B.C., were

hostile to Antony, but they had no armies before their entry on their office and they could not at once gather an adequate force. An army could be formed immediately only from Caesar's veterans, and among the partisans of the senate there was no one who could appeal to them. Under these circumstances when Octavian, having gathered a considerable force, offered his sword to the senate, Cicero could see no alternative but to accept his services. He could and did write earnestly to the East to urge upon the senate's champions there the need of coming with all possible haste to Italy with the troops that they could bring, but till they arrived he must use such soldiers as were at hand. Thus a coalition was brought about between Octavian and the murderers of Caesar. Suppressing his misgivings, Cicero declared himself Octavian's friend and persuaded the senate to accept him as its general and to vote him the necessary powers. This done, Octavian joined his forces to those which the two consuls had succeeded in raising, and set out to meet the common foe.

While the forces of the senate were being strengthened by the swords of Caesar's veterans, Antony pushed his operations against Decimus with vigour and succeeded in shutting him up in the town of Mutina. The first task of the senate's army was to raise the siege of this place and deliver Decimus from the hands of his enemy. The brief campaign therefore centred around Mutina and Antony sustained a sharp reverse. Finding himself unable to hold his lines longer, he released his prey and sought to escape across the Alps into Transalpine Gaul, where he hoped to find support from the armies which were stationed in that region. The news of his retreat elated the senate beyond measure. Cicero tells us that the first reports were that ' Antony had fled with a small body of men, who were without arms, panic-stricken, and utterly demoralized '.[1] Had this been true, he would have been doomed to speedy destruction, and even though the first reports exaggerated

[1] *Letters*, iv. 242 ; *Fam.*, xi. 12.

his plight, he might, perhaps, have been completely crushed had the pursuit been pushed with energy. This was not done, however. The forces of Decimus, just released from a long siege, were, as he himself says, ' most wofully reduced and in the very worst condition from want of every kind of necessary '.[1] They were quite incapable of acting with vigour against their retreating foe, and Octavian would not follow up his victory. Why he refused to move cannot be said with certainty. Perhaps he had no wish to free the senate from all danger. He must have realized that the republicans did not give him their entire confidence and that nothing but necessity had forced them to accept his services. If all such pressure were removed, they might be but too ready to discard him, and he may have felt that a decisive victory would be his own undoing. Another explanation is suggested by a letter from Decimus to Cicero in which he wrote : ' But if Caesar had listened to me and crossed the Apennines, I should have reduced Antony to such straits, that he would have been ruined by failure of provisions rather than by the sword. But neither can any one control Caesar, nor can Caesar control his own army—both most disastrous facts.' [2] This may well have been the truth, for after all, the soldiers of Octavian were veterans of Julius and they can hardly have been eager to defend the murderers. They had their own plain reasons for a profound distrust of the senate which they were serving, and, if Octavian had presumed too far on their obedience, he might well have found himself deserted by his men. It is improbable that they felt any enthusiasm for a war against their former comrades and it seems quite possible that they would have refused to hunt down one of the ablest of Caesar's lieutenants even at the bidding of Octavian. If such was, in any degree, the sentiment of his army, it can only have strengthened his own doubts.

The senate in its folly gave Octavian little chance to hesitate. Misled by the first exaggerated reports of a great

[1] *Letters*, iv. 236 ; *Fam.*, xi. 13.  [2] *Ibid.* 230 ; *Fam.*, xi. 10.

victory, the conscript fathers showed themselves quite blind to the realities. Octavian had saved them, as Cicero freely confessed, but they had no real confidence in him and little or no gratitude. Now that they thought him no longer necessary, they made haste to cast him aside. The war had cost both consuls their lives and new ones must be chosen. A suggestion that Cicero and Octavian should be elected found little favour with the nobles and was dropped. The senate transferred the forces of the late consuls to the command of Decimus, thus pointedly ignoring Octavian, and appointed a commission of ten members to review the acts of Antony's consulship. This was certain to affect the interests of the veterans, but neither Octavian nor any other in whom the soldiers had confidence was named among the ten. By these ill advised measures the senate contrived both to slight Octavian and to enrage his men. The youthful Caesar could no longer hope for anything from the senate, and his army was ready to support him in any course he chose to take.

For a time Octavian still pretended to negotiate. He was already feeling his way toward a compromise with Antony and he also wished to save appearances. Accordingly he let the senate blunder on until, when action came, it might seem forced upon him by the army. The soldiers, as might have been foreseen, refused to serve under the command of Decimus Brutus, stained as he was with Caesar's blood, and sent an angry deputation to Rome to demand the rewards that had been promised them and the consulship for Octavian as well. The conscript fathers attempted to evade their demands and thus threw away their last chance, if any still remained. Octavian had assured himself that terms were possible with Antony and he was now ready to let the army act. Without further delay the soldiers broke up their camp and marched swiftly upon Rome.

While in Italy the senate and its general were thus drifting into open war, Antony was recovering from his defeat and becoming more formidable than ever. In the Trans-

alpine province and the newly conquered parts of Gaul were
stationed important armies under the command of Lepidus
and Plancus.  When Antony, escaping from Italy, crossed
the Alps, his fate depended upon the action of these two.
Cicero had long seen their potential importance and all that
his pen could do to insure their loyalty to the republic had
been done.  But letters, however eloquent, could not determine their decision.  In truth they were not the masters of
their own course but were dragged along by their armies.
Perhaps they were quite willing to follow the lead of their
men, but in any case they could hardly have resisted.
Neither Lepidus nor Plancus had a strong hold on his
soldiers, and Antony could safely appeal to the latter over
their heads.  Lepidus made no attempt to prevent the appeal,
probably because he wished it to succeed, and, after his
troops declared for Antony, he promptly combined his forces
with those of the fugitive.  Such a combination was far too
strong for Plancus to resist, even if he wished, and he accordingly threw in his lot with the other two.  As a consequence
all the troops on the further side of the Alps were united
under the actual control of Antony, who thus found himself
at the head of a large army and in a position to invade Italy
at any time.

While Antony was thus regaining his power in the North,
Octavian had ended his alliance with the senate by a rapid
march on Rome.  In vain the conscript fathers sought to
renew negotiations and offered to concede all his demands.
If he still felt any lingering inclination to accept their offers
a final act of folly on the part of the nobles must have swept
it away.  The frantic appeals for help which Cicero had long
been sending to the provincial governors brought a response
which completed the ruin of the senate.  Neither of the
republican leaders in the East made the slightest move, but
the propraetor of Africa dispatched some troops to Italy.
Two legions arrived at Rome just after the sweeping concessions had been offered to Octavian.  With this unexpected
support at hand, the senate's hopes suddenly revived and

hurried preparations were begun for a defence. Octavian merely hastened his advance, and when he reached the city the African legions came over to his side without a blow. Taking possession of the city, Octavian caused himself to be at once elected consul. This done he gratified military sentiment, and doubtless his own, by passing a law to punish the murderers of the great dictator. Few of the conspirators were within his reach at the moment, but they were all solemnly condemned to death in their absence. No voice could be raised in their favour while the troops of Octavian dominated the city, and the people and the juries registered his will without the slightest opposition. Having in this manner thrown down the gauntlet to the republicans, Octavian left the capital and marched north to encounter Antony. This time the meeting was to be a friendly one, however. The previous negotiations had prepared the way for an agreement and all that remained was to arrange the final terms.

The motives of Octavian in forming this coalition seem fairly clear. Perhaps he had never meant to fight for the senate longer than would suffice to bring the overbearing Antony to terms. Even if he had been sincere in his alliance with Cicero, recent events had taught him that any real friendship with the republicans was impossible. By continuing on their side he could achieve nothing but his own ruin. In the event of victory they would certainly cast him aside, and, by fighting their battles for them, he might easily forfeit the loyalty of his army. Besides all this, Antony was much the stronger of the two since he had gained the legions of Gaul, and in a war had every chance to win. Octavian had, therefore, little choice but to combine with Antony if possible.

On his side Antony had equally strong motives for compromise. Although he had the stronger army, he could not afford to overlook the fact that in the East large forces were gathering under the command of M. Brutus and Cassius. If Caesar's veterans should fight among themselves, Antony might crush Octavian, but it was very probable that he would find his army so much weakened by the victory that he in turn would fall an easy victim to the republicans. Even had he been sure of his men, he might well think a contest under such conditions too dangerous. But now that Octavian had broken with the senate and had proscribed the conspirators, would Caesar's veterans have been willing to fight against his adopted son, the bearer of his name, supported as he was by followers who were their former comrades? We may well suspect that the pressure of the army was added to the other considerations and that all combined to point in the direction of a union of the Caesarians against their common foes.

Both Antony and Octavian were, therefore, in a mood for compromise, and Lepidus served as a convenient mediator. A meeting was arranged and the three agreed to the formation of the second triumvirate. Unlike the first this was to be a legal institution. They resolved to pass a law creating a triple dictatorship for themselves and to combine their armies for a war with the republicans. The East they had yet to conquer, but the West they divided among themselves. Lepidus was to keep his provinces of Spain and Narbonensis,[1] Antony took the newly conquered parts of Gaul together with the Cisalpine province, and Octavian got only Africa and the islands of Sardinia and Sicily. Italy itself was to be kept under the joint rule of the three, but, while the other two should be absent in the East, Lepidus was to remain there as their representative.

One other measure was decided on at the conference which has left a lasting stain on the triumvirs. They determined to revert to Sulla's methods and to open their administration by a sweeping proscription of their enemies. The motives which they avowed in public have been preserved in Appian. In their proclamation they dwelt much upon their wrongs and pointed out that, while they marched against their open foes,

---

[1] Narbonensis was the old province of Transalpine Gaul. After the conquests of Caesar it had lost its old importance, since it was no longer a frontier province.

they could not safely leave their enemies at home to strike them from behind. They called attention to the disastrous results of Caesar's clemency and sought to justify themselves by an appearance of indignation at his murder.[1] Beneath the surface there were other motives which could not be avowed with decency. All three had made reckless promises to their soldiers and now the time had come to pay. From the treasury of the state they could not hope to meet their obligations, and the confiscations which accompanied the proscription were necessary to enable them to satisfy the most pressing of their men's demands. Cupidity and vengeance thus joined hands, and, while they struck down their personal and political foes, they took into account the rich as well. Each of the three gave up those of his friends who had incurred the resentment of his partners, and thus Octavian was obliged to sacrifice Cicero to Antony. But the death of the great orator was only one of many ; some three hundred senators and two thousand knights perished in the massacre. The republicans in Italy were thus wiped out in blood. Their refusal to accept the dictatorship of Caesar was paid for by their complete destruction at the hands of his successors. Of those who had slain Caesar and of those who had approved and condoned the act, only such survived as found their way as fugitives to the camp of their last remaining champions in the East or with Sextus Pompey in the West.

In later years, when Octavian had become the emperor Augustus and had reverted to a policy of clemency, it was his natural course to shift the blame for the proscription to the shoulders of the vanquished Antony. This version of events, although official, is probable enough, and the strongest of the three must bear the heaviest responsibility since without his consent such a massacre would have been impossible. But there is also a tradition that Octavian, though reluctant at the start, was far more ruthless than his colleagues after the decision had been made. This would be highly characteristic, at any rate ; from boyhood he displayed a cool astute-

[1] Appian, iv. 8–11.

ness and a calm, deliberate policy which contrasted strongly
with the recklessness of Antony. He was less likely to
sacrifice expediency to passion or to pity than was the impulsive and not ungenerous soldier, and he was far too able
not to see clearly that a proscription which failed to destroy
the party at which it was aimed was a blunder as well as
a crime.

The thorough destruction of the republicans in Italy had
two immediate results : all danger of revolt was at an end,
and means were found to quiet temporarily the clamours of
the soldiers. The three could now turn to meet the armies
which their opponents had gathered in the East. Leaving
Lepidus in charge of Italy, Antony and Octavian embarked
their legions for Greece, where Cassius and M. Brutus were
awaiting them. These two conspirators, fleeing from Rome
while Antony was consul, had taken possession of nearly all
the East without having, or needing, the slightest legal right.[1]
Brutus had seized Macedonia after the bulk of the troops had
been withdrawn by Antony, while Cassius had gained complete control of Syria. They had succeeded in raising large
forces but took no part in the decisive events in Italy.
Turning a deaf ear to Cicero's frantic appeals for help, they
stood passive during the last agony of the republic to restore
which they had murdered Caesar. The cause of their inaction
cannot be fully known. Cassius was probably too far away to
act in time and it is on M. Brutus that the chief responsibility
must fall. It is possible that the condition of his army was
such as to prevent any other course, but the impression given
by his letters to Cicero suggests narrow-minded obstinacy as
the explanation. He had a profound distrust of Octavian
and was bitterly opposed to the alliance with him. He disapproved of extreme measures against Antony and Lepidus,
and was firmly convinced that he in Macedon could judge
the situation better than the men in Rome. When the break
between Octavian and the senate began, he answered Cicero's
appeals with a complacent ' I told you so '. Quite probably

---

[1] See the article by Schwartz in *Hermes*, xxxiii.

he did not appreciate the full extent of the danger, or anticipate the proscription till it was too late, but seemingly he
held aloof and left his party to its fate because it would not
follow his advice.  Apparently what he desired was that the
senate should abandon Rome to take refuge in his camp, as
had been done in Pompey's day.[1]  Then, in due time, he
hoped to bring them back and re-establish the republic.
Such a course would probably not have altered the result,
and Cicero was right in feeling that, if the republic could not
be saved in Italy, it was lost beyond recall.

Now that the tragic end had come in Rome, nothing remained for the two tyrannicides in the East but to unite
their armies and fight a last battle for their lives.  In reality
the nobles who had murdered Caesar, or approved the deed,
had perished, and with them the republic they had thought
to restore.  The future government must be one resting upon
the swords of the soldiers and not upon the votes of the
senate.  A victory for Brutus and Cassius might change
the personnel of that government but could not change its
character.  Whichever party won, their power would have
no basis but the sword.  If Brutus and Cassius had prevailed,
they might have undertaken to restore the republic, but the
wishes of the senate would have counted for little in the
decision.  Their rule would have been set up by the legions
and would have depended for its existence upon their support.
The senate might have been restored to nominal supremacy
again, but this was destined to be the policy of Octavian in
the years to come after the fall of Antony had left him sole
master of the Roman world.  There is no reason to suppose
that the senate as reconstituted by Brutus and Cassius would
have been in any way more capable of governing than was
the senate of Augustus.  Underneath the surface its position
would have been much the same.  Placed in nominal control
by a successful general, it could have retained that control
only so long as its restorer kept possession of the sword for
its defence.  If the author of its authority laid down the

[1] Meyer, 543–4.

command of the army, the conscript fathers would be at the mercy of some new military chief.   Real power the senate could have only if some means were devised to give it a strong hold upon the loyalty of the legions.   The army had paid little heed to the conscript fathers since the reforms of Marius, and to alter this condition of affairs a reorganization of the military system was required.   It seems impossible to imagine that such sweeping changes could have come from the conspirators.   The murder itself is conclusive evidence of their narrow pedantry.   The war which ended at Philippi was, therefore, in no real sense a struggle for the old republic ; in its essence it was only a battle between rival pretenders to the throne.

The issue was soon decided.   The battle of Philippi crushed for ever the hopes of the great party which had followed Pompey, and, after Caesar's death, had made a last effort to regain control of the state.   That this result was fortunate for the world there can be little doubt.   Nothing that we know of Brutus or of Cassius would seem to indicate that they possessed better qualifications for the task of reorganization than did either of the victors.   Octavian must be accounted a great statesman and Antony displayed a far clearer insight into realities than was shown by the conspirators.   The men who killed Caesar without a thought of what their next step was to be had shown themselves so blind to obvious consequences, so unable to look beneath the surface of things, that it cannot be a matter of regret that the work of restoring order to the world should have fallen into other hands.   Even Antony was better qualified to rule than men who combined such violence and such short-sightedness.   Their fate is hardly likely to provoke much sympathy ; their crime was atoned for with their lives, and in their ruin they dragged down their whole party.

## VII. THE TRIUMPH OF OCTAVIAN

ALTHOUGH the battle of Philippi destroyed the last serious opposition to the triumvirs, the task which confronted them was, nevertheless, one of extreme difficulty. The whole world had been thrown into confusion and now urgently demanded reorganization at their hands. Their soldiers were clamorous for pay but their treasury was empty. In the West the silence and submission showed that the proscription had achieved its purpose, but the war with the republicans had produced chaos throughout the East. The triumvirs found themselves obliged to deal at once with two distinct problems. The West must be kept quiet and their soldiers pacified by being paid a part, at least, of their demands ; and, while this was being done, a new settlement of the East must be undertaken. It was obvious that the soldiers could not safely be ignored, and Caesar's experience warned them that to postpone dealing with the regions which the republicans had held might lead to a renewal of the war. Caesar's delay after Pharsalia had prolonged the civil war, and, as the victorious triumvirs had no desire to fight a Thapsus or a Munda, they determined to divide the double task between them.

In the arrangements after Philippi, Antony showed himself decidedly the predominant partner. The credit of the victory belonged to him rather than to Octavian, and he could impose his will in the division of responsibility. He took for himself the lion's share of the spoils and the more alluring of the tasks before the two. The East was the richest part of the Roman world, and the settlement of its affairs promised to present few difficulties and to yield enormous profit. The triumvirs hoped to fill their exhausted treasury in this region, and to have this money in his own hands would obviously be a great advantage to Antony.  In the West the task of settling conditions abounded in difficulties, owing to the demands of the army and the bankruptcy of the three. The confiscations which had accompanied the proscription had been but a drop in the bucket, and new confiscations would be necessary to satisfy the troops.  Whoever under-took this was certain to rouse the bitter resentment of those whom he despoiled, and it was not by any means sure that he would be able to content the army.  It seemed not unlikely that he might alienate all parties and every class, while his colleague in the East would be engaged in the easy work of settling the affairs of the richest provinces of the empire, in doing which he might possess himself of an immense sum of ready money.  If the triumvir in the West should fail, it was probable that all parties would turn with one accord to his partner in the East, those who were being robbed as the only man who could save their property or compensate them for its loss, the soldiers as the only man who could pay them the rewards so often promised.  These considerations were so obvious that there can be little wonder that Antony selected the East as his share of the world and turned over to the weaker Octavian the dangerous problems of the West.  It is possible that Antony already dreamed of carrying out Caesar's plan for the conquest of Parthia, but such an enterprise, if successful, would only serve to make his advantages the greater by giving him new military glory and the immense plunder of the Farther East.  Appian represents Octavian as choosing the West of his own accord on account of his health,[1] but this seems hardly credible.  It is quite true that Octavian had been ill at the time of the battle of Philippi and that he was still far from strong, but it is not easy to see why the task awaiting him in Italy was any better adapted to an invalid than that in the East.  Even if Appian be right, it would seem certain that the other arrangements were such as Octavian would never have accepted willingly.  Antony not only assumed full authority over all Eastern affairs, but

[1] Appian, v. 3.

he retained control of a large part of the West as well. He kept what he had held under the first division and added to it a portion of the share of Lepidus. The latter had been from the start the weakest of the three and his two partners now determined to despoil him. Antony took the province of Transalpine Gaul, and Octavian received the two provinces of Spain. If Lepidus objected and it should seem dangerous to set him aside entirely, it was agreed that he should be given Africa and Numidia in exchange for the provinces which he was required to surrender. These arrangements were distinctly favourable to Antony. He held all Gaul across the Alps as well as the Cisalpine province, and, though Octavian was given all of Spain, this was far less important from a military point of view than Gaul since it was completely cut off from Italy by the regions held by Antony. Besides all this the army of Antony was the larger, and while a portion of it would follow him to the East, strong forces under his generals would remain behind in Gaul and even in Italy itself. Such a dispersal of his legions might prove dangerous in the future, but at the moment he undoubtedly occupied a far stronger position than Octavian.

As soon as the triumvirs had completed these arrangements each set about the work allotted to him. Octavian returned empty-handed to Rome with clamorous veterans in his train to undertake the formidable task of satisfying them without entire ruin to himself. The soldiers demanded land and none was available without some fresh spoliation. Octavian, reluctant to increase his unpopularity, sought to make his new demands as moderate as possible. In this endeavour he very nearly fell between the two horns of the dilemma by rousing to fury those who felt their property in danger, while leaving the army, on which he must rely for power and safety, still unsatisfied. He had scarcely set about his task when the inevitable discontent began to show itself in a particularly menacing form because of the leaders around whom it gathered. These were none other than the brother and the wife of his own colleague. Declaring that the new acts of plunder were contrary to the absent triumvir's wishes, Lucius Antony and Fulvia put themselves at the head of a violent agitation against Octavian and his policy. In the face of this opposition the latter hesitated at first, fearing to act with decision lest Antony's generals should come to the support of his relatives. However, when his own men began to desert him, he dared no longer temporize but struck boldly as his only chance of escaping shipwreck. Mustering his troops, he shut his foes up in the city of Perusia and there besieged them, while watching anxiously to see if Antony's forces would march to their relief. Fortunately for him the officers of his colleague were in great perplexity. Both sides in Italy claimed Antony's sanction for their course, and each could do so with some show of reason. It would have seemed natural to trust his wife and brother, if it had not seemed equally so to trust his partner, who produced a written agreement with him duly signed and sealed. This might have been decisive if men could have felt sure how Antony would take the defeat of his relatives. Such an event might rouse his resentment, agreement or no agreement. Thus Antony's officers, doubtful of his wishes and fearful of responsibility, hesitated and did nothing. Another factor in the situation was that the forces of Antony were divided among several generals who were without a common plan, and, in their uncertainty, no one of them ventured to make a stand against Octavian single-handed. Under these circumstances Fulvia and Lucius failed to obtain any assistance and were finally compelled to surrender.

While the crisis was still acute, immediately after the fall of Perusia, Octavian made earnest efforts to detach some of the Antonian armies from their allegiance. Two legions commanded by Plancus came over to him, but the rest rejected his offers.[1] Fate, however, suddenly came to his assistance. Fufius Calenus, the general whom Antony had left in command of Gaul[2] with a considerable army, died, and Octavian, hastening there in person, succeeded in taking

---

[1] Appian, v. 50.　　　　[2] Jullian, *Histoire de la Gaule*, iv. 53.

H

over both the provinces and the army from the son of Calenus, whom he found in charge.[1] Thus circumstances had enabled him to upset the unfavourable arrangements made after Philippi and to gain the control of practically the entire West. Yet his position was by no means free from anxiety, since Antony still had considerable forces in Italy. After the fall of Perusia these had hastened to the coast to await the coming of their leader or the arrival of definite orders from him. Octavian had gained the army in Gaul, but seems to have been doubtful of its loyalty.[2] A war with Antony was something which he dreaded and did his best to avert. When Perusia surrendered, he was careful to avoid giving his colleague any cause for complaint by treating with gentleness and courtesy the relatives and particular friends of Antony. If vengeance was taken upon any, it fell on none whose fate would rouse the absent triumvir's resentment. Fulvia and Lucius departed unharmed for Greece, there to lay their complaints before Antony, while Octavian prepared to stand on the defensive if a break should come. For a time it seemed improbable that Antony would permit the wrongs of his relatives, and especially the seizure of his provinces and legions, to go unavenged, and Octavian prepared gloomily for the struggle that seemed inevitable.

Yet the inevitable did not happen, and this for several reasons. Antony cared little for the wrongs of his wife and brother and seemed disposed to believe those who affirmed that they had brought them on themselves by their own recklessness and folly. He had agreed to the policy of Octavian in advance, and he could not decently protest against it now. These reasons for moderation might have been overborne by resentment at the seizure of Gaul, but they were reinforced by other motives which he dared not disregard. In the Perusine war the sympathies of the soldiers must have been with Octavian rather than with his enemies. His difficulties must have seemed to the army to be due to

---

[1] Appian, v. 51 ; Dio, xlviii. 20.
[2] Appian, v. 66. The fact might be inferred in any case.

his well-meant efforts to provide for his troops, and Fulvia
and Lucius cannot have been regarded with much sympathy
by the veterans whose rewards they were trying to hold
back.  In such a cause his soldiers were not likely to support
Antony with enthusiasm against their former comrades.
The influence of the army was, therefore, exerted strongly
in favour of peace.  The sentiment of the legions was something that neither of the two triumvirs could disregard,
even if they had been desirous of war.  But both had private
reasons for avoiding it if possible.  Octavian was at the head
of a large army, but a considerable part of it was composed
of troops whom he had just taken from his rival and of whose
loyalty he was doubtful.  So anxious was he to avoid
hostilities that he had sought earnestly to refrain from any
act which would make the break irreparable and dispatched
friends to his colleague to explain and justify his course.
On his side, Antony was by no means ready for a decisive
conflict.  The East was still so far from settled that ominous
clouds were gathering in that quarter where the Parthians
were threatening an invasion of Syria, and, under these
circumstances, he was reluctant to involve himself in a war
in the West.  The news of the Perusine war had reached him
in Alexandria, but he displayed no eagerness to return to
Italy.  Instead of hastening home to settle with Octavian,
he lingered in Egypt until the Eastern situation itself compelled him to return.  The forces he had with him in the
East were inadequate to deal with the Parthians so that it
was necessary to bring up reinforcements, and a large part
of his army was in Italy itself.  Moreover, though he showed
little sympathy with the complaints of Fulvia, he was not
disposed to overlook the seizure of his legions and his
provinces.

When Antony arrived in Italy, his intentions were still
so uncertain that Octavian prevented him from landing
at Brundisium, but, in spite of this, a peaceful settlement
was finally reached.  The influence of the soldiers who were
reluctant to fight each other prevailed, and when at length

Antony landed, it was to negotiate rather than to fight. An agreement was soon brought about and a treaty, known as the treaty of Brundisium, was arranged between the two triumvirs. The terms of peace could hardly fail to be greatly to the advantage of Octavian. He was, indeed, obliged to hand back to Antony the legions he had taken from Calenus, but he kept the provinces of Gaul which he had seized at the same time. Perhaps his colleague agreed to this the more readily since, if he remained for any length of time in the East, Gaul could be of comparatively little use to him. As soon as he had sailed for Italy the Parthians had invaded Syria, and a serious war with them was unavoidable. For this Antony required soldiers and not provinces too remote to be of much importance in the conflict. Accordingly he insisted that his legions should be restored to him, and, in addition, he reserved the right to recruit soldiers in Italy on an equal footing with Octavian.[1] By this new division of the provinces Antony retained the East while giving up nearly all the West to his partner. Lepidus, who can hardly be considered as a partner though he bore the name of one, was to keep Africa. To make the treaty seem more binding to the soldiers, who had largely dictated it, Antony married Octavia, the sister of Octavian. This was made easier by the death of Fulvia, rumour said of a broken spirit because of her husband's indifference to her wrongs.

The peace concluded, Antony paid a brief visit to Rome, but the affairs of the East were calling for attention, and with his new wife he soon set out for Greece. Here news arrived that the Parthians had been disposed of by his officers, at least for the moment, and he remained for a considerable time in Greece, busy with preparations for the conquest of Parthia which he intended to attempt.

In the West Octavian was soon confronted with a new foe in the person of a son of the great Pompey, who had turned pirate and become dangerously strong. After the battle of Pharsalia had overthrown his father's party in the field

[1] Appian, v. 65.

the young Sextus Pompey succeeded in making his escape
to Spain. After Munda he had taken to the sea and gathered
around him a large number of reckless men. At first no one
had thought him worthy of serious attention, but while the
world was occupied with other matters his power grew
steadily, recruited from all sides. To him had fled runaway
slaves, pirates, refugees from the proscription and their like,
until at length his forces became so strong that he was able
to play a part of greater dignity. He seized the islands of
Sicily and Sardinia and ravaged the western seas at pleasure.
At the time of the treaty of Brundisium he had been in
alliance with Antony, but that leader abandoned him in
order to come to terms with Octavian. The latter had at
first intended to proceed at once to war against him, but the
pressure of popular feeling at Rome, and doubtless that of
Antony as well, led him finally to agree to a peace with
Sextus. This peace, known as the treaty of Misenum, proved
to be only a brief truce, and hostilities soon flamed out again.
It matters little which of the two was the more to blame
since Sextus held a position that Octavian could not tolerate
permanently. Master at once of Sicily and of the sea, the
food-supply of Rome was at his mercy. Neither party to the
treaty could trust the other very far, and Sextus had but an
imperfect control over his followers. Under such conditions
war was certain before long, and Octavian resolved to crush
an enemy who was potentially so dangerous. Antony promised help in ships, but they failed to come at the expected
time, so Octavian resolved to build a fleet of his own and
put the work in charge of his ablest lieutenant, Agrippa.
After much difficulty and delay that capable officer was
finally in a position to take the sea against the foe, and in a
naval battle he broke the maritime power of Sextus for ever.
It only remained to stamp out the last remnants of the young
Pompey's forces in Sicily, and to assist in this Octavian called
on Lepidus to bring his legions from Africa. Lepidus did
so, but he resented the way in which his nominal colleagues
had set him aside and came looking for an opportunity to

reassert himself.  His forces, joined to those of Octavian, were speedily successful in reducing Sicily, and Sextus Pompey, escaping from the ruin of his power, sought refuge in the East with Antony, where he was put to death not long afterwards.  Meanwhile the conquerors were left face to face in Sicily, and Lepidus, taking advantage of the circumstance that he had a large army under his command, attempted to regain his old position as an equal partner in the triumvirate.  But he had not been so long ignored without good reason.  Instead of meeting him with the concessions which he demanded, Octavian appealed to his soldiers. On them Lepidus had little influence, and they were readily prevailed upon to abandon their general.  Deserted by his men, Lepidus found himself helpless.  Octavian spared his life but sent him into exile, and from this time he disappears from history.  With him the last independent power in the West was eliminated, and that part of the Roman world passed wholly into the hands of Octavian.  The East and West now faced each other and a final struggle between them was inevitable.

While his potential rival was gaining the control of the Occident, Antony was pursuing his oriental policy.  The real nature of that policy is worth a brief consideration because the reasons for its failure were not without a serious lesson for Octavian.  From modern eyes the underlying causes of the downfall of Antony at Actium have been in part concealed by the glamour of romance, but the astute statesman who saw and profited by his rival's blunders can hardly have been deceived.  It was not the beauty of Cleopatra that ruined Antony, except in so far as this was one of the factors that lured him into a fatal policy.  It was the political errors which she persuaded him to commit that destroyed him and not the mere fact of his connexion with her.  His infatuation was of importance only as it led him into blunders of statesmanship.

When Antony chose the East after the battle of Philippi, he probably already dreamed of completing Caesar's work

by carrying out that war against Parthia which the dictator
would have undertaken had he lived.  All Caesar's plans
for that enterprise fell into the hands of Antony after the
Ides of March, and he believed that he could execute the
designs formed by his master.  For such a task he needed
to secure his hold upon the East by a thorough reorganization of that region, and he was engaged in this when the
Perusine war occurred.  In all probability this fact played
a part in persuading him to make peace with Octavian.  If
the war which he was planning resulted in the conquest of
Parthia, the loss of the provinces of Gaul would be a minor
matter, and Antony was confident of victory.  He returned
from the compact of Brundisium to continue his career of
glory in the East.

As has been seen, the Parthians had not waited till their
would-be conqueror was ready to attack.  During his absence
in Italy they invaded Syria, and Antony dispatched against
them an officer by the name of Ventidius Bassus who successfully drove them back.  This victory procured a breathing
space and enabled Antony to proceed at leisure with the
preparations.  The treaty of Brundisium was concluded in
the autumn of 40 B. C., and it was not till the next summer
that Antony left Italy.  He spent the remainder of that year
and all the next with Octavia in Greece.  During this time
the war between Octavian and Sextus Pompey had broken
out and Ventidius had been winning victories in Syria.  In
the early part of 37 B. C. Antony made a hurried visit to
Syria, his critics said because he was jealous of the glory
which his lieutenant was gaining.  He accomplished little
there, as he was soon recalled to the West, partly perhaps by
Octavian's appeals for help, but doubtless more because the
law creating the triumvirate was about to expire and it
seemed desirable to have a new understanding with his
partner.  In any case he returned to Italy with a large fleet
and at Tarentum concluded his last compact with Octavian.
By the terms of this agreement the two decided to renew
the triumvirate (Lepidus was not deposed till the next year)

for a period of five years, and arranged an exchange of resources by which Antony was to furnish ships for the war against Sextus Pompey and in return was to receive a force of 20,000 Italian soldiers for his projected war with Parthia. As soon as this bargain was concluded, Antony sailed for Syria, leaving Octavia in Rome with her brother.[1]

Up to this time Cleopatra had played no important part in Antony's career. After the battle of Philippi, he had met her at Tarsus, where she had been summoned to appear before him, and he accompanied her to Alexandria where he spent some time in 40 B. C. The Perusine war had forced him to return to Italy, where he had married Octavia, and he paid no further attention to the Queen of Egypt until, in 36 B. C., he set about the Parthian war in earnest. Up to this time she cannot be said to have exerted any influence upon his policy. As soon as he assumed the command of his army in Syria, he summoned her to meet him in Antioch. For this step there were political as well as personal reasons. For such a war as he was planning he needed ample funds, which he could not hope to get from his bankrupt partner. Such sums as he had so far been able to extort in the East had melted away, and he still needed money. The richest district in the East was the kingdom of Egypt, which still remained nominally independent of Rome. Towards Egypt and its wealth the eyes of Antony naturally turned. He wanted gold, while the government of Egypt was in need of military force, though well supplied with money. The triumvir might have seized the kingdom, but he did not care to take a violent way to reach his ends, since, if he did, it was quite possible that the country would revolt as soon as he had gone, or would require to be held down with a large force of men. If, however, he respected the legitimate government, the peace could be maintained with a much smaller force and with a much better chance of success. The Egyptian government desired his support to keep itself in

---

[1] Appian, v. 95 ; Dio, xlviii. 54.

power and could readily be induced to pay for it. An alliance with the reigning queen of Egypt seemed the wisest course, and such a policy he now adopted. When Cleopatra, responding to his summons, met him in Antioch, there seems to have been little difficulty in arranging terms. She was to furnish money for the Parthian war, and, in return, was to receive the recognition and support of Antony. In addition he ceded to her the island of Cyprus and a district in Coele-Syria.[1] Both had in former times been dependencies of Egypt and their cession does not seem to have aroused any great opposition, although Cyprus was then a Roman province. If Antony had fallen in love with the Queen, his passion had not yet betrayed him into any very serious political error.

Having supplied himself with funds, Antony set out on his carefully prepared campaign. But in the war that followed the plans of Caesar broke down in the hands of his disciple. A single year of fighting shattered all Antony's dreams of conquest, and his invasion of Parthia ended in disaster. One cannot altogether escape the question of whether Caesar would have failed in the same way. A definite answer is of course impossible, but it is clear that he would have had advantages which his successor lacked. Caesar had allotted several years to the task, but Antony could not afford so long a time. He dared not turn his back upon his brother-in-law, who had already shown himself astute and ready to take prompt advantage of any favourable circumstances. If Antony allowed himself to be drawn into a long and difficult campaign in Parthia, he might find the East slipping through his hands as completely as the West had done. To succeed at all it was necessary that he should succeed at once, and this he failed to do. Part of the failure must be attributed to disasters which the far greater Caesar might have avoided. In any case the result was that Antony returned, not as a laurelled conqueror laden with the spoils of the remoter East, but as an unsuccessful general who had saved his

[1] Bouché-Leclercq, ii. 254-5.

army from entire destruction by a masterly retreat. To this new situation he had now to adjust his policy.

To understand the new policy which Antony adopted requires but a brief consideration of the circumstances, yet there are one or two preliminary factors to be borne in mind. The first of these is the fascination which the East possessed for that generation of Romans. The countries of the eastern Mediterranean were at that time not only richer and more populous than those of the West, but they represented a far older, more luxurious, and subtler civilization. Within their borders, and especially in Egypt, the ancient civilizations of the inhabitants, dating back to millenniums before the foundation of Rome, had, after the conquest of Alexander, taken on a veneer of Greek culture which made them singularly attractive to the ruder and more practical Roman. In the fields of art and of the intellect the peoples of Italy admitted themselves inferior to the Greeks, and had long been accustomed to accept the superiority of that highly gifted race. Though Rome had conquered Greece, she in her turn had been vanquished by the weapons of the spirit, by the fascination of Greek thought and literature. The average Roman of the upper class was sent to finish his education at the famous schools of Greece and returned with more or less enthusiasm for the Hellenistic culture of the East. This influence was deepened by the wars which had flooded Italy with eastern slaves, who filled the households of the great. With them there came strange gods whose cults began to take root in the West.

In addition to the fascination of the oriental world for the Romans, the political structure of the eastern states should also be kept constantly in mind. When first the Roman legions crossed the Adriatic, the states with which they came in contact were for the most part kingdoms that had arisen out of Alexander's empire and had taken shape in the period of confusion that followed his death. There is a striking analogy between the conditions which followed the death of the great Macedonian and those which resulted from the Ides of March. In both cases a great soldier had been suddenly struck down, leaving behind him a legacy of war. In both cases the strongest power then in existence was to be found in the now leaderless army. The vital question in both cases was soon seen to be whether these armies could unite in choosing a single successor to their dead general. This in both cases proved to be impossible, and several chiefs arose, each able to secure the support of a portion of the veterans and so to claim some part of the inheritance. This in both cases led to struggles between the rival generals before a final solution could be reached. In the wars which followed Caesar's death, however, the cause of unity was destined finally to prevail and his entire empire passed to his adopted son. The bitter struggle between the successors of Alexander had the opposite result. No one of the pretenders was strong enough to overcome all rivals, and in the end the empire of the Macedonian was divided among his generals. Thus arose three important kingdoms in the East which still controlled the greater part of that region when Rome appeared upon the scene. They were the kingdom of the Antigonids in Macedonia, that of the Seleucids in Syria, and that of the Lagids, or Ptolemies, in Egypt. Of these Macedon stood somewhat apart, much smaller in size than the others but more compact and homogeneous. The other two were empires, rich and extensive indeed, but without natural unity. Their structure was very similar and was the natural result of the circumstances which had given them birth. Both Ptolemy and Seleucus were generals of Alexander who after his death had gained the support of an important section of his army. Both depended for their power upon their Greek soldiers, and neither could venture without the certainty of ruin to offend his troops beyond a certain point. Both, therefore, although able to seize rich and populous provinces, were forced to rule them as Greek sovereigns and to depend for the stability of their thrones upon Greek mercenaries. Yet in both cases an enormous majority of their subjects belonged to other races. Each, therefore, was compelled by his position to seek to gain and hold some districts which could serve as a recruiting ground for the army on which his power rested. Thus the Seleucids strove to annex Asia Minor and even to push their conquests into Greece itself, while the early Ptolemies, realizing that they could not afford to remain shut up in the Nile valley, sought to acquire an empire outside.

The Ptolemies, who alone concern us here, met with a large measure of success, and they were able not only to hold Egypt firmly, but to gain extensive provinces beyond its borders. To numerous possessions among the islands of the Mediterranean and on the coasts of Asia Minor they added the important district of Coele-Syria. Such an empire furnished them a fairly stable basis for their power. Egypt supplied the money to fill their treasury, while the outlying provinces furnished the soldiers for their army and Coele-Syria contributed the materials for the fleet on which they depended to bind the rest together. But their success was destined to be temporary. Reverses soon arrived and the seemingly solid structure fell to pieces. A naval battle broke their maritime supremacy, and before they had recovered from this blow, another fell upon them. In the last days of the Second Punic War the two chief rivals of the Ptolemies, Antiochus of Syria and Philip of Macedon, taking advantage of a regency at Alexandria, united to despoil them. Antiochus seized Coele-Syria and Philip threw himself upon their other outlying possessions. The unexpectedly sudden defeat of Carthage enabled Rome to intervene in favour of the Ptolemies, who had previously shown themselves her friends. She protected Egypt from attack, and, crossing into Greece, she easily crushed the power of Philip and forced him to give up his plunder. The Ptolemies, however, gained nothing by his defeat, for, whether from craft or from a failure to understand their importance to her Alexandrian ally, Rome did not restore to Egypt the places seized by Philip. Thus the Ptolemaic empire passed away and with it the real strength of the Lagid dynasty. The later members of that house were suffered to remain as kings at Alexandria, but their military power was broken and the stability of their throne was undermined.  Shut up in the valley of the Nile, their army rapidly rotted away.  They had from the first relied on foreign troops and most of these had been provided for by lands assigned to them in Egypt, upon whose soil they were thus quartered.  The result of this was that they soon became a militia and lost more and more their military character and effectiveness.[1]  The standing army of the Ptolemies was a force of royal guards, and, in case of war, they trusted to recruiting mercenaries.  This was easy enough as long as they were in close communication with all the ports of the Aegean and the Greek world had an abundant supply of soldiers of fortune ready to take service with any one who could pay them.[2]  The native Egyptians were only employed in time of crisis and under pressure of necessity.[3]  With the loss of their empire and the changed conditions due to the advent of Rome in the eastern Mediterranean, an effective army could no longer be created by these means, and they found themselves dependent on a handful of Greek guards who proved unable to keep down the turbulent mob of their capital.  If Rome had not given them a certain measure of support they must have fallen long before they did.  As it was, the last rulers of the dynasty were driven from their thrones at intervals, but, upon each occasion, were restored by Rome—for a consideration.  The senate, unwilling to annex Egypt, was content to see it in the hands of a line of rulers too weak to stand alone.

Thus when Cleopatra mounted the unstable throne at Alexandria, her house retained only the shadow of its former greatness.  It was natural that a young and ambitious queen should dream of the possibility of reviving the glory of her ancestors and of making her gilded mockery of rule once more

---

[1] Bouché-Leclercq, iv. 2-3.  See also Ferguson, *Greek Imperialism*, for an admirable discussion of the Ptolemies.

[2] Bouché-Leclercq, iv. 10.

[3] At the battle of Raphia Ptolemy IV had employed a large number of Egyptians successfully, but this had resulted in a series of rebellions on the part of the natives.  Bouché-Leclercq, iv. 5-7.

a thing of solid reality. Nor did such a dream seem impossible of realization. The cause of the present weakness of her house was so plain that the remedy was obvious. The Lagid power had declined with the loss of the empire outside of Egypt, and it might revive if that could be restored. But to make such a revival possible she clearly needed force. The troops at her disposal were a mere handful, and she had at hand no means of creating an efficient army. She had money, it is true, but Rome now controlled the regions from which in the past her ancestors had drawn their mercenaries. Even if the troops could be obtained, how could she hold off Roman intervention until the raw recruits had been turned into disciplined soldiers? In any plans which she might form she must allow for Rome, and she boldly resolved to use Rome as an instrument by which to realize her ambition. If she could gain the support of the Roman legions the restoration of the glories of her house would present few difficulties. The Queen, therefore, spared no pains to win the help she needed. She had wooed Caesar when he came to Egypt in pursuit of Pompey and she now wooed Antony. Nor had her wiles been without success in either case. Tradition and popular rumour believed that even the great Julius had so far yielded to her charms as to meditate giving effect to the policy she urged. At Rome before his murder he had been credited with the design, after his conquest of Parthia was completed, of making Alexandria his capital. There was probably no truth in such reports, but their existence is enough to show that the idea was in the air, that men had guessed the policy which the Queen of Egypt incarnated.

Then came Mark Antony, and the Queen perceived in him another who might play the part which she, perhaps, had once assigned to Caesar in her imperial dream. She set herself to win him to her purpose and to obtain from him the force she needed to make her policy prevail. She must secure his sanction and the support of his military power to regain the lost possessions of her house across the seas. With the wealth of Egypt at her disposal and recruiting grounds in her control, she might in time create a powerful army and an empire strong enough to stand alone.

To the Roman she could offer not only herself but a grandiose dream of oriental empire. That vision, alluring in itself, could be presented as the only way out of the difficulties which were crowding upon Antony. After the failure of his Parthian expedition that general found himself in a position of real peril. The disaster had been costly of men, and the means of replenishing the depleted ranks of his legions were not ready to his hand. Under the treaty of Brundisium he had reserved the right to recruit troops in Italy on an equal footing with his fellow triumvir, but a short experience undeceived him as to the value of this stipulation. It proved easy for Octavian to prevent recruits from reaching him upon a dozen plausible pretexts; so, at Tarentum, he sought to bind his slippery colleague by a definite bargain. By this new treaty he had agreed to furnish Octavian with ships for his war on Sextus Pompey in return for 20,000 Roman soldiers. But the young Caesar promptly found excuses for delay, and, without waiting, Antony marched against the Parthians. Returning from that expedition defeated, he looked anxiously for the 20,000 men to reinforce his army. But when at length, in 35 B.C., Octavian bestirred himself to redeem his engagement, instead of the promised soldiers he sent back the borrowed ships accompanied by his sister and a paltry force of some 2,000 men. The meaning of this was clear enough, and it is not to be wondered at that Antony in anger ordered Octavia to return to her brother. But the need for men remained as pressing as before, and, if Antony could not get them from Italy, he must seek them elsewhere. His rival plainly hoped to destroy his army by cutting off recruits, and war had been declared between them in everything but name. Under these circumstances Antony was compelled to turn to the East for men to fill his ranks, and the imperial dreams of Cleopatra might seem to offer the best means of obtaining them. If he adopted her policy it might be possible to arouse the East to rally

round his standard.  Orientals were not likely to be enthusiastic for the weaker party in a war, and he might believe
that the best way to overcome their hesitation would be to
place by his side the one remaining Hellenistic sovereign.
Besides this, if disaster came and he were beaten by his
rival, Egypt was the easiest of eastern lands to defend against
a foe.  Sheltered behind the deserts he might hope to hold
the valley of the Nile in any event, and this would be the
easier if the rightful queen to whom the people had long been
accustomed to look up as a goddess reigned by his side.[1]

To all these varied influences Antony at length yielded,
and his downfall was the consequence.  For in the policy
of Cleopatra there lay one element of weakness that proved
fatal in the end.  To create the eastern empire of which she
and her lover dreamed the Roman legions were indispensable;
but Roman soldiers would not consent to play the part
marked out for them.  The vital defect of the whole plan
was, not that what Cleopatra proposed was obviously impossible, but that to realize her design it was necessary to
employ forces which would not knowingly support it.  The
visions of oriental empire that fascinated the general made
no appeal to the common soldiers.  They were Italians, and
throughout their service they looked forward to an allotment of land in Italy as the ultimate reward of victory.[2]
This, if he lost control of the West, their general would be
powerless to give.  More than this, his eastern policy would
make necessary the prolonged sojourn of his men in the East
and postpone indefinitely their return to their native country.
While thus demanding the sacrifice of their interests, he
offended their sentiment as well.  There was in them enough
of the stern pride of the old Roman character to prevent
them from viewing with any degree of favour a scheme

---

[1] For Antony's final policy and his campaign against Octavian, see the
brilliant articles by Kromayer in *Hermes*, xxxiii and xxxiv ; and Strack's
article on Cleopatra in the *Historische Zeitschrift*, cxv.

[2] Antony made it one of his grievances against Octavian that the latter
had distributed all the available Italian land to his own men and so left
none for the army of the East.  Plutarch, *Antony*, 55.

which would separate the eastern lands from Rome. To them
the very thought of an eastern empire independent of the
West was repugnant, and any idea of making Alexandria
supreme over Italy unthinkable. To carry out Cleopatra's
plan by means of such an army was difficult at best, and
would be clearly impossible if the purpose in view were
frankly set before the soldiers. The only chance of success
was for Antony to conceal his real aims from his men. This
would involve grave contradictions and the danger of a
sudden collapse if the course of events should at any time
reveal the secret intentions of their leader too clearly to his
troops. These difficulties were so obvious that Antony
did not yield until his rival's measures had left him little
choice. It may reasonably be assumed that Cleopatra had
tried to persuade him to adopt her policy from the very first,
but for a long time she met with small success. The only
concessions she had been able to obtain were made on the
eve of the Parthian expedition, and these were not of great
importance. It was only when hope of reinforcements from
the West was gone that Antony came over completely to
her side. Already he had been induced to marry her and
so become legitimate king of Egypt. This had taken
place in Syria just before the war with Parthia, but he
had carefully avoided taking the royal title lest he should
alienate his men. Nevertheless Cleopatra had issued coins
in Alexandria bearing his head side by side with hers.[1] After
the Parthian disaster he took his place more openly as
sovereign of Egypt, but still refrained from styling himself
king in any official way, at least to Romans. Neither did
he divorce his Roman wife Octavia. His position was thus
highly ambiguous. At war with the young Caesar in all but
name, he seized the occasion when his rival was involved
in a war in Pannonia to launch a swift and successful campaign against Armenia in order to secure his rear from danger
in the coming struggle. Returning victorious to Alexandria,
he took the last decisive step, and, after celebrating a splendid

[1] Bouché-Leclercq, ii. 256.

triumph for his victories, he solemnly proclaimed a new distribution of the eastern lands. To Cleopatra and her eldest son Caesarion he assigned the territories of Cyprus, Libya, and Coele-Syria ; to his own children by her he gave kingdoms formed from his new conquest and from the Asiatic provinces of Rome. To one he handed over Armenia and Media with the promise of Parthia when it should be conquered, and he bestowed upon the other Syria, Phoenicia, and Cilicia. ' All this,' Mahaffy says quite truly, ' was evidently suggested to Cleopatra by the traditions of her house ; she only claimed in the Greek world what had formerly, and had long, belonged to Egypt '.[1] The Ptolemaic empire was thus boldly revived under the sovereignty of Antony, although he did not dare to assume the crown himself.

The new empire created by these measures, known as the Donations of Alexandria, could be viewed by Romans with nothing but alarm. Rome was not likely to surrender quietly her provinces of Cilicia and Syria to the Ptolemies in addition to Cyprus. Octavian eagerly seized the opportunity to turn the sentiment of the West against his rival. At first, however, he was less successful than might have been expected. In spite of his recent acts Antony retained the loyalty of his soldiers and that of many partisans in Italy. This may have been due to the unpopularity of Octavian, or it may have been that men did not yet regard Antony as an eastern monarch. His rival naturally insisted that he was the tool of Cleopatra, but the world apparently was not convinced. It was just possible to construe his policy in a Roman sense and to argue that it relieved Rome of a heavy burden while leaving her such of her eastern possessions as were really valuable. Thus the province of Asia, so dear to Roman financiers, was still hers, and, if Syria was ceded to Egypt, that province had never been of much advantage and had involved Rome in a war with Parthia. It might

[1] Mahaffy, *History of Egypt*, 249–50. See also to the same effect Bouché-Leclercq, ii. 278–9.

prove cheaper in the end to hold the Parthians in check by creating a strong buffer-state between them and the Roman provinces.

Perhaps the Romans excused Antony on some such grounds as these, or they may have hoped that once in Italy he could be induced to modify his policy. In any case the Donations aroused less anger in Rome than might have been expected.[1] Antony had still a strong party and he addressed a long letter to the senate professing his desire to restore the republic and requesting the sanction of the conscript fathers for his new arrangements. This Octavian would not, of course, allow, but he was not strong enough to prevent the consuls and large numbers of the nobles from leaving Italy to join Antony in the East. Nevertheless the Donations of Alexandria produced a deep impression and one disastrous to Antony ;[2] they had not been greeted by any outburst of anger, but the tide of public sentiment ran more in favour of Octavian. Even in the ranks of Antony's army a deep distrust was forming in the minds of his soldiers. Under these circumstances, if Antony was to retain his hold upon his Roman supporters for any length of time, it was essential to dispel the growing suspicions. Unfortunately for himself he did the exact opposite, and Octavian found his strength daily increased by the blunders of his rival. The first great blunder, and the source of all the rest, was that Antony permitted Cleopatra to accompany him upon the campaign. While she was with him in his camp it was difficult for Antony to pose as a Roman general, and his Roman supporters urged that she should be left behind in Egypt. This, however, was not at all what she desired. It is clear that she feared the influence over Antony of his Roman officers and partisans whom she knew to have no sympathy with her ambitions. Not only did she insist upon accom-

---

[1] Octavian found it necessary to seize and publish Antony's will in order to heighten the effect.

[2] Antony's partisans tried to prevent the reading of that part of his letter to the senate dealing with the Donations ; evidently they feared the effect on public opinion.

panying him, but she made every effort to isolate him from his supporters and to surround him wholly with counsellors on whom she could rely. In this she was successful, and her success was all to the advantage of Octavian, for it furnished a visible justification of his charges against Antony, which many hitherto had disbelieved.

At the outbreak of the war the position of Octavian was precarious. His legal status was obscure, neither his fleet nor his army was ready for the struggle, and Italy was seething with mutinous disaffection.[1] If Antony had taken the offensive and invaded Italy at once he might have won the war, but this he failed to do. His delay has been attributed to Cleopatra, in whose company he squandered the precious time in luxurious idleness, but a closer study does much to clear his fame. To concentrate his army and to transport it to the West was a task of such magnitude that it seems very doubtful if Antony could have struck more quickly than he did.[2] In any case the opportunity slipped by, and when at last he led his forces into Epirus, Octavian was prepared to meet him there.

Into the details of the campaign it is unnecessary to enter. In the end the two armies found themselves face to face on the shores of the bay of Actium, directly across the Adriatic from Italy. For some time neither side was ready to risk a battle, at any rate on such terms that the other side would accept the challenge. Antony's land forces outnumbered those of Octavian, but his fleet was the weaker of the two. As the days passed without a battle the position of Antony grew steadily worse ; his fleet was blockaded in the bay and his army was so far cut off by land that its supplies began to fail. More ominous still, the dissensions among his followers grew constantly more violent. The Roman officers in the camp waged a bitter struggle with the partisans of

---

[1] For the difficulties of Octavian, see Ferrero, iv. 69–86. See also the article of Caspari in the *Classical Quarterly*, v. 230–5.

[2] Kromayer in his articles on the campaign of Actium has shown that the things that Antony is known to have accomplished were enough to occupy his time fully.

Cleopatra. Disgusted beyond measure at her influence over the general, his supporters began to slip away to join his rival. Under these circumstances his position was fast becoming untenable, and his officers advised him to fall back from the coast so as to draw his adversary after him, as Caesar had done not many years before. This would have entailed the sacrifice of the fleet, and Cleopatra strongly opposed it. Antony finally decided that his ships should make a desperate effort to break through the blockade, and that he and the Queen should sail for Egypt, while the army attempted to retreat by land.

That this was the strategic plan behind the battle of Actium Kromayer has shown beyond all reasonable doubt.[1] But the battle proved a decisive defeat for Antony. In the first place his plan miscarried, and, instead of breaking through, his fleet was defeated and almost utterly destroyed. Only a small squadron bearing Antony and Cleopatra with their treasures succeeded in passing through the hostile lines and sailed away to Egypt. This flight has been traditionally ascribed to faint-heartedness, or treachery, on the part of the Queen and to a love-sick infatuation on the part of Antony. The facts, however, furnish an overwhelming refutation of this interpretation. That the flight was premeditated is made clear beyond dispute by the preparations for the battle. Dio, indeed, expressly states as much,[2] and adds that Octavian was fully informed of the design in advance by deserters from Antony's camp.[3] But, though the flight to Egypt was carefully planned beforehand, the circumstances under which it happened were quite other than Antony intended and its results were wholly unforeseen. Instead of finding himself at the head of the greater part of his fleet with a large force of men on board sailing for Egypt after having triumphantly broken through the blockade of his enemies, he found himself a fugitive who had succeeded in escaping from a disastrous battle. This in itself irretrievably shattered his prestige in the East.

<hr />

[1] See his articles in *Hermes*, xxxiii and xxxiv.    [2] Dio, l. 15.    [3] Ibid., l. 23.

While thus his hold upon the orientals was broken, his army in Greece promptly abandoned him.  In forming his design Antony had allowed himself to overlook the sentiments of his Roman soldiers and had failed to take account of the psychological effect upon them of his acts.  His departure with the Egyptian squadron and the Queen opened the eyes of his men to his real policy.  After a brief hesitation his army surrendered to his rival.  So far as can be seen it was quite able to obey his orders and retreat to the East.  It was not merely the disgrace of his flight that decided his men to abandon him, for they rejected during seven days the offers of Octavian, alleging that their general was absent on some military business.  This seems to show that if he had returned promptly to his army and separated himself from Cleopatra, his men would still have followed him.  Probably one reason for his blunder was his failure to realize how deeply his soldiers resented the presence of the Queen in his camp and his manifest yielding to her influence.  For this she was in some part to blame, since she had made a consistent effort to surround him with her partisans while keeping all unfriendly counsellors at a distance, and, as a result, Antony had in some degree lost touch with his men.  When his army learned that he had fled with her to Egypt, their loyalty to him broke down.  It was no longer possible to entertain a doubt as to his policy ;  he was not a Roman general, fighting to restore the republic as he had pretended hitherto, but a king of Egypt, fighting for an eastern empire against Rome.  If his men should still follow him, they must renounce their nationality and give up all hope of seeing Italy again.  Face to face with realities that could no longer be misunderstood, they soon reached a decision.  The powerful army of Antony, unbeaten in the field, laid down the sword without another blow.  Octavian had only to accept its surrender and his rival's power was broken for ever.

Antony for a time cherished a hope that he might hold Egypt even yet.  He sought to rally round him such forces as had been left in the East when he started on his fatal campaign. But Roman loyalty to Antony was gone, and his soldiers no longer felt an interest in his fate. The legions in the East followed the example of the army in Epirus and deserted at the earliest opportunity. Octavian, as he advanced, encountered no resistance. For Antony and Cleopatra nothing remained but death. The battle of Actium, which from a military point of view was wholly inconclusive,[1] had none the less by its political consequences given the world to Octavian. The problems of that world the victor had now to face. Above all the problem which had baffled even the great Julius must be met, that of providing a government for the world which men could accept without too keen a sense of degradation.

[1] It has been suggested that Antony's army was forced to capitulate after Actium. The account of Dio does not give this impression ; it is expressly stated that no battle occurred. It seems incredible that an army which outnumbered its opponents should have allowed itself to be cut off and should have surrendered without a blow if it had had any real desire to fight. Its retreat may have been blocked, but the absence of any effort to break through can only be explained by the supposition that it no longer felt any wish to support Antony. The flight of that general from Actium to Egypt had made it all too clear what his real purpose was. The account in Plutarch is in harmony with this. Like Dio, he makes no mention of any fighting, but implies that the army of Antony surrendered voluntarily. Kromayer, whose views have in general been accepted in the text, seems to adopt the view here rejected as to the surrender. See Hartmann and Kromayer, *Römische Geschichte*, 156.

## VIII. THE RESTORATION OF THE REPUBLIC

AS a result of the fall of Antony and Cleopatra the whole East had been thrown into confusion, and Octavian found himself obliged to undertake a general reorganization of that part of the Roman world. As soon as this was finished, he returned to Italy to face the task of establishing a stable government. What actually existed was little better than an organized confusion. The triumvirate had expired in 32 B. C. and had not been renewed, but Octavian continued to exercise practically dictatorial powers; and to gain some semblance of legal justification for this, he had himself elected consul year by year. Yet it was obvious that he was no ordinary consul, and that all constitutional forms were more or less suspended. However obscure the legal situation might be, Octavian was in fact the sole commander of the legions, and now that peace had come the proper course would have been to disband the army until such time as a new war broke out. Under the actual conditions this was no longer possible, nor could Romans, even if attached to the customs of their ancestors, desire it. Recent events must have convinced all but the most shortsighted that the conquests of the last thirty years had created a new situation.

Since the destruction of Carthage it had been the singular good fortune of the republic to have on its frontiers no formidable enemy. In the East the weak and declining power of the successors of Alexander, so far from being dangerous, had long served Rome as a shield against the restless forces of Asia; while in the West the tribes of Spain and Gaul and Africa were too ill organized to cause serious apprehension. The frontiers could be protected against any probable enemy by a comparatively small force, and Rome no longer needed

to fear revolt within her borders. The last uprising of the
Spaniards had been suppressed, and as much of Gaul as Rome
essayed to hold was reasonably quiet. In such circumstances
men might persuade themselves that a large army was super-
fluous. Now, however, conditions had materially changed.
When Pompey annexed the province of Syria, he not only
extinguished the Seleucid dynasty, which had grown too
weak to serve any longer as an adequate protection, but he
brought the Roman frontier into contact with a new and
dangerous foe. The Parthians, now immediate neighbours,
were a menace that Rome could not ignore, and they must
be held in check by a strong force stationed in the East. It
may be doubted if the people of Italy fully realized this, for
Syria was remote and conditions there may not have been
clearly understood by men who stayed at home. Nearer at
hand was another peril to which they could not shut their
eyes, for the conquest of Gaul had created a new situation
on the northern frontier. The vast territories which Caesar
had added to the empire were still too new to Roman
sovereignty for any confidence to be felt in their loyalty to
their new rulers. If the military forces there were too much
diminished, a revolt was likely to occur. The annexation
had, moreover, entailed responsibilities from which the
Romans could not escape. If the newly conquered Gauls
were allowed to retain their arms, they would in all probability use them against their conquerors at the earliest opportunity. If they were disarmed, the duty of protecting them
against their enemies was plain, and along the Rhine frontier
the restless Germans could be kept off only by a powerful
army. No one could reasonably propose to strip the great
river of defenders and to wait till the invaders had made
havoc in the newly acquired provinces before beginning preparations for defence. Under the circumstances it must have
been clear that the great force then under Octavian's command could not be entirely disbanded, but that a considerable part must remain under arms for an indefinite period.
That at some future day Rome could dismiss her soldiers and

return to a peace footing may have been the dream of many, but they could not imagine that that time had yet arrived. The Romans, therefore, found themselves compelled to accept a standing army as a necessity of the present, at least, and, if this were granted, there could be no serious question that Octavian must be its commander.

Public opinion seems to have been unanimous in calling on Octavian to remain at the head of the army. His problem did not lie in reconciling men to that necessity, but rather in finding some means of retaining his position without offending too deeply such other sentiments as had a strong hold on their minds. If the world was eagerly demanding peace and order, it was no less insistent on a revival of the old republic. The force of this demand was such that Octavian could not safely ignore it. Even if he had been far less astute than he was, the events within his memory would have sufficed to convince him that public opinion was still a force that no leader, if he hoped to possess stable power, could venture to despise.

The story of Caesar's life must have been full of meaning to his adopted son. He knew how Caesar and Pompey before the civil war had manœuvred to put each other in the wrong. He could not be blind to the fact that Caesar's victory in the negotiations had made his march on Rome successful. His strategy in the first part of the war would have been quite impossible if the sentiment of Italy had been resolutely hostile to his cause. Had the towns of the North resisted his advance, Pompey might have rallied his forces and have defended Italy. If the peninsula had been seething with discontent, Caesar would not have dared to take his army off to Spain as he had done. If Pompey's diplomatic defeat had thus influenced the first part of the war, so in his last days when the world was at his feet Caesar had found himself embarrassed and perplexed. It proved impossible for him to organize a government that men were willing to accept, and this led directly to the Ides of March. That tragedy showed clearly that the Roman world would not consent to be long governed by the sword alone, and that the man who tried to rule it thus would walk in daily peril of his life, trembling at the shadow of conspiracy on every hand and depending for his safety on the vigilance and fidelity of his armed guards.

Although the control of the legions might be the only thing that mattered at the moment, Octavian felt the need of building on some more stable foundation for the future. This was only made the clearer by his recent victory at Actium, since the war with Antony had shown that even the legions could not be depended on to act indefinitely against the sentiment of the world around them. Subject though they were to an iron discipline, the soldiers were yet Romans drawn from the ranks of the common people, and it was impossible that in the long run any strong drift of sentiment should fail to influence the army. That this was true the sudden collapse of Antony's power after Actium had placed beyond all doubt, and Octavian could hardly miss the moral of his rival's downfall. Antony's ruin had been due to the fact that he had adopted a policy for which Roman soldiers would not fight. Octavian cannot have imagined that he possessed a stronger hold upon the loyalty of his men than Antony had had in earlier years. Plutarch bears eloquent testimony to the passionate devotion of Antony's soldiers, even in the midst of the Parthian disaster, declaring that their loyalty had never been surpassed and that the approval of their general was valued more than life itself by officers and men alike.[1] Yet even this loyalty had failed, because the object of it had blindly ignored the drift of public sentiment. If the victor at Actium should venture to defy the deeply rooted feelings of the Roman world, he too might see his power suddenly collapse. The very circumstances under which he had become supreme constituted a warning that he must find

---

[1] Plutarch, *Antony*, 43. Plutarch was not a contemporary, of course, but he doubtless drew from contemporary sources. In any case his testimony is borne out by all we know of Antony's career up to the last campaign.

a way to reconcile men to his authority if it was to be permanent.

If the position of Octavian was such as made compromise appear necessary, this policy was wholly congenial to his temperament.  By nature cautious and averse to extremes, he had a real sympathy with the feelings of his subjects and a strong love for the old Roman customs and traditions.  The world was now demanding a return to regular government, and this, to Roman minds, implied of necessity a restoration of the old republic.  It was not liberty in the modern sense for which men yearned so much as law.  The mass of the Roman people had never had a voice in public affairs except in theory.  The voting on all questions had always taken place in Rome; and the vast majority of the citizens, who lived scattered about in Italy, could never hope to cast a ballot in an election or to vote upon a law.  The decision had been in the hands of the rabble of Rome and of the handful of voters from the country towns of Italy who might chance to be there on the appointed day, or who were rich enough to make a journey there for the purpose.  As a consequence, under the republic the greater part of the people had never taken any active share in the government.  It would hardly seem that they can now have been deeply interested in the restoration of privileges which they had never used in the past and could not hope to use in the future.  But to bring back the reign of law was a very different matter.  Under the law men knew what acts were held permissible and what acts were forbidden.  They could demand, as an unquestionable right, a public trial in which they had an opportunity to plead their cause and where definite evidence of a definite offence must be presented and weighed according to known rules.  To this the only alternative was the arbitrary action of individual men.  In the days of the triumvirate, during the proscription, men were put to death without any public charge being brought against them, were condemned on vague and general grounds, were sentenced without trial, on no one knew what evidence, and with no chance whatever to reply to the unknown accusation.  While such things were done no man could feel himself secure in either person or property. All men were anxious that government by arbitrary force and individual caprice should now give place to the known processes of law.

But the entire body of Roman law had grown up under the republic and presupposed that form of government at every turn.  If the law were to be restored to its supremacy, it would entail the restoration of the republic as well.  This was the more true because the Roman system had bound the military, administrative, and judicial functions together in one body of institutions.  It was impossible to return to legality without reviving the old system of which the courts were but one part.  It was useless to attempt to meet the universal demand for legality by devising some new system, however excellent, since what the world passionately craved was precisely a return to beaten tracks which had the supreme merit of familiarity.  It was, perhaps, this feeling which caused the Romans to regard the name of king with such intense aversion.  The word *rex* seemed the symbol of arbitrary power and hence the negation of all law.  The future was to show that they felt no such violent hatred for a monarch who could contrive to bring his supremacy within the known forms of the Roman law.

Nor could Octavian ignore the immense force of the sentimental associations which clustered around the old republic. Whatever its defects had been, all that was glorious in Rome's past was closely bound up with its traditional forms ;  the newer institutions, dictatorships and triumvirates, were odious and discredited.  Although the military power had seized control, thrusting aside the old nobility, the circumstances attending the predominance of the army had produced a revulsion of feeling in favour of the vanquished aristocracy. Just as in England the execution of Charles I threw a halo around the memory of that king and did much to bring about the restoration of his son, so in Rome the proscription produced a strong reaction.  The Romans were a people of an eminently conservative and aristocratic temper, and the massacre of the old nobility had filled them with pity and with horror.  They had found it difficult to submit patiently to a government of upstarts stained with the blood of the great houses, and they turned with all the more deference and respect to such of the old families as survived, desiring earnestly to see them restored to a position of dignity and honour in the state.

If Octavian hoped to build a stable government he must take into account these demands of public opinion, and must discover some way of meeting the necessities of the present without doing too much violence to the traditional usages of the past.  In particular he must effect a reconciliation with the old nobility and persuade them to lend to his authority the lustre of their names.  In his struggle with Antony he had made repeated professions of his desire to restore the republic, and the world was now demanding that he should make good his promises.  Accordingly in 27 B. C., having carefully set the whole machine in order, he proclaimed the restoration.  His own description of that event is worthy of quotation.  On the monument at Ancyra is recorded the view which he wished men to take of his career. To his establishment of the principate, as his government has come to be called, he alludes in these words (vi. 13 sqq.) :

In my sixth and seventh consulships, when I had extinguished the flames of civil war, being by universal consent the master of all things, I transferred the commonwealth from my own power to that of the senate and the Roman people.  For which service of mine I was called Augustus by a decree of the senate, laurels were placed upon the door-posts of my house, a civic crown was fixed above the door, and a golden shield was placed in the Curia Julia on which was an inscription testifying that it was given to me by the senate and the Roman people because of my valour, clemency, justice, and piety.  After that time, while excelling all others in dignity, I possessed no greater power than did those who were my colleagues in the magistracy.[1]

[1] The text of the Ancyra monument has often been reprinted.  The latest and best edition in English is that of Hardy.

There is here no suggestion of any new constitution for the Roman world, but rather it is implied that the old republic was set up again without serious change. That this view of the case does not accurately represent the facts the whole history of the early empire bears emphatic witness. Even in the reign of Augustus—as Octavian should be called after 27 B. C.—the lack of harmony between his theory and his practice became sufficiently glaring. From this the conclusion has sometimes been drawn that he was simply a hypocrite playing the leading role in an elaborate farce. On the face of it this seems too simple an explanation ; it can hardly be believed that a political settlement that lasted for several centuries had no better foundation than the whim of one man. But even if it be accepted, there is still a problem to be solved in explaining why the farce should have been so well received and so successful, and how the world could be so readily deceived by forms which were obviously devoid of substance. In considering the government established by Octavian in 27 B. C. there is one fallacy against which it is essential to guard, and it is one into which the historian is especially liable to fall. Knowing what did actually result from any given act, it is easy to assume that it was part of the conscious purpose of the act, which is not always the case. Even though it is true that the restoration of the republic was unreal, this is not of itself an adequate proof that Augustus meant it to be unreal or was entirely to blame for its unreality. Indeed it can be shown that to a large degree the unreality was due to causes for which he was not in any way responsible. The critics of Augustus have sometimes demanded of him the impossible ; thus Gardthausen, his chief modern biographer, asks bitterly why he did not restore the republic in a real sense, if he had any desire to do so, and concludes that his professions of republican sentiment were wholly hypocritical.[1] But this seems hardly fair to Augus-

---

[1] Meyer has argued in favour of the sincerity of Augustus in his essay on that emperor published originally in the *Historische Zeitschrift* for 1903, but now included in his *Kleine Schriften*. Gardthausen replied in the *Neue*

tus, since much was involved in the matter besides his personal will. The republic had fallen long before he was born, and whether he could restore it or not would obviously depend upon the underlying causes of its fall. To all the Romans of that day the terms republic and senate were almost synonymous. The vital weakness of the senate since the time of Marius had been the fact that it had no real hold upon the loyalty of the army ; such a hold no mere imperial edict could give, and without it the supremacy of the senate could never be much more than nominal. What Augustus had it in his power to restore to the conscript fathers he did in fact restore, and the Romans, more reasonable than some of his modern judges, accepted what he offered them as a satisfactory solution.

The vital point in the new settlement was obviously the command of the army. Here there was little room for discussion as to the course to be pursued ; it was clear that a powerful standing army was necessary for the present, and Rome had but one method of dealing with such an army. Since the republic had first become engaged in distant wars, the great command had been an essential part of its machinery. This device was not, as has been sometimes held, in any way peculiar to the democrats at Rome ; it was the only means that existed for carrying on war on any large scale, and it was used equally by both parties. The senate, no less than the people, created great commands, but the manner in which it was done differed in the two cases. Since the senate ordinarily had control of both foreign and provincial affairs, that body could create a great command by a manipulation of the provincial assignments from year to year. This process did not entail the necessity of any startling or unusual procedure ; for example, when the second war with Mithridates broke out and the senate wished to send Lucullus to take charge of it, it was comparatively easy to arrange the matter. Lucullus was consul at the time and had already been assigned a province under the Sempronian law. This he straightway resigned, and the senate was then free to allot him a new province in Asia. Once he had been placed in command of the war it was a simple matter for the senate to keep him there as long as might be thought desirable. All that was necessary was to omit the Asiatic provinces each year from the list of those to be assigned by lot and to prolong his *imperium*.

When, however, the people wished to send Pompey to supersede Lucullus, they could only do so by passing the Manilian law. Such a law, although perfectly constitutional, was unusual and was thus open to criticism ; moreover, it attracted much more attention, both then and since, than did the annual assignment of the provinces by the senate. It is this that has given rise to the impression that it was the people who were responsible for the development of the great command. In fact the Manilian law did not create such a command, for it already existed ; all that it did was to transfer the command from one general to another. The question between the parties was not how the war should be carried on, but simply who should have charge of it.

That the great command involved a possible peril to the commonwealth was obvious enough, and it had been often found that it met one emergency by creating another. The general who won an important war was almost as serious a problem to the state as the enemy whom he had defeated. Yet though alive to the dangers of the great command, no Roman regarded it as an institution which was inconsistent with the existence of the republic. Such commands had been repeatedly created without serious consequences. In the days of Cicero, Pompey had held one of vast extent, and yet, if men were to believe the most eloquent of republican orators, the republic had continued to flourish.

The only method of controlling a strong army, therefore, was by creating a new great command. No party had any alternative to propose, since it was plainly impossible for the legions to be distributed equally among the provinces,

I

as circumstances required their concentration along the frontiers. The only point open for discussion was whether there should be several great commands or only one. On this question Romans could hardly hesitate ; experience, dearly bought by two long civil wars, had shown the probable result of several simultaneous commands. All men were ready to concede that, if a large standing army must be maintained, the army as a whole should remain subject to the *imperium* of Octavian. What public opinion demanded was not that he should lay down his command, but that he should exercise it in accordance with the old republican forms.

The republic without the senate was unthinkable to the Roman, and, unless the senate included among its members the great noble families, it lost all claim to his respect. But membership in the senate had always been closely connected with the magistracies of the republic ; and so a revival of the republic, if it were to have enough reality to be deceptive, must entail a return to office of the aristocracy. On this point there was little room for hypocrisy ; Augustus could not persuade the Roman world that the republic existed at all unless what survived of the republican nobility took a large apparent part in the government. It was necessary for him to associate the senate with himself, at least in name, and to allow the old families to hold many of the high positions in the state. In the last analysis his sovereignty might rest upon the swords of his legions, but only if he gave it an aristocratic appearance would it be accepted by the world.

If a reconciliation with the aristocracy was thus imposed upon Augustus, recent events had made such a reconciliation much easier for him than it had been for Caesar. In the case of the latter the defeat of the nobles had been too recent for them to forgive the victor, and it was still possible for them to dream that the yoke of the army could be shaken off and that the senate could recover its control. What followed Caesar's death had proved this to be impossible, and the greater part of the generation that had known the days of freedom had perished. The great families which had survived the proscription and the civil wars were broken and impoverished, and were ready now to accept with gratitude a system which restored them, at least outwardly, to their former splendour.

Circumstances and the weight of public opinion, therefore, clearly dictated to Augustus the general form his settlement must take. He was to be commander of the Roman army, but the senate was to be a partner in the government and the nobility was to be given a prominent place in the state. It only remained to work out the details by which this general result could be most readily attained. Here Augustus was very careful to follow republican precedents in all particulars where this was possible, and so to make his government appear a continuation of the old republic. According to the usage of the past, if Augustus was to be the head of the army he should be given the governorship of the provinces where that army was stationed, because the Romans made no distinction between the civil and the military functions. It seemed, therefore, entirely natural when a law was passed by the assembly conferring on Augustus the proconsular *imperium* for ten years over the principal frontier provinces of the empire. The position thus created for him was not materially different from that held by Pompey under the Manilian law.[1] It is true that the army given to Augustus was larger, but since the military power intrusted to Pompey had been practically irresistible, this could hardly seem important. It is also true that so many provinces had never before been subject to one man, but the provinces counted for little except for the legions

[1] Meyer is right in saying that Augustus was rather the heir of Pompey than of Julius Caesar (*Caesars Monarchie*, 548). It might be questioned, however, whether he has not attributed too definite a design and too clear a purpose to Pompey. If he had been successful, the position of Pompey in the Roman world would have been very similar to that afterwards held by Augustus, but this does not prove that Pompey had any notion of what he was seeking to gain or of the inevitable consequences of his acts.

stationed there. A Roman might, therefore, regard the position of Augustus as substantially the same as that of Pompey in the days of the republic.

There were many obvious differences in detail in the two cases, but they would hardly strike a contemporary as of vital significance since, in most cases, this significance lay chiefly in the future, which the contemporaries of Augustus, unlike the historian, did not know. They were bound to judge by their own past experience and this alone ; and judging thus, the differences cannot have seemed of much importance. For example, the provinces assigned to Augustus were widely separated, and, instead of residing in them, he found it convenient to remain in Rome and from this point to carry on their administration by means of deputies. This could hardly be called an innovation, since Pompey had governed Spain from Italy with the sanction of the senate. But if this were to be done it must have seemed childish to try to prevent Augustus from entering the city limits, as Pompey had been prevented. It would be absurd for the senate to meet in the suburbs every time Augustus wished to attend the session, and no one could reasonably object to permitting him to come within the city while retaining the *imperium*.

Serious discussion only became possible when it came to determining the precise relations that should exist between the princeps, as the holder of the new great command came to be called, and the restored republic of which he was to be nominally one of the magistrates. If their functions could have been clearly separated, the princeps might have administered his provinces, while the republican magistrates and pro-magistrates under the advice and direction of the senate governed the remainder of the Roman world according to the old republican tradition. In actual fact the princeps found himself so vitally concerned in the working of the republic beside him that he was inevitably driven to seek to direct and control it. In the first place he derived his own authority from the senate and the people, and what

they gave they could revoke. Then too, like all Roman generals,
he was forced to promise rewards to his soldiers, and to secure
the redemption of his pledges he was compelled to interfere
in politics. Moreover, many of his acts required formal
sanction from the senate and assembly, and might, in theory,
be reversed or modified by them. Perhaps the most important point of all, however, was the fact that he drew many
of his officers from the ranks of the republican nobility, which
necessarily gave him a keen interest in the results of the
elections ; if he wished one of his deputies to have consular
rank, he must see to it that the man in question was elected
consul. In a word, the princeps was so closely concerned
in the working of the republican machine that he could not
permit it to work freely, but was obliged to some extent to
direct and control it.

The Romans had already learned by experience that the
holder of a great command could not remain a mere spectator
in politics. Pompey was certainly no politician, yet he had
never been able to let politics alone, not because of any
personal desire to meddle, but because of his position. While
he was engaged in the war with Mithridates he had been
forced to keep an eye on Rome, because measures were
constantly brought forward there which were certain to
affect him. He had been obliged to seek some weapon with
which to ward off the blows aimed at him by his enemies ;
this he found in the tribunate. If he could secure the
election of one or more of his trusted agents to this office,
they could protect his interests by the use of their veto and
could bring forward any new proposals which he might desire.
This connexion between the general invested with a great
command and the tribunes had been carried even farther
by Caesar during his term as proconsul of the Gauls, and it
must have been an association very familiar by that time
to Roman minds.

Past experience had shown the necessity for some connexion between the princeps and the machinery of the
republican government, and this could be established in two

ways. One was by permitting the princeps to select some
of the regular magistrates and use them as his agents, as
had been done by Pompey : the other was to allow the
princeps to act in person rather than by deputy, since he
intended to reside in Rome the greater part of the time.
For this purpose Augustus could be given one of the regular
offices of the republic, or the special powers which he wished
to have could be conferred upon him without his holding
such an office.  Both methods were at first employed.  In
view of the recent precedents of Pompey and of Caesar it
was natural that men should think of the tribunate for this
purpose.  Augustus, being a patrician (by Caesar's creation
though not by birth),could not hold this office directly, and
hence he had the tribunician power, detached from the office,
conferred upon him.  This can hardly have struck the
Romans as a very important innovation ; it must have
seemed little more than allowing Augustus to do in person
what preceding holders of a great command had been in the
habit of doing by deputy.

The conditions of the case required more than this, however.  In order to control the republic more easily, especially
in the first days of its restoration, Augustus had himself
elected one of the consuls every year.  He was thus at the
same time the holder of a great command (his proconsular
*imperium*), was invested with the tribunician power, and
was one of the two chief regular magistrates.  This, in brief,
was what may be called the first draft of the imperial constitution ; but to the Romans of that day it seemed a partial
and imperfect restoration of the old régime.

Augustus soon found that the arrangement he had made
was unsatisfactory.  The stricter republicans still held aloof
and would take no part in public affairs.  They felt that
while one man thus held the consulship year after year, the
state of affairs was little better than a tyranny, and that
all talk of a restoration of the republic was a mockery.  In
addition to such opposition as this, Augustus had doubtless
become conscious of several less apparent objections to the

practice. If he held the consulship, a large amount of routine
business would necessarily devolve upon him. His health
was feeble, and he may have regarded this as a serious waste
of the time and energy which were sorely needed elsewhere.
Another inconvenience lay in the fact that if he held the
consulship each year, he would be forced to deny to many
men a distinction which they had come to claim almost as
a right, and would thus give bitter offence to those old
families that survived and to the public that had come to
look upon them with a sentimental affection. Partly to
rid himself of a troublesome burden, and probably even more
to conciliate the republicans, Augustus in 23 B. C. suddenly
resigned the consulship and refused to hold it any longer.
This concession won over to his side the last of the obstinate
upholders of the past, and their chief leaders accepted
office under the new régime. With this event the reconciliation of the republic and the principate seemed final and
complete.

But when Augustus laid down the consulship and so
divested himself of any of the regular magistracies, the need
for some close connexion between the princeps and the
republic acquired an added force. This difficulty was
promptly solved in a new fashion. Augustus began to lay
greater stress upon the tribunician power than he had
hitherto done, but something more than this was necessary.
Accordingly he had certain of the consular powers which he
desired to retain conferred upon him by special laws. He
was given the right to summon the senate and to bring
matters before that body. He could do both these things
by virtue of the tribunician power, but only subject to annoy-
ing restrictions. If he convened the senate in this way the
summons of the consuls had precedence over his, and, when
the senate met, it was the consuls who presided and controlled the order of business. This would offer opportunities
for vexatious obstruction and delay, which the powers now
conferred upon Augustus would remove. Another special
law gave him the right to preside over the elections ; this

would furnish him a chance to influence their results without too great a break with the traditional forms. He was furthermore permitted to retain his *imperium* even within the city of Rome. When he renounced the consulship he could not otherwise have entered the city without forfeiting the *imperium*, and must have spent his time in the suburbs and country villas round about as Pompey had formerly been obliged to do.[1] These changes involved no actual innovation since, while he held the consulship, he had possessed all these powers by reason of his office. All that was done was to permit him to lay down that office and yet retain some of its rights and privileges which seemed more or less necessary to secure the convenient transaction of the public business. No alarm seems to have been felt at these reservations on his surrender of the consulship. The fear of anarchy was still strong, and men were disposed to quarrel with the princeps because he took so little, rather than because he asked too much. Confident that what he had gained was ample for his purpose, he steadfastly refused the still more sweeping powers pressed upon him.

With the changes made in 22 B.C. the principate was given its final form in point of legal theory. Throughout the early empire this theory was destined to undergo scarcely any alteration. It is true that the actual working of the government was speedily and radically transformed, and, after a brief vision of a restored republic, the drift toward monarchy overwhelmed the constitution. Even in the lifetime of Augustus the principate had been profoundly modified in point of fact, and he had come to be, not the first citizen of the republic, but an emperor in the modern sense. This transformation was brought about by causes far deeper than

[1] It has usually been held that at this time the *imperium* of Augustus was declared *maius* and extended to include the senatorial provinces. McFayden, in an able article in *Classical Philology* for January 1921, has shown—conclusively as it seems to the present writer—that this is a mistake. If Augustus received any right to interfere in the senatorial provinces, he made practically no use of it, and such control as he had over them he obtained in other and less direct ways.

his personal volition. In the main it was not his fault that the republic that he had restored failed to maintain itself. Its vital weaknesses were not those that any single man could remedy, and it was far less the conscious choice of Augustus than the irresistible pressure of imperial necessities that transformed the principate into a despotism.

# IX. THE TRANSFORMATION OF THE PRINCIPATE

THE settlement toward which Augustus had been feeling his way ever since the battle of Actium may be regarded as complete in 22 B. C. In that year a sort of partnership, sometimes called a dyarchy, had been arranged between the republic (officially restored in 27) and the princeps, as Augustus now began to be styled. In theory there was no suggestion of a monarchy or of a monarch ; the emperor [1] was simply a general of the republic to whom certain exceptional powers had been intrusted for a term of years. Although no formal change was ever made in this legal theory, yet before his death Augustus had come to be the absolute ruler of the entire Roman world. The purpose of the present chapter is to call attention to some hitherto neglected causes for this striking transformation.

Although in point of law a general of the republic, the powers conferred upon the princeps were so sweeping as to make him a partner of the senate rather than a subordinate magistrate. To his sole control had been committed a number of provinces, and over these he ruled by virtue of a formal law of the Roman people. These provinces embraced most of Spain and the newly conquered part of Gaul in the West, while in the East they included Cilicia and Syria, as well as the former kingdom of Egypt. Great as were the powers thus given, the charge of these regions involved yet other responsibilities. The provinces of the princeps had been so selected that they carried with them the control of the army and of the foreign policy of the empire. Most of the Roman legions were stationed in his provinces, and by his

---

[1] Everything that could suggest monarchy to the Roman was carefully avoided by Augustus. The title *imperator*, from which our word emperor is derived, was one bestowed on any victorious general of the republic.

proconsular *imperium* Augustus had sole command of them.
The governors of the senatorial provinces enjoyed an *imperium* which was legally independent of the princeps, but
they seldom found themselves possessed of a sufficient number of troops for serious military operations. The proconsuls
of Africa alone were an exception, since they sometimes
carried on campaigns of some importance against the tribes
of that region, and, if victorious, they were allowed the
honour of a triumph. This in itself shows that they commanded the forces there, not as officers of the princeps, but
by a commission direct from the state and independent of
him. Their armies were too small, however, to make them
a serious factor in the situation ; it was to the emperor that
nearly the entire army looked up as its commanding general.
It is, therefore, correct to characterize Augustus as the war-
lord of the Roman standing army,[1] but he held this position
indirectly because of the particular provinces subject to his
proconsular *imperium*. With these provinces went also the
control of foreign policy. The relations of Rome with other
states were largely in the hands of the governors of the
frontier provinces. Whether there was war or peace with
Parthia would be determined, in so far as it rested with Rome
to decide the matter, by the course pursued by the governor
of Syria, who was now the deputy of Augustus, removable at
his pleasure, and bound to carry out his orders.

Yet, though a large extent of territory and powers of great
importance were committed to the sole charge of the new
commander-in-chief, he did not control the entire Roman
world ; the republic stood by his side and retained the management of all the older and more settled provinces. To
govern these the old machinery was employed without change
except that Pompey's law, fixing a five-year interval between
the magistracy and pro-magistracy, was now enforced, and
that Caesar's practice of allowing the proconsul to remain for
two years in his province was likewise observed. In 27 B. C.
ten provinces had been reserved as senatorial, and this was

[1] Gardthausen, vol. ii, pt. 1, 522.

almost as large a number as the republic could provide with governors. In 22 B. C., when the final settlement was made, two other provinces, Narbonensis and Cyprus, were ceded to the senate by the princeps, and at about the same time the number of the praetors was increased by two.[1] Approximately half the empire was thus subject to the conscript fathers, and within this half they held very nearly the position which Sulla had given them, while they were freed from the responsibility for the turbulent frontier provinces which a painful experience had shown they could not govern.

The policy which Augustus followed in his portion of the Roman world was in the main a peaceful one. At first sight it seems almost paradoxical that Rome should have ceased to be a conquering power as soon as she was really organized for war. Without a genuine standing army she had won the world, yet now, with a permanent war-lord, the legions halted and stood still. The paradox, though striking, is not difficult of explanation. Many of the motives which have led modern states to adopt a policy of expansion were of little weight in the empire of Augustus. The world he governed was not overpopulated and stood in no need of new territories for colonization. It was not industrial in any modern sense, and required no new sources of raw materials or new markets for its goods. Even if these needs made themselves felt, the system of land transportation was so clumsy that markets were of little use to the manufacturer unless they could be reached by sea, and all such markets Rome already held. The surplus capital available could find an ample field for profitable investment in the newly annexed regions of Gaul or in the older provinces. Thus none of the causes which have led to the imperialism of our days exerted much influence in Rome. Since the Second Punic War there had been little desire for expansion on the part of the Roman

[1] Making ten in all. I have followed Mommsen, *Staatsrecht*, ii. 202, in the view that in 27 Augustus reduced the number of praetors from sixteen (the number under Caesar) to eight and that in 23 he raised it to ten, the new praetors being given charge of the treasury. With the five-year interval there were doubtless some ex-praetors who could not take provinces.

government ; the recent conquests had been made by the over-great proconsuls whom the senate was unable to control. Caesar and Pompey had extended the empire, but both had consulted their own pleasure rather than the wishes of the conscript fathers. The possibility of such aggressive wars as they had waged was now abolished, since the princeps controlled the frontiers, and he had no intention of permitting his officers to act in any way contrary to his policy. That policy was essentially the same as that of the senate, but with the vital difference that Augustus could enforce his will whereas the senate could not.

In addition to lacking most of the modern motives for expansion, the emperor had strong reasons of his own for desiring to keep the peace as far as possible. By temperament and natural ability a statesman and administrator rather than a soldier, Augustus felt little inclination for military adventure. New conquests would require large armies, and he hesitated to intrust too great a power to any man whose loyalty was not above suspicion. Moreover, war would entail heavy expenses. In the past, when Roman arms had been directed against civilized or semi-civilized peoples, the plunder had not infrequently been more than sufficient to defray the cost. Now, however, there were upon the frontiers only rude and barbarous tribes from whom such profits could not be expected. There was but one quarter where a successful campaign might be remunerative, and that was in the East. The conquest of Parthia promised a rich booty, but experience had shown the Romans that this would prove a difficult and perilous venture. If Augustus undertook it, he must either lead his armies in person or intrust then to a deputy. If he assumed the active command, defeat might easily cost him his throne ; if he sent one of his generals, failure would diminish his prestige and glory, while success would inevitably create a most embarrassing situation. The conqueror of Parthia would be a dangerous subject and might readily become a rival. It was natural that the princeps should avoid an enterprise where success or failure seemed almost equally damaging to his position and should prefer, if possible, to keep the peace upon the eastern frontier.

But if Augustus put aside dreams of conquest, he still had work enough before him. Spain had never been completely subdued, and the turbulent mountain tribes gave constant trouble. In Gaul the work of organization was still far from finished ; Caesar had begun the task of setting up a systematic administration, but the civil war had interrupted him. To the settlement of the West Augustus turned his attention as soon as he had restored order in the East. In this he found a vast and necessary task, and one entirely adapted to his temper and abilities. Hardly had he officially restored the republic in 27 B. C. than he set out for Gaul and Spain, leaving his colleagues in the consulship to manage affairs in Rome during his absence. He did not return to the city till the end of 24, after having completed the provincial organization of Gaul and quieted Spain, where serious fighting was found necessary. Augustus remained in Rome over two years and used the opportunity to revise the settlement of 27 B. C. and make the changes in the principate that have already been discussed. After giving to his government what was destined to be its final form, he turned his attention once more to the East, leaving the city in 21. During his absence his trusted general Agrippa represented him in the capital. After the princeps returned to Italy in 18 he had his proconsular powers renewed for five years, and in 16 set out again for Gaul, where he remained for the next three years.

The work of organizing and pacifying the West had been fairly well completed by 16 B. C., so that Augustus could devote his attention to another phase of the problem committed to his care. The northern frontier of the empire was in a most unsatisfactory condition ; everywhere it bordered on turbulent and warlike tribes and for much of its length it rested on no natural barriers. If peace and security were to be obtained for the Roman world, this boundary must be rounded out and rendered easy of defence. From Macedonia to Gaul Rome held only a thin strip along the shores of the Adriatic, and from the mountain fastnesses of the interior the barbarians swept down in constant raids upon the settled districts. Unless the Romans were willing to withdraw from the coast they had little choice but to push their frontier forward to the Danube. In Gaul, too, there were frontier difficulties. Caesar had carried his conquests to the Rhine, but the Germans on the other side of that river gave continual trouble, and the best method of dealing with them was still an open question. In both these regions Augustus decided to consolidate the Roman possessions by an advance. The Germans were to be conquered and Gaul protected from their raids by pushing the frontier to the Elbe, while farther East, by the addition of Pannonia and Moesia, the boundary was to be brought forward to the Danube. These lines would be much easier to defend than the old ones, and the wars resulting from this rounding out of the frontiers might have a political value to the princeps. His office was in theory a temporary one, and it might be a matter of shrewd policy to silence all objection to its continuance. The commander-in-chief could hardly be dispensed with in the midst of war, and an aggressive policy on the frontiers might make the renewal of his powers seem necessary even to the stern republicans. This is suggested, at least, by the fact that in 18 B. C. Augustus had had his *imperium* prolonged for only half the original term, and when this time expired had taken it again for but five years. As soon, however, as the new policy was inaugurated on the frontiers he reverted to the earlier precedent, and in 8 B. C. had his powers renewed for ten years.

While he was thus occupied with the organization of his provinces and the rectification of the frontier, Augustus exercised his proconsular *imperium* largely through his own immediate family circle. At the start he shared his burden with his general Agrippa. In 23 B. C. he dispatched this trusted officer to Syria and gave him charge of all—or most

—of the eastern part of the empire. When he himself undertook a journey to the East he recalled the general to Rome to act as his representative. Upon the return of Augustus to the city, Agrippa, after suppressing a revolt in Spain, went back to Syria in 17 and remained in charge there until 13 B. C. In the early years of the principate Augustus and his ablest lieutenant thus divided the responsibility for the management of the imperial provinces between them. The fidelity of a general so trusted was naturally a matter of concern to the emperor. To make doubly sure of his loyalty, Augustus sought to bind him to the imperial family, and with this end in view a marriage was arranged between Agrippa and the only child of the emperor, his daughter Julia. Augustus then conferred upon his general powers second only to his own and recognized him as his probable successor.

For such other officers as he needed to administer his provinces and lead his armies Augustus employed but few of the old nobility. Among his officers whose names are preserved the majority—previous to 16 B. C.—were men whose rank had been acquired since the civil wars. During this time the higher republican aristocracy played only an insignificant role in the imperial provinces.[1]

A list of the known officers of Augustus from 30 to 16 B. C. may be of interest.

T. Statilius Taurus (cos. 37 and 26), Dalmatia 33–28. A new man.

Sex. Appuleius (cos. 29), Spain before 26. On his father's side of no distinction, but on his mother's a nephew of Augustus.

M. Appuleius (cos. 20), an officer in the army in 23. Brother of above.

C. Antistius Vetus (cos. 30), Spain 26. A member of a praetorian family.

C. Furnius (cos. 17), Spain 22. His father was given consular rank by Augustus.

M. Vinicius (cos. 19), Germany 25. The son of a knight.

P. Silius Nerva (cos. 20), Spain after 25. A member of a praetorian family.

M. Lollius (cos. 21), Germany 16 and in Thrace before. A new man.

T. Carisius—never consul—Spain 25–22. A new man.

L. Aemilius Paullus Lepidus (cos. 34), Spain 24. Noble.

M. Licinius Crassus (cos. 30), Macedonia 29. Noble.

M. Tullius Cicero (cos. 30), Syria 27. Noble.

M. Valerius Messalla Corvinus (cos. 31), Gaul before 27. Noble.

All statements may be checked by Liebenam's or Klein's edition of the

Augustus made use of his sojourn in Gaul from 16 to 13 B. C. to inaugurate his new policy on the frontiers. Several incidents combined to furnish an excuse for the change. On the Rhine the legate of the emperor, M. Lollius, had been defeated by the Germans and at about the same time the tribes of Noricum and Pannonia had made an attack on Istria. The senatorial governor of Illyricum, P. Silius, met the incursion of the barbarians successfully, and Marquardt is probably right in supposing that the conquest of Noricum was the direct outcome of the raid and its repulse.[1] The situation on the frontier was, perhaps, dangerous, and could in any case furnish an excuse for a more vigorous policy. Augustus set out for Gaul, taking with him his two stepsons, Tiberius and Drusus, with the intention of giving the two young princes a trial; and, if they displayed capacity, of placing the solution of the frontier difficulties in their hands. His stepsons were first employed in the minor task of subjugating the mountainous region known as Raetia. In this they were successful and demonstrated their fitness for command. More serious responsibilities followed, and they were placed at the head of the aggressive defensive on which Augustus had resolved. When the emperor returned to Rome in 13 B. C. he left Drusus to carry on the campaign against the Germans, while in Illyricum Tiberius undertook the definite conquest of Pannonia. Thus, when Augustus set about the task of securing natural frontiers for the empire, he was able to place the active management of his share of the Roman world very largely in the hands of his immediate relatives. Agrippa, his son-in-law, controlled Syria and the East, and his two stepsons had charge of almost the whole northern frontier. Up to 13 B. C. he had made little use of the higher republican nobility. As if by way of compensation the latter had been permitted to control the republic and the portion of the empire assigned to the senate.

While the princeps was thus occupied, the restored republic

---

*Fasti*, and a reference to the *Prosopographia*, where the authorities a cited.          [1] Marquardt, *Römische Staatsverwaltung*, i. 290

was functioning in Rome. A brief examination of such
scanty facts as have been preserved will serve to show that
during this time the restoration had considerable reality
and that the republican machine was working with some
degree of freedom. It is true that by the settlement of
22 B. C. the princeps held powers which gave him ample
opportunity for interference. He had the right to summon the senate and to preside at the elections, and
his tribunician power gave him a sweeping veto which
he could employ to check at once any policy that
might seem dangerous to his position in the state. Of
these powers the right to preside over the elections carried
with it a vast indirect influence, since by the Roman system
the magistrate who presided at the polling had the duty of
determining the eligibility of the candidates.[1] Such a power
placed the career of every politician more or less at his mercy,
and so gave him a potent means of influencing their conduct.
He could also recommend to the people any candidate in
whose success he felt an especial interest, and such an indication of his will was always followed by the voters. Yet there
seems no reason to think that Augustus availed himself of
these powers to interfere with the freedom of the republic
more than was strictly necessary. Political life certainly
revived in Rome and ran a sometimes turbulent course. In
21, while the princeps was absent, the consular elections were
so hotly disputed that disorders broke out in the city.[2] It
was this that led Augustus to send Agrippa to Rome to act
as his representative there during his sojourn in the East.
In spite of this, when in 19 the emperor returned from Asia,
he was met by news of further troubles at the consular
elections, and deputies waited on him in Greece to ask him

---

[1] That the presiding magistrate had such a power and responsibility
has been generally held. Willems argues in favour of some restriction of
this right, but his view would hardly touch the point here involved. That
such a right was recognized under the empire is shown by the conduct of
Sentius Saturninus in 19 B. C. as reported by Velleius, ii. 92. See Willems,
*Le Droit public romain*, 221 ; and Destarac, *La Brigue électorale à Rome*,
25–32.                                    [2] Dio, liv. 6.

to settle the dispute.[1] These recurrent difficulties led him
in the next year to enact a new law against bribery, and
another law on the same subject was passed in 8 B. C.

The impression given by these disorders and the resulting
legislation is confirmed by an examination of the consular
fasti for the period. These fasti are simply tables of the
consuls for each year. As the Romans commonly indicated
the year by the names of the consuls it was of great importance to preserve such lists, and it is still possible to
reconstruct them in a practically complete form. A study
of them in the reign of Augustus reveals several very suggestive facts. After the battle of Actium, as we have seen,
public opinion demanded a return to aristocratic government. The significance of this needs to be clearly understood.
The aristocracy under the later republic was essentially
a nobility of office, and every man who attained a curule
office by virtue of that fact ennobled his descendants. The
precise rank of the family depended upon the dignity of the
office he had held ; among the nobles there would thus be
several grades, but, disregarding small groups, we may consider the aristocracy as divided into consular and praetorian
families. Such rank was not hereditary in law, but popular
sentiment and the strong class spirit of the aristocracy combined to make it so in fact. From this it came about that
a member of one of the noble houses felt himself entitled to
hold in his turn the magistracies which his ancestors had
held, and this claim was accepted by the Roman voter. The
natural consequence was the formation of a ring of noble
families who practically monopolized the offices in the last
century of the republic. It was but rarely and under special
circumstances that a new man could force his way to the
consulship. The praetorship was somewhat more open to
talent apart from birth, but the consulship was almost wholly
confined to the aristocracy. The civil war and the second
triumvirate shattered the monopoly of the noble families,
but, with the restoration of the republic, the popular reac-

[1] Dio, liv. 10.

tion in their favour was bound to bring them back to office.
Men were wearied of seeing upstarts receive the highest
dignities and longed to bestow the honours of the state on
such of the old families as had survived the storm. Augustus,
safely intrenched in his own provinces, had little need to
quarrel with this feeling even if he did not share it. He could
well afford to let the nobles dominate the republic and
administer the senatorial provinces while he concerned himself with his own special problems.

The use of the fasti to determine the position actually
held by the nobility is unfortunately attended with some
difficulty. The Roman system of family names was so
irregular that in some cases a son did not bear the same
family name as his father ; thus Aemilius Paullus was the
son of Aemilius Lepidus and Asinius Gallus of Asinius Pollio.
Moreover, the same gentile name was often borne by several
unconnected families. Furthermore, while the fasti usually
indicate the given name of the father and often of the grand-
father, the civil war and the proscription make such a break
that it is not always possible to pick up the links. Yet
enough can be gathered for our present purpose.

The administration of the triumvirate had exhibited a
marked preference for new men in the consulship. Even
counting as a noble every man who bore a gentile name that
had appeared in the fasti for two hundred years before
Actium, the new men formed a majority.[1] The proscription had shattered the aristocracy, and the old families
were doubtless as a whole too profoundly alienated for the
triumvirs to trust them. Here and there a noble who had
adhered to their side or had made his peace with them was
advanced, but in the main they relied on men of undistin-

[1] Of the forty-five men who held the consulship after Octavian marched
on Rome only twelve were certainly nobles ; of the rest twenty-four were
certainly new men and the remaining nine are doubtful. These nine
bore gentile names that had occurred in the fasti in the last two hundred
years, but their family names were new to the highest office. Some of
them may have been members of old families under a new name, but it
seems unlikely that they were all so connected.

guished birth. When, however, Augustus sought to establish a stable government he found so marked a reaction in favour of the fallen nobility that he at once attempted to come to an understanding with them. This policy was doubtless congenial to his temperament and in accord with his convictions, but it was attended with some difficulty and he reached his goal only gradually.

In the years from 30 to 23 B. C. the aristocratic names become more frequent in the fasti. During these eight years Augustus himself held the consulship each year and associated with him in the office thirteen other men. Of these, six were members of noble families or had been prominent among the republicans, four were officers of Augustus, and one, Saenius Balbinus, was perhaps a new man, but may also have been a son of a senator mentioned by Sallust and a member of the lower ranks of the old nobility. When the emperor laid down the consulship in 23 he named two prominent republicans, one of whom was a noble, to the office, and this event may be taken as indicating that the reconciliation was complete.

In 22 B. C. the restored republic began to function with comparative freedom and the nobility took prompt possession. From 22 to 13 B. C. some twenty-two persons held the office. Of these, twelve were, either certainly or probably, members of consular families.[1] Of the rest, one was a member of a family of praetorian rank and three were adherents of the republican party who had been proscribed by the triumvirs. The imperial family furnished three consuls, of whom one, Tiberius, was also by birth a member of an old aristocratic house.[2] Among the consuls for this period there were but three who seem to be new men, and they were all soldiers

---

[1] One was a son of a supporter of Antony to whom Augustus had given the consular rank without the actual consulship. This son was C. Furnius, and he had served Augustus as legate in Spain in 22. He was consul in 17 B. C.

[2] The other two were M. Appuleius, a new man, and P. Quinctilius Varus, a member of a praetorian family. From the name of his father Appuleius would seem to have been a brother of Sex. Appuleius (cos. 29).

who had served under Augustus and whose promotion to the highest honour was probably a reward for such service. It will thus be seen that the old nobility was distinctly predominant.  Of the nine consuls taken from a lower rank three had been so identified with the aristocratic party and had suffered so greatly for the cause that it may reasonably be conjectured that the nobles regarded them as members of their class.  Of the remaining six consuls, two were men promoted from the lower ranks of the senatorial aristocracy. Some such result as this is precisely what might be expected if the princeps allowed the republican institutions to work freely.  The effects of the proscription and the years of furious civil strife would amply account for the promotions that actually occur.

While thus the restored republic was functioning with comparatively little interference, the princeps, as has been shown, was carrying on his own department of the state with the help of his immediate family.  Under these conditions he had no strong motive for meddling with affairs in Rome, as long as order was preserved there and the regular authorities did not require his help.  All that was necessary was for him to protect himself against any acts which might injuriously affect his own position, to reward a competent officer from time to time, or to give a fitting and appropriate rank to some one of whose ability he was anxious to make use.  These latter needs he probably found it easy to provide for in the depleted state of the old aristocracy ; the known facts give no reason to assume any continuous, or even frequent, interference on the part of the emperor.  Moreover, such interference would be clearly to his disadvantage.  If Augustus thought it worth while to pose as a constitutional magistrate, he must have felt it desirable to act the part with care and make the comedy successful.  Such facts as are available

and thus a son of Octavia Major, the half-sister of Augustus.  Varus was related to the emperor through his marriage with Claudia Pulchra, though the date of the marriage is unknown and it may have taken place after his consulship.

would seem to show that this was actually his course ; he busied himself with the work assigned to him and allowed the nobles to manage their republic very much as they pleased.

Yet the conditions which made it possible for the emperor to restore some sort of liberty were essentially unstable. The Romans were a people little likely to look with favour on men possessed of neither illustrious birth nor high official standing in important posts, even in the imperial service. This mattered little while the princeps could conduct his administration through his near relatives. If these should fail him, Roman sentiment would force him to call on the nobility to govern his share of the Roman world, and this necessity would give him a far stronger interest in the working of the republican government. A time might come when the pressing demands of his own administration would compel more frequent interference and would oblige him to diminish in fact the liberty which he had ostentatiously restored. The transformation of the principate into a slightly veiled despotism was due to many causes, but among the most direct, although hitherto almost ignored by historians, was the close dependence of the emperor on the republican machine. He could not permit it to work freely when its working came to affect seriously his own administration. He was then forced to interfere, and thus, in the end, to reduce the restored republic to a sham.

The aggressive frontier policy inaugurated after 16 B. C. led directly to such a transformation in the government. When the work of consolidating the borders of his empire was undertaken by Augustus he could intrust the bulk of it to his own family ; in the East his son-in-law was in charge of affairs, while in the West his stepsons carried on the wars which were the inevitable result of the new policy. At first everything went well, and the Elbe-Danube frontier was successfully reached, though only after some hard fighting. Then fortune seemed to turn against the princeps, and the situation grew rapidly more difficult. The hand of death fell heavily upon the imperial house, and the management of the republic became steadily less easy for the emperor. Both of these factors deserve a brief consideration.

In 13 B. C. Agrippa left Syria to take command on the Danube, where revolt was threatening ; he was not destined to see active service, however, for early in the following year he died in Italy. This event compelled the emperor to find governors to replace his son-in-law in the East, and for them he turned to the senatorial nobility. But the death of Agrippa was only the first blow ; three years later—in 9 B. C.—Drusus, the younger of his stepsons, died in Germany and in 6 B. C. the other, Tiberius, resigned his position and retired into voluntary exile at Rhodes.

This rapid narrowing of his family circle was rendered the more serious by the new responsibilities which Augustus had assumed. To furnish a convenient base for his advance to the Danube he had taken over the province of Illyricum from the senate, and the success of his campaigns on the frontier left in his hands a vastly increased extent of territory to administer. His need of officers was thus greater than ever, while the number of his relatives diminished. The consequence of this was that he found himself depending on the republican aristocracy much more than in the past. At the beginning of his reign as princeps, the emperor had but two consular provinces (Tarraconensis and Syria) among those assigned to him, but by the time of his death three others had been added (Pannonia, Dalmatia, and Moesia), and in addition to these the command of the army along the German frontier usually called for several generals of consular rank. Under these circumstances the retirement of Tiberius brought the problem, already becoming serious, to a crisis, and this serves, in part at least, to explain the anger of the emperor at the ' desertion ' of Tiberius. Unable to persuade his step-son to renounce his purpose, Augustus saw himself obliged to undertake a readjustment of his relations with the republic and its aristocracy.

The more extensive employment of the senatorial nobility

in the imperial service which the changed situation made
necessary was not without its difficulties. To understand
these it must be borne in mind that, while the Roman nobility
was essentially one of office, it had acquired a hereditary
character in fact, so that when a man had held one of the
higher offices, his descendants after him claimed in their
turn, as a matter of natural right, to hold the same office,
and such claims met with general support throughout the
Roman world. Thus every new man elevated to high office
might become the founder of a new noble house, and his son
in due time would come forward to demand that he should
be advanced to the same position that his father had attained.
In this way the aristocracy, even though badly shattered at
the beginning of the reign, would soon renew itself and the
princeps, before many years had passed, would find himself
surrounded by a group of claimants numerous enough to fill
the offices. It would be inevitable that many of these should
be men who inherited the rank of their ancestors rather than
their ability, and to such men the emperor would be reluctant
to intrust his armies or his provinces. If he desired to use
new men in these positions he felt it necessary to give them
standing by elevating them to the nobility. If the emperor
wished the chief posts in his service to be held by men of
consular rank—as in actual fact he did—he found himself
compelled to take a keener interest in the consular elections.
In the first years of the reign he had met with little difficulty
since he needed but few consulars, and the ranks of the
aristocracy were so depleted that he could readily find places
for such men as he desired to reward or use. But by the
middle of his reign the matter became less simple, and as
time went on he faced a serious dilemma. The number of
noble claimants had increased so much that new men could
be advanced only by the exclusion of a corresponding number
of nobles. Such exclusion was certain to be angrily resented,
and Augustus, whether from temperament, or policy, or
both, was unwilling to offend the aristocracy. Yet, on the
other hand, he was equally unwilling to restrict his choice

of officers solely to the existing noble families. It was this problem which the retirement of Tiberius in 6 B. C. had made acute.

The increasing dependence of the emperor on the senatorial nobility is attested by such records as have been preserved. Unfortunately the lists of the imperial officials are incomplete, and most of the information that is now available must be gathered from the narrative histories of the period. In these the interest is centred on the imperial princes and the court, and the provinces are treated only incidentally. Unquestionably the names of many of the princeps' officers have failed of record, especially when their service was attended by no striking incidents. But if we make allowance for this, the facts which can be gleaned from an examination of the sources seem obviously significant. From 22 to 13 B. C. only three men of consular rank are mentioned as serving in the imperial provinces; of the three, two were new men and only one was connected with the old nobility. From 12 B. C. to A. D. 3 the names of nine such consulars are found,[1] who

---

[1] The names of the active consulars in the two periods may be of interest. They were as follows:

From 22 to 13 B. C.

    M. Lollius (cos. 21), legate in Germany in 16 and in Thrace just before.

    M. Vinicius (cos. 19), in Pannonia 13.

    L. Calpurnius Piso Frugi (cos. 15), in Pamphylia in 13 and in Thrace 13–11.

From 12 B. C. to A. D. 3.

    L. Calpurnius Piso Frugi, as above.

    L. Domitius Ahenobarbus (cos. 16), in Pannonia and Germany, perhaps continuously from 9 to 2 or later.

    M. Vinicius (cos. 19), in Germany 1 B. C.–A. D. 2.

    P. Sulpicius Quirinius (cos. 12), in Syria 11–9.

    M. Titius (cos. 31), in Syria 9–8.

    C. Sentius Saturninus (cos. 19), in Syria 8–6.

    P. Quinctilius Varus (cos. 13), in Syria 6–4.

    C. Caesar, in Syria 1 B. C.–A. D. 4 with

        C. Marcius Censorinus (cos. 8),

        M. Lollius (cos. 21),

        P. Sulpicius Quirinius, as counsellors.

For Quirinius I have followed Bleckmann, *Klio*, xvii. 104–10. The *Prosopographia* dates his governorship as 3–2. All agree that he was governor

appear upon the scene as the members of the imperial family drop out. The death of Agrippa leads—after a short gap in the list of governors—to the appointment of six consulars, one after the other, as legates in Syria ; while on the northern frontier Drusus and Tiberius had to be replaced a little later. Of the men thus called into the imperial service only three were members of old families of high rank, and of these three, but one held a position of the first importance,[1] and he was connected with the emperor by marriage. Augustus evidently preferred to fill the most important posts with men whose nobility was recent and who owed their rise to him.

As the emperor's need for men of high rank thus steadily increased, he could no longer look on indifferently at the consular elections. He might not care who presided over the republic in Rome, but when the holding of the consulship became a qualification of his officers, that magistracy acquired a new and serious importance. If he were to govern Syria by means of consulars, it was essential that the men he wished to send to that province should be successful in the elections. It is not surprising, therefore, that the consular fasti for this period contain some indications of an increased inter-ference by the princeps with the working of the republican machinery.

In the thirteen years preceding Agrippa's death (25–13 B.C.) there seem to have been but six new men and men from praetorian families advanced to the consulship, if four men

---

again in A. D. 6. I have accepted the earlier dates partly because the reasons of Bleckmann seem strong and partly because they are slightly less favour-able to some of my conclusions than the later ones (see p. 252, n. 1).

[1] Domitius seems to have taken over the command on the northern frontier from the emperor's stepson. He was married to Antonia Major, the daughter of Augustus' sister. The other nobles of old families were L. Calpurnius Piso Frugi, who continued to command in Thrace from the preceding period, and Marcius Censorinus in Syria. Piso can hardly have had an army at all comparable to that commanded by Tiberius in Pannonia at the same time. Censorinus was only one of the counsellors of C. Caesar. With him were associated M. Lollius and Sulpicius Quirinius, both new men.

closely identified with the republican party are considered
nobles.[1]  In the thirteen years which followed that event
(12 B.C.–A.D. 1) there were ten such ;[2] not only was the
number nearly twice as great, but they were advanced in
spite of the increasing pressure of aristocratic claims upon
the office.  This pressure is clearly attested by the fasti.  In
the thirteen years in question there were at least six consuls
whose families had acquired consular rank since the outbreak
of the civil war between Caesar and Pompey.[3]  To satisfy the
claims of this nobility and of the ancient aristocratic houses
that survived, and, at the same time, to promote the new
men whom he needed, Augustus was forced to find some way
of increasing the number of the consuls.  A method of accomplishing this was ready to his hand.  In the days of the
republic it had sometimes happened that a consul died during
his term of office ; when this occurred a *consul suffectus* had
been elected for the remainder of the year.  During the
government of the triumvirate the resignation of consuls had
been rather frequent, and extra consuls had been appointed
to fill the vacancies thus made.  After 28 B.C., when Augustus
began the attempt to establish a stable government, there
had been but three occasions when such extra consuls were
chosen, and one of these was in 23 when the emperor laid
down the office.  As the need of consulars and the pressure
of aristocratic claims increased, Augustus reverted to the

---

[1] The men from praetorian families were P. Quinctilius Varus, who was
related by marriage to the imperial house, and P. Silius Nerva.  Of the
new men M. Appuleius was probably a brother of Sex. Appuleius (cos. 29)
and so related to Augustus ; the others were M. Lollius, M. Vinicius, and
L. Tarius Rufus.  The republicans were L. Sestius Quirinus, L. Arruntius,
Q. Lucretius Vespillo, and C. Sentius Saturninus.

[2] The ten were L. Volusius Saturninus, Q. Aelius Tubero and M. Plautius
Silvanus from praetorian families, and P. Sulpicius Quirinius, C. Valgius
Rufus, A. Caecina Severus, D. Laelius Balbus, L. Passienus Rufus, and
Q. Fabricius, new men ; the tenth new man was C. Fufius Geminus
(cos. 2) who is given in Liebenam but not in Klein.

[3] The six were C. Caninius Rebilus, C. Asinius Gallus, C. Antistius Vetus,
L. Vinicius, C. Calvisius Sabinus, and L. Caninius Gallus.  Possibly
M. Herennius Picens should be added.  The name Herennius had occurred
in the fasti before, but the name Picens is new.

precedents of the triumvirate, though with apparent caution. In the year of Agrippa's death the emperor induced the consuls to resign in the middle of the year and thus made place for two *consules suffecti*. Of the consuls for the year, two were afterward active in the imperial service ; one of these was a new man and the other a member of a praetorian family.[1] In 9 B. C. the death of Drusus, who was one of the consuls for the year, enabled Augustus to promote another new man destined to hold high office in his provinces without any break with the republican tradition. The retirement of Tiberius in 6 B. C. rendered the situation more acute. Of the four years from 9 to 6, inclusive, there were three when— if members of the imperial family are excluded—only one noble of the highest rank held the consulship. The claims of the aristocracy were, perhaps, becoming pressing, for the emperor himself took the office for 5 B. C. on the ground of giving greater splendour to his grandson's assumption of the *toga virilis*, and shared the consulship with four members of the high nobility. In 2 B. C., when his second grandson came of age, Augustus held the consulship for the last time and again with a larger number of colleagues than was normal, though on this occasion two of his three associates were new men.[2] In this way the emperor was able to increase considerably the number of consuls in the period under discussion. So far he had done so only tentatively and under circumstances more or less exceptional ; the difficulty was a permanent one, however, and he needed to find a permanent solution. There were four such solutions possible : Augustus might govern without the help of consulars ; or he might take his officers exclusively from families already of the highest rank ; or he might advance new men while excluding a corresponding number of nobles ; or he might increase

---

[1] The death of one of the consuls made another vacancy, which was filled by a new man.

[2] One of them, M. Plautius Silvanus, was of praetorian family. C. Caesar was consul in A. D. 1, but as he was absent in Syria his consulship was honorary and it may be doubted if the appointment of two consuls in Rome seemed a break with the republican tradition.

the number of the consuls in some regular and systematic fashion. Of the four the emperor chose the last ; beginning with A. D. 2, for the remainder of his reign one or both of the consuls regularly resigned in the middle of the year and thus made place for one or two *consules suffecti*.

The dilemma which had led to the new system can be clearly seen in the last thirteen years of the reign. Under the old practice there would have been but twenty-six consuls during this time. Excluding one member of the imperial house, the office was held by twenty-six men who belonged to consular families, either certainly or probably. There would thus have been no opportunity to promote a single new man without refusing the coveted honour to a noble. But during this period Augustus advanced a number of new men whom he afterwards used in his provinces and army. There are no less than six or seven such men whose names have been preserved.[1] These promotions alone required either a considerable increase in the number of the consuls or a rather extensive exclusion of the aristocracy. If extra consuls were to be introduced, however, it might be well to go beyond the strict necessity of the case. It was desirable to have at hand a few capable men of high rank to use if an emergency arose. It was usual too to allow a few years to elapse between the consulship and active service in the provinces. Thus it happened sometimes that the emperor advanced a man to the consulship intending to employ him in the imperial service without actually doing so. There can also be little doubt that a number did serve in his provinces whose names have failed of record. In addition it was necessary to have a considerable number of consulars in Rome to give distinction to the deliberations of the

---

[1] They were C. Poppaeus Sabinus, L. Aelius Lamia, L. Nonnius Asprenas, C. Vibius Postumus, L. Apronius, Q. Junius Blaesus, and Sex. Aelius Catus. The last named held an active command in Thrace, probably soon after his consulship (Hardy, *Mon. Ancyr.*, 142–3). An eighth consular, C. Ateius Capito, held an important administrative post in Rome, that of *curator aquarum*, under the emperor in the last year of the reign. Of the new men three, including Capito, were from families of praetorian rank.

conscript fathers, and to assist the princeps with their advice and (what he probably wanted far more) the support of their names and their exalted rank. Thus in A. D. 6, when the finances and the food supply were both in difficulties, the emperor was assisted in the task of supervising the expenditures by three consulars, and at the same time he appointed others—though how many is unknown —to take charge of the situation in respect to grain and bread.

The increase in the number of the consuls was accompanied by a tightening of the emperor's control over the elections, as is made evident in several ways. No more is heard of disorderly campaigns, and the last law against electoral corruption was enacted in 8 B. C. This would seem to mean that, as the interference of Augustus increased, the motive for either riot or bribery disappeared. At first he seems to have availed himself of his right to preside over the elections to influence their results, but as he grew older he found this troublesome, and after A. D. 8 he made his recommendations (*commendatio*) to the people by an official notice. He seems also to have extended his control so that but few places were now left to be filled by popular choice.[1] The voting in the comitia thus became little more than an empty form, and Augustus was planning to transfer this form to the senate at the time of his death.

The motives for this increasing control of the elections, which ended by depriving the populace of all share in the government, have been already indicated. As the emperor depended more and more upon the consulars for his chief officers, he must make sure that the men he wished to use received the qualifying office from the people and that they did so at the time required. As evidence of this it is only necessary to note the marked increase in the number of men who are found in the imperial service very shortly

---

[1] Dio, lv. 34, and Tac., i. 15. The language of Tacitus seems clearly to imply that most of the places were filled by the use of the right of *commendatio* in the last years of the reign.

after their consulship.[1] In the case of the senatorial provinces there was regularly, though with an occasional exception, an interval of at least five years between the holding of a magistracy in Rome and a provincial command. In the imperial service such an interval, though it often occurred, was in no way obligatory, and, when in the latter part of his reign, Augustus came frequently to hurry men from Rome to important posts in his administration, he found a stricter control of the elections necessary. A single illustration of this will, perhaps, suffice. In A. D. 3 the consulship was held by L. Aelius Lamia, a member of a praetorian family, and in the following year he was an officer in the imperial army in Illyricum. If he had been defeated in A. D. 2 he must either have waited a year before beginning active service, or else have held his command without the prestige of consular rank. The emperor had, therefore, an obvious motive for making sure of his success at that particular election.

The deaths of Lucius and Gaius Caesar, the two young grandsons of Augustus, led to the return of Tiberius to public life, but made no essential change in the situation. The emperor had again a general of his immediate family to place in high command, and in the young Germanicus a second prince was soon available for service, but one or two

---

[1] A list may be of interest. The existing records show that at a given date a man was in a certain province but not when he went to it, which must always have been earlier, perhaps a year or two earlier, than the time when the casual mention of some historian reveals him there. From 27 to 1 B. C. we find only two or three consulars, L. Calpurnius Piso Frugi, M. Lollius, and probably P. Sulpicius Quirinius, in the imperial service in less than five years after their consulship. After A. D. 1 there were three, L. Aelius Lamia, L. Nonius Asprenas, and C. Silius Caecina Largus, so employed the next year; two, M. Aemilius Lepidus and C. Poppaeus Sabinus, in two years; four, C. Vibius Postumus, Q. Caecilius Metellus Creticus Silanus, P. Cornelius Dolabella, and Q. Junius Blaesus, in four years. Perhaps we should add two others, Sex. Aelius Catus, who may have been in command in Moesia soon after 6 (see Hardy, *Mon. Ancyr.*, 142-3), and L. Apronius, who came from the Dalmatian war to the consulship in 8, and may have returned to the frontier at once, as he was a legate of Germanicus in 14.

members of his house were not enough. The soldiers had become accustomed to being led by officers of the highest rank, and the princeps deemed it wise to adhere to this tradition. Although he placed his relatives at the head of his chief armies, their immediate subordinates were mostly consulars. Perhaps the seriousness of the wars had something to do with this. The Elbe-Danube frontier proved much easier to reach than to hold, and in the last years of the reign a furious revolt broke out in the newly annexed regions. From A. D. 4 to 13 hard campaigning was almost continuous in Pannonia and Germany, and at this time the imperial arms met their greatest disaster in the defeat of Varus and the loss of Germany which followed it. Faced with military operations of so serious a character, Augustus made greater use than ever of the senatorial nobility. If from 12 B. C. to A. D. 3 he had employed nine consulars, from A. D. 4 to 14 there were no less than seventeen in his service.[1] The principate was now hopelessly entangled in the republican machine, and the result was the rapid destruction of the republic's independence, accompanied by an inevitable drift of the government in the direction of despotism.

The final form of the imperial government may be said to have been reached in A. D. 2. The constitutional basis remained unchanged, but in the actual working of its institutions several important modifications were to be found. Most of the consuls now held office for a term of six months only, and the control of the elections had passed wholly into the hands of the princeps. Both these changes could not but have far-reaching consequences  The control of the elections not only diminished the part played by the Roman people in the state, but was fatal to the independence of the

[1] In addition to those given in a preceding note we find C. Sentius Saturninus, L. Volusius Saturninus, P. Sulpicius Quirinius, A. Caecina Severus, M. Valerius Messalla Corvinus, M. Plautius Silvanus, P. Quinctilius Varus, and perhaps Cn. Cornelius Lentulus (cos. 18), for whom see Hardy, *Mon. Ancyr.*, 142–3. Hardy is wrong, however, in identifying him with the consul for 14 (see *Prosopographia*). Cn. Calpurnius Piso was governor of Spain, but, as the date is wholly uncertain, I have not counted him.

K

senate as well. Since every senator was classed according to the dignity of the office he had held, it followed that whoever had the least ambition to rise in rank must court the favour of the man upon whom, more and more, his promotion would depend. Ambitious men were little inclined to oppose the emperor under such conditions, and men destitute of ambition were not likely to give trouble.

If the control of the elections was bound to make the senate less independent, this effect was emphasized by the increased employment of consulars. In the early days of the reign a senator's career was likely to lie wholly within the republican machine ; only in rare instances could he look forward to receiving an appointment in the emperor's service. The average noble could only hope to rise through the regular round of the republican magistracies, with one or two terms as governor of one of the senatorial provinces, and when this was finished, to enjoy a dignified retirement from active service in the highest rank of the nobility. Such a career was almost identical with that provided by Sulla's constitution, and after the disasters of the civil wars the secure enjoyment of all the rights and privileges which their greatest champion had given them must have seemed to the broken aristocracy a true restoration of the republic. For success it would no doubt be well not to offend the emperor too seriously, but some degree of independence might reasonably be ventured. The outlook was now profoundly altered ; numerous attractive and important posts in the imperial service were within the reach of the senator who gained the imperial favour. A purely republican career was not to be compared with that which was now possible. Nor was a senator required to make a choice between them ; he could enjoy all the honours the republic could bestow, and yet, if he pleased the princeps, he might receive imperial distinctions in addition. A remark of Dio shows the situation in a flash ; speaking of the imperial as contrasted with the senatorial provinces, he tells us that in the former the emperor could name a man as governor whenever he pleased and that many praetors and consuls

secured such appointments during their term of office.[1]
Under these circumstances the conscript fathers and the
magistrates grew steadily more and more subservient to
the princeps. Nor was this change displeasing to the senators;
if they lost in freedom they gained in the splendid careers
now opened up to them, and the gain was far more obvious
and immediate than the loss. Dio expressly says that in his
latter years Augustus, growing milder with age, became more
reluctant to offend the senators or to incur their enmity.[2]
This change in the emperor's character has often been com-
mented upon, and has been variously explained, sometimes
as burnt-out cruelty. A study of his administration in its
practical workings suggests another motive; in proportion
as he drew his officers more and more from the nobility, the
emperor wished less and less to quarrel with them.

Another consequence of the new system was an obvious
decline in the efficiency of the republican government. With
the chief magistrates in office for so short a term, anything
like a continuous policy became impossible and the administration of affairs was bound to suffer. Where this could not
safely be allowed to happen, the only course open was to
invoke the help of the princeps. Thus in the last years of the
reign several important departments of the public business
in the city of Rome itself were transferred from the republic
to the emperor. He was given charge of the police and the
maintenance of order as well as the food and water supply of
the capital. In this way the really vital matters passed into
the hands of the monarch, and the republic more and more
became a thing of pageantry and empty honour. Not all the
powers thus transferred were taken directly from the consuls,
but the weakening of that office must have made encroachment easier because it took away any alternative. If affairs
were badly managed, the magistrates could obviously provide
no remedy, and nothing was left but to have recourse to the
emperor. This undermining of the republic has been pointed
out as furnishing the explanation of Augustus' policy. But

[1] Dio, liii. 14.          [2] Dio, lv. 12 ; also Tacitus, *Annals*, i. 2.

this seems hardly adequate since for nearly thirty years he had tolerated the show of freedom, and in the requirements of his own administration may be found another motive ; the pressing need of consulars which must be met, no matter at what cost to the republic. That he may have foreseen the consequences is quite possible, but he was by temperament an opportunist and was inclined to meet a difficulty in the way which gave least trouble at the moment. He was little likely to seek to save the republic by quarrelling with its guardians ; if it declined, the nobility must bear their share of the responsibility.

While thus the power of the princeps grew steadily greater, the view men took of the office was also slowly changing. Little by little the world came to look upon it as a permanent part of the government. In point of law it had at first been nothing more than a great command, created to meet an exceptional condition. In strict accord with precedent this command had been conferred only for a fixed term of years, but as time slipped by it grew more and more evident that it must continue. If the Romans ever cherished any dreams of disbanding their army, the repeated wars on the frontier must have dispelled the illusion. It became gradually clear that the legions could not be dispensed with save at the price of immediate disaster. But, if a great standing army must be maintained, the state required a war-lord to take charge of it. The principate could only be abolished if a substitute were found, and the only substitute was to appoint another princeps. If the senate and people shrank from making the selection they merely left the choice to the arbitrament of civil war. Since he must have a successor, the emperor might reasonably feel that it was his duty to give the Roman people the benefit of his experience in determining a matter of such vast importance. Better than any other man he knew the situation on the frontiers and could judge the real capacity of any general. The question of the imperial succession came, therefore, naturally to engage the attention of Augustus. By the theory of the constitution his death should have left the senate and the Roman people free to consider whether they had any further need of a war-lord in their government. They might abolish the office altogether, or if this was impossible, they might intrust such powers as they saw fit to any person they might choose. In spite of this, Augustus could influence or determine their decision. He might content himself with pointing out the man he thought most worthy of the place, but it was in his power to make the acceptance of his nominee inevitable. He could induce the senate and the people to confer such powers on the man of his choice that nothing short of revolution could keep him from the throne. Such a colleague might obviously be dangerous to the reigning emperor, and it was natural that Augustus should seek to minimize the risk by making his selection from the circle of his own family. Family pride and affection had no doubt a part in this, but he may have believed such a choice more likely to prove successful than any other he could make. The republican aristocracy had lost little of its exclusiveness, and, while the nobles acquiesced in the supremacy of Augustus and accorded a certain deference to his family, they might have been extremely reluctant to see one of their own number raised above their heads. The house of the Caesars had been so long upon the throne that its continuance in power would arouse less jealous resentment than the advent of a new dynasty. Thus the emperor might feel that the choice of a near relative was almost a necessity, and that any other solution of the problem of the succession was an invitation to a new civil war. From the beginning of his reign Augustus was occupied with the question, but the hand of death on several occasions thwarted his designs. Marcellus, Agrippa, and Gaius Caesar all preceded him to the grave, and, in the end, he was forced to fall back upon his surviving stepson, Tiberius, as his heir. All he could do to secure the ultimate succession to his own blood was to have Germanicus marry his granddaughter and to cause Tiberius to adopt this prince as his son. In this way his descendants would inherit the throne and he would thus give a dynasty to Rome.

When this prospect had become fully apparent, the principate had become a monarchy in everything but name.

Whatever the establishment of the empire may have meant in Rome and Italy, it conferred vast benefits upon the world at large. That the republic had shamefully oppressed the provinces is beyond dispute. From this misgovernment the empire to a considerable extent relieved them since the princeps could not afford to shut his eyes to tyranny and pillage as the senate had too often done. If the provinces were misgoverned they might be impoverished, or goaded to revolt, and either result would create difficulties for the emperor. If for no other reason than to avoid trouble the monarch was inevitably a champion of decency and justice. Even the senate had feebly striven in the same direction, but the princeps had better means of making felt his good intentions. It had been one weakness of the republic that while it might occasionally punish an exceptionally bad governor, it had no reward to offer to a good one. His conduct in the provinces seems to have counted little, either for or against a candidate, in the eyes of the Roman voter. But with Augustus in power the situation was at once altered ; good government in the provinces was distinctly to the emperor's advantage, and by the very fact that he presided at the elections, he could exert a powerful influence in its favour. The princeps could reject the name of any candidate for office, and so had means of stopping the career of any man who made a bad record for himself. Moreover, as the use of consulars in the imperial service increased, the rewards of just and efficient administration became splendid and alluring. Thus the establishment of the principate was an enormous gain to the provincials quite apart from any definite reforms. Such reforms were made and were of great value to the empire, but the mere existence of the monarch was, very possibly, well worth them all.

The improvement which the principate brought with it in the government of the provinces has long been recognized, but it is often said that this gain was purchased at the price of Roman liberty. That the part of the people in the government became a farce has been already shown ; but to the bulk of Roman citizens this was no real loss, because they never had possessed a voice. All voting was done in Rome, and those who lived at any distance from that city had always been disfranchised in practice. The populace of Rome might lose their bribes and riots, but the citizen at a distance merely lost in theory what he had never had in fact, and the tightening grip of the princeps on the republic deprived him of nothing valuable. The sort of liberty which he really prized remained untouched, the right to control the affairs of his own municipality. Italy was a great confederacy of towns with whose self-government the emperor had no desire to interfere, and in which a vigorous local life went on quite undisturbed for many years. When at length this form of liberty died out, it was from causes for which the imperial government was not responsible and which a genuine republic could not have cured.

It may be objected that the early empire soon degenerated into a gloomy tyranny, and that under such sovereigns as came after Augustus the imperial despotism weighed like a nightmare on the world. While partially true, such a criticism overlooks some fundamental features of the case. Let the reigns of Tiberius, Caligula, Nero, and Domitian be painted in the darkest colours, yet their oppression was restricted within very narrow limits ; their tyranny fell almost exclusively upon the senatorial nobility in Rome and did not touch the great mass of their subjects. Their courtiers may have gone in terror of their lives, but the ordinary citizen was not in any way disturbed. Hence the personal character of the emperors mattered very little to the world at large, and there is no reason to doubt that under the worst of the Caesars mankind in general was better off than under the republic.

In conclusion it may be well to mention a reform which Augustus considered, but which he finally rejected. This was a scheme to extend the franchise in an effective way to all the Roman citizens in Italy. To do this the ballot, instead of being taken exclusively in Rome, would have been cast simultaneously in all the towns of the peninsula ; the votes were then to be sent to Rome and counted there. At first it might appear as though this was a promising reform and one that might have kept alive some elements of genuine popular government. There were, however, serious objections to the change. Unless the new system of conducting the elections proved an empty form, it would have made it far less easy for the princeps to control them. This would have made the task of governing more difficult if the close connexion between the republican offices and rank in the nobility were permitted to continue. It was probably not this consideration, however, which had most weight with Augustus. In the restoration of the republic he was seeking to conciliate public opinion, and he found a conservative reaction in full swing. The reform would probably have been unpopular just because it was a violation of usage and tradition ; the world could be most readily satisfied by the simple restoration of the old forms, and the emperor was doubtless wise to lay the scheme aside. To have preserved the republic as a reality would have required far more sweeping reforms than a mere modification of the machinery of voting. The whole system which made rank depend on office must have been done away with, and the sentiment of the Roman world which called for men of exalted rank in all the greatest positions, even in the imperial service, must have been modified. Above all, the character of the army must have been profoundly altered, so that the common soldier would have remained a citizen. For such sweeping changes the Romans were wholly unprepared, even if Augustus had possessed the genius and originality to think of them. Had he conceived such designs it is extremely unlikely that he could have carried them out in the face of the opposition of all classes of his subjects. What was possible he did. He conciliated public opinion by setting up again the old machinery of government with such slight modifications as men in general were willing to accept.

This machinery, when once it had been set up, he worked with a minimum of friction. The fact that he was able to rule the world for forty-four years without serious opposition and after death to live on in men's memories as a divine and resplendent figure is a striking testimony to the skill and tact with which he had met the world's most pressing needs while satisfying its dominant desires.

# APPENDIXES

# I. THE LEX VATINIA

THE view of the Vatinian law taken in the text differs from that usual among historians, and it seems desirable to state briefly the reasons for it.

It is generally held that the language of Cicero in his oration on the consular provinces proves beyond serious question that by the Vatinian law Caesar was given the province of Cisalpine Gaul for a term of five years beginning March 1, 59.[1] This date is explained by assuming that the bill was passed on the last day of February and took effect immediately, as was usually the case with Roman laws. But these facts, which may be taken as established, raise at once two questions : why was the law passed so early in Caesar's consulship, and why did it make his governorship in Gaul begin during his year of office in Rome ? The two problems here stated seem obvious once they are raised, but Ferrero was apparently the first to feel their full force and to attempt a solution. The explanation which he gave has met with considerable favour[2] and is therefore deserving of consideration. He accounts for the Vatinian law on the ground that the sudden death of Metellus Celer left the governorship of Cisalpine Gaul vacant and that Caesar took prompt advantage of the opening thus provided to seize the province and so forestall any possible intrigues on the part of the conservatives. This explanation encounters serious difficulties, however.

In the first place, the probable date of the passage of the agrarian bill[3] does not fit the theory. Ferrero and the others are

---

[1] Guiraud has questioned this, but has met with no apparent support. Recently Lacqueur has offered a new interpretation of Cicero, but Holmes (*The Roman Republic*, ii. 300, note 5) has, as it seems to me, refuted his views.

[2] Ferrero, i. 290, note. Heitland has adopted the theory of Ferrero in his work, *The Roman Republic*, iii. 135, and note 2. Jullian appears to accept it somewhat tentatively in his *Histoire de la Gaule*, iii. 166, note 4. It has finally been adopted in a recent text-book on Roman history : Boak, *A History of Rome*, 166.

[3] There has been some discussion of whether there were two agrarian laws or only one. Ferrero, Heitland, and Meyer (to name only the latest

forced to assume that the bill was passed in February ; the evidence of the sources is against this, however, and—unless some of the evidence is rejected—is decisively against it.  We are expressly told by Dio that the law imposed an oath on all the senators and that Metellus was one of the last to take this oath. He did finally take it, however, after much hesitation.[1]  Now it is certain from Cicero's letters that Metellus was dead by the middle of April.[2]  So far the facts would agree well enough with the theory of Ferrero.  But Dio and Suetonius make Bibulus retire to his house immediately after the passage of the agrarian law [3] and Plutarch says explicitly that he did not appear in public during the remaining eight months of his year of office.[4]  If this statement is true, his retirement must have taken place in April and not in February.  If it did take place in April, Metellus must have lived till then, and the first agrarian law must have been passed in that month.  If so, the death of Metellus can have had nothing to do with the Vatinian law, which was carried at the end of February.

Even if this difficulty should be cleared away, and it can only be done by the rejection of Plutarch's statement, there remains another difficulty.  It is not by any means certain that Metellus had the province of Cisalpine Gaul, in fact the probability is that he did not.  In the preceding year the senate, alarmed by the news of an impending war in Transalpine Gaul, directed the two consuls for that year, Metellus and Afranius, to draw lots for the two Gauls.[5] In all probability they first resigned the provinces previously assigned them under the Sempronian law, though there is no definite statement to that effect.  Unfortunately, we do not know how the lots fell, but later in the year Cicero speaks of Metellus

writers) hold that there were two ; Drumann maintains that there was only one.  I believe the evidence is overwhelming in favour of two.  It has not seemed necessary to discuss the point, however, since unless there were two laws the theory of Ferrero falls at once.

[1] Dio, xxxviii. 7.

[2] .Letters, i. 90 ; Att., ii. 5.  That the passage refers to the death of Metellus is made certain by passages elsewhere.  See Letters, i. 98 ; Att., ii. 9 ; and the Oration against Vatinius, 8.  The first two passages rather suggest that the death of Metellus was very recent.

[3] Dio, xxxviii. 6 ; Suetonius, The Deified Julius, 20.

[4] Plutarch, Pompey, 48 ; Meyer, Caesars Monarchie, 71, and note 3, accepts this as fixing April as the date for the passage of the agrarian bill.

[5] Cicero, Letters, i. 54 ; Att., i. 19.

as greatly disappointed at the peaceful news then arriving from Gaul because he was desirous of a triumph.[1] Since the war that had been threatening was in the Transalpine province, this suggests strongly that this was the province drawn by Metellus. Of course a very serious war might involve the governors of both Gauls, but this is certainly not the natural implication of the passage. Before Ferrero all scholars held that Metellus received the Transalpine province, and this seems much the more probable supposition.

The data furnished by the sources, therefore, fail to support the theory of Ferrero either as to the date of Metellus' death or as to the province which he held. There is still another objection to it. Although intended to explain the Vatinian law, it fails to achieve its purpose. Even if it be granted that Metellus died in February and that he had the Cisalpine province, his death does not adequately explain the haste with which the Vatinian law was carried or the reason for making Caesar's proconsulship begin early in his year of office as consul. Ferrero thinks that both were due to a desire to forestall possible intrigues of the conservatives, but it is difficult to see what they could do. After the agrarian law was passed and Bibulus was shut up in his house, the opposition was cowed. Even if Bibulus convened the senate in spite of Caesar, the conscript fathers could only assign the vacant province to one of the consuls or praetors of that year. The consuls were out of the question, since they had already been assigned provinces, and Caesar could probably have prevented a new assignment to his colleague. The assignment of the province to one of the praetors was impossible, since here the veto of the tribunes would hold good and Caesar had Vatinius ready for that or any other purpose.[2] In spite of all this, if the senate did succeed in

---

[1] *Letters*, i. 60 ; *Att.*, i. 20. Metellus never left Rome, but died there after an illness of only three days. See Dio, xxxvii. 50 ; and Cicero, *Oration for M. Coelius*, 24.

[2] The tribunes could not veto the assignment of the provinces under the Sempronian law ; but this had been made and Bibulus had received, along with Caesar, the care of the roads and forests in Italy. This assignment the senate could only alter if the consuls, or one of them, resigned the province so assigned. If this were done a new province could be decreed for him by the senate. It seems probable that this decree could be vetoed by the other consul, and there is no reason to think that the tribunes did not have a veto against such a special assignment. The praetorian provinces were always subject to the veto of the tribunes.

getting through an arrangement contrary to Caesar's interests, he could set it aside at any time by an act of the assembly. Why then did he show so much anxiety to forestall intrigues which could not, as it would appear, do him the slightest harm?

Groebe suggests that the reason for making the governorship of Gaul and Caesar's consular term run concurrently was to enable Caesar to assume the command during the year 59 if circumstances should require.[1] This might do as an explanation if the province assigned to Caesar by the Vatinian law had been Transalpine Gaul. So far as we know there was no likelihood of war in the Cisalpine province, and it is difficult to see any reason why Caesar should suppose that he might be obliged to hurry to the valley of the Po before his term of office had expired in Rome.[2] It seems certain that, even if he did think it possible that he might wish to leave the city before the year was up, he cannot have intended to do so for several months after the Vatinian law was passed. He was then in the midst of his legislative programme, even if the first agrarian law had been carried; and it seems clear that he would not dare to leave, nor would his partners dare to let him leave, till the elections had been held. Why then did he bring in the Vatinian law so early? If the purpose was to take advantage of the disorganization and discouragement of the conservatives after his first great victory over them in the agrarian law, why did he make his term as proconsul begin at once? It was surely possible to make the proconsulship of Caesar begin at any date that might be specified, and unnecessary to fix a date months before Caesar could take advantage of it. It seems impossible to explain in this way why Caesar should have been authorized to assume command of a province where there was no particular danger at a time several months earlier than he can have had any intention of acting upon the permission.

It seems to me that the only real explanation of the Vatinian law is to be found in the political conditions in Rome. From this point of view one of its main purposes was to provide Caesar with a military force with which he could overawe the conservative

[1] Drumann, *Geschichte Roms*, edition revised by Groebe, iii. 720.
[2] It should be borne in mind that the governor of the province was probably Afranius. He was a competent soldier, at least he was one in whom Pompey felt confidence, since he served as Pompey's legate both before and after this time. It is not unlikely that his military reputation was quite as good as Caesar's. With Pompey it was probably better.

opposition and prevent them from attempting to defend the constitution, which he was planning to violate. To this supposition there are two obvious objections; the first is the comparative ease with which the law was carried, and the second is the absence of any explicit statement of such a purpose in the sources. Neither of these will be found upon examination to be as serious as it may at first appear.

As to the first point, there was opposition, but it seems to have contented itself with rendering the law technically invalid by religious obstruction; this was the only way in which Bibulus could act, since he had no veto against a tribune. Three of the tribunes joined Bibulus in the attempt to stop Caesar by raising religious obstacles to the meeting of the assembly. We get this information from Cicero's oration against Vatinius,[1] and from his silence as to actual violence we must conclude that none was offered to the hostile tribunes. This seems to show that on this occasion they did not appear in the forum, but merely announced unfavourable omens. Later, when the agrarian bill was carried, these same three did interpose a veto and were nearly killed in consequence. It is not unreasonable to conclude that they did not try direct intervention at first from fear of the mob, and perhaps also they had faith in the effect of the *obnuntiatio*. When it had been made clear that religious scruples would not check Caesar, they used their veto with the support and backing of the other consul. So far as the records show, Cato alone had the courage to resist the Vatinian law in person and he warned the people that by their own votes they were setting up a tyrant in their citadel.[2] This utterance is entirely in harmony with the conjecture here offered as to the purpose of the law.

As to the second objection, if the Vatinian law were used as a means of establishing in Rome a military tyranny, why was not the point brought out explicitly by ancient writers? It does not seem impossible to suggest a reason. In the case of Cicero it would be natural that he should refrain from writing to his friend what the latter already knew; the facts of Caesar's rule were as familiar to Atticus as to Cicero. Under these circumstances what we should expect to find would be allusion and implication rather than plain statement in definite language. This is exactly what we do find; indeed, he makes the case quite clear if we will only

---

[1] *Oration against Vatinius*, 6–7.    [2] Plutarch, *Cato Minor*, 33.

take his language at its face value. In his orations he could not
speak out because of the risk involved in offending Caesar and
Pompey. In the case of the later writers, such as Dio, Appian,
Plutarch, and Suetonius, they all wrote after the empire had been
established for a considerable time. It would be quite natural that
they should fail to grasp the full significance of a body of troops
camped at the gates of Rome, since they were thoroughly familiar
with such a situation. They *do* concur in representing Caesar's consulship as a period of violent usurpation, but they do not see any
occasion to emphasize this particular point in his method. If that
was not grasped, it would be natural for them to treat the Vatinian
law as they do and discuss it in connexion with the end of Caesar's
consulship and as looking toward his future career in Gaul rather
than his present position in Rome. Dio, indeed, places his account
of the law in the middle of his narrative of Caesar's consulship,
but he discusses it from this point of view, and his arrangement
is clearly logical and not chronological. He deals first with the
legislation and then takes up the other events of the year. Under
the head of legislation he places first the laws introduced by
Caesar himself—the Julian laws—and then those that he insti-
gated and inspired but which were brought forward by others.

When these considerations are borne in mind neither of the
objections will seem decisive, and the positive evidence which the
sources contain that the Vatinian law was actually used for the
purpose indicated is fully as strong as could be reasonably expected. Our only contemporary source is Cicero ; his letters show
plainly that after the law was passed he regarded the government
of Caesar as a military despotism. It is not a question merely of
mob violence overriding technicalities of the constitution, for he
twice refers explicitly to Caesar's army. Once he represents
Pompey as meeting all criticism of the triumvirate's measures by
saying ' I shall coerce you by means of Caesar's army.'[1] This was
written at the beginning of May. Again, some time between July
and October, he pictures Clodius as rushing wildly about threatening now this party and now that : ' When he sees how unpopular
the present state of things is, he seems to intend an attack upon
the authors of it ; but when he again recalls their power and
armies, he transfers his hostility to the loyalists.'[2]

Moreover, Cicero applies to Caesar's government the Greek

---

[1] *Letters*, i. 106 ; *Att.*, ii. 16.　　　　[2] *Letters*, i. 118 ; *Att.*, ii. 22.

term tyranny and the Latin term *regnum*.[1] It is hardly likely
that he would have used these terms on several occasions unless he
meant them, and, if they were seriously intended, they can mean
nothing but an illegal despotism resting on force. Was the force
in this case merely that of the mob reinforced by Pompey's
veterans ? The orator's references to Caesar's army show quite
clearly that it was more than this. If the power of the triumvirate
had depended on the populace, the conservatives might have
rallied if the three lost the favour of the mob in any marked degree,
but this was not the case. Unless Cicero was egregiously deceived,
the three did lose the popularity with which they began, and even
the rabble turned against them. A single quotation in addition
to those given already in the text will suffice to illustrate the point.
In July Cicero wrote to Atticus, ' They hold no one by affection,
and I fear they will be forced to use terror. . . . The feeling of the
people was shown as clearly as possible in the theatre and at the
shows. For at the gladiators both master (*dominus*) and supporters were overwhelmed with hisses.' The younger Curio ' received
an ovation such as used to be given to Pompey when the constitution
was still intact (' ut salva re publica Pompeio plaudi solebat '). . .
They are at war with everybody.' But Cicero does not imagine
that their unpopularity will make any difference. ' Men are
indignant at what nevertheless must, it seems, be put up with.
The whole people have indeed now one voice, but its strength
depends rather on exasperation than anything to back it up . . .
What else is there to say ? What else ? This, I think : I am
certain that all is lost. For why mince matters any longer ? ' [2]
If we are to regard Caesar as a popular leader who simply brushed
aside senseless technicalities and obstinate obstruction, Cicero's
evidence must, at the start, be thrown out of court.

If the only contemporary writer is thus clear in testifying to a
military tyranny, this view is supported by two of the four later
authorities. Plutarch confirms the evidence of Cicero, though he
is inaccurate in the details. He states explicitly that Pompey—
and to contemporaries he seemed the real head of the triumvirate
—filled the city with soldiers and carried Caesar's laws with a high
hand.[3] He also quotes the warning of Cato in regard to the Vati-

---

[1] He uses the term tyranny in *Att.*, ii. 14 and 17, and the term *regnum*
in *Att.*, ii. 12 and 13. He uses a quotation calling the three kings in
*Att.*, ii. 8 ; in a letter to his brother he calls them kings himself (*Q. Fr.*, i, 2).
[2] *Letters*, i. 112–13 ; *Att.*, ii. 19.     [3] Plutarch, *Pompey*, 48.

nian law,[1] and he narrates the story of Considius, an aged senator, who replied to Caesar's question as to why the conscript fathers did not meet by saying that they were in fear of his soldiers.[2] Appian asserts that at the very beginning of their year of office both Caesar and his colleague Bibulus proceeded to arm secretly. He interprets the conciliatory bearing of Caesar at the first as intended simply to throw Bibulus off his guard, and says that Caesar had gathered a large band of soldiers before he presented his agrarian bill to the senate. When Bibulus appealed to the senate against Caesar, Appian says that the conscript fathers did nothing to oppose the preparations and force of Caesar.[3] It is quite true that Appian does not show how Caesar used the force he had gathered, but it can hardly be doubted that both Appian and Plutarch drew upon sources wherein the consulship of Caesar was represented as a military tyranny. Neither makes the mechanism of that tyranny very clear and neither connects it with the Vatinian law, but both bear witness to its existence. The other two sources are much less definite. Suetonius is very brief and merely says that Bibulus was expelled from the forum by Caesar, who resorted to arms.[4] This might mean no more than simple rioting, which undoubtedly played a part, and a large part, in the first days of Caesar's consulship. Dio does not imply military violence. Neither of these writers, however, asserts anything inconsistent with the interpretation of the Vatinian law adopted in the text.

It has so far been assumed that the beginning of Caesar's pro-consulship was determined automatically by the date of the passage of the Vatinian law. This has been questioned [5], and it is quite conceivable that the law distinctly stated that Caesar's five-year term was to be reckoned from March 1. This would leave us free to fix some other day as that on which the law was finally voted by the people.[6] It is hardly possible to place its enactment earlier

---

[1] Plutarch, *Cato Minor*, 33.

[2] Plutarch, *Caesar*, 14. Cicero refers to the incident but does not quote the remark of Considius. *Letters*, i. 124 ; *Att.*, ii. 24.

[3] Appian, ii. 10–11.   [4] Suetonius, *The Deified Julius*, 20.

[5] For example by Sage in the *American Journal of Philology*, xxxix. 367–83. His arguments, however, leave me, at least, unconvinced.

[6] It cannot have been carried later than July, when Caesar offered Cicero a legateship in his army (*Letters*, i. 113 ; *Att.*, ii. 19). It was almost certainly passed before the end of April, since in the first days of May

than March 1; and if it was passed later and yet this date was specified in the bill, we should have to suppose that Caesar's proconsulship was deliberately dated back and made to begin at a time then already past. The account in Appian would serve to suggest a possible motive for this. If Caesar began gathering troops *before* he had a legal right to do so, he might think such a retroactive statute worth while. Appian, indeed, states that the recruiting began at the very beginning of the year, but he may have thrown it back two months too early, or it may have been that up till March the recruiting had not involved any definitely illegal act that could be proved in court. One question will at once suggest itself, however. Why did Caesar suddenly become scrupulous at some time during his stormy consulship, and that, apparently, upon this single point? It seems not impossible that the somewhat erratic conscience of Pompey was the source of the scruple. Pompey had shown himself extremely careful to disclaim any responsibility for Caesar's acts, but he may have felt the accusation that he was supporting and sanctioning a military tyranny. All ancient moralists regarded resistance to a tyrant as a duty of the citizen, and if Caesar was becoming something very like one, Pompey may not have been able to quiet his conscience with evasions and quibbles. If this were so the Vatinian law, whenever passed, may have relieved his troubled mind by dating back the beginning of Caesar's proconsulship and so legalizing *ex post facto* Caesar's acts. Such a conjecture would not, as it seems to me, matter greatly. The purpose of the Vatinian law is practically the same, and it is intended to cover the highhanded and despotic acts of Caesar with a show of legality. Whether those acts were past or future makes very little difference, since it would still be true that his consulship was a military tyranny.

It may be worth while to say in conclusion that I am far from holding a brief against Caesar. That the republic had become unworkable is, I believe, entirely true, and one main purpose of this book is to point out some of the reasons why this was so. Nevertheless, it is an obvious duty of the historian to try to understand the point of view of those whom he holds to have been in the wrong. It was natural that the Roman conservatives should fail

Cicero speaks of Caesar's army (*Letters*, i. 106; *Att.*, ii. 16). See also *Letters*, i. 91–2; *Att.*, ii. 6.

to see that the republican machine was unequal to the task imposed upon it, and this especially since they could find a plausible explanation of the obvious breakdown of the constitution. The republic *had* managed to work after a fashion up to the moment when the triumvirs threw a wrench into the machinery. The disorders that followed, the anarchy of the next few years—for these they had a very simple explanation. The three held the military force of the state in their hands, and while they did not themselves employ it to keep the peace, they would not permit the senate to take any vigorous action. In the days of Catiline the propertied classes, under the leadership of Cicero and the senate, had had little real difficulty in putting down the disturbers of the peace. Under the triumvirate they were not allowed to try, and they might very well think, and perhaps rightly, that the same thing could be done again. Under such circumstances they would naturally feel that the republican constitution was not seriously wrong in any part, but that it had been stopped by lawless violence, and that this same violence was all that stood in the way of its working again. There seems to me so much of justice in this view that, while I do not believe that the republic could have continued for any length of time, yet it seems impossible to prove that it would have broken down in 59 B C. had it not been for the action of the triumvirs. Cato was literally right when he laid the ruin of the constitution, not to the civil war, but to the combination of Caesar and Pompey.

## II. THE LEX POMPEIA-LICINIA

AS the question of the exact date at which Caesar's pro-consulship in Gaul came to an end has given rise to much controversy, a brief consideration of the matter and an indication of the chief contending views may be of interest. It was long supposed that Mommsen's study on the subject had definitely settled the date as March 1, 49. Guiraud in 1878 disputed this view and propounded another, but it met with little or no favour, and it is only within comparatively recent years that the controversy can be said to have been really begun. The date supposedly established by Mommsen held the field till 1904, when it was attacked by Hirschfeld, who contended that the renewal of Caesar's *imperium* in 55 by the *lex Pompeia-Licinia* was for no definite period, and that the only limits set by that law to his proconsulship were indirect and such as were involved in the clause that forbade the discussion of a successor before March 1, 50. This new theory gained very considerable acceptance in spite of opposition, until in 1913 Judeich advanced another, namely that Caesar's term as renewed in 55 ended in December of 50. In general, German scholars have accepted the year 50 while English scholars have adhered to the view of Mommsen, which has recently been very ably defended, and the arguments of Hirschfeld and Judeich answered by Holmes and Hardy.[1]

In this controversy it appears to me that both sides have established some of their contentions. The view of Hirschfeld that no date was fixed for the end of Caesar's proconsulship seems to have been shown by his opponents to be untenable, and the date

---

[1] Mommsen, *Die Rechtsfrage zwischen Caesar und dem Senat.*
Guiraud, *Le différend entre César et le sénat.*
Hirschfeld, in *Klio*, iv and v, with answers by Holzapfel in the same.
Judeich, in *Rheinisches Museum*, lxviii.
Holmes, in *Classical Quarterly*, x.
Hardy, in *Journal of Philology*, xxxiv.

I regret keenly that circumstances have prevented my having access to the articles of Hirschfeld and that I have been obliged to depend upon the answers of his critics for my knowledge of his views. I sincerely hope that I have done him no serious injustice in consequence.

fixed by Judeich seems to have been equally disproved. So much the adherents of the view of Mommsen have accomplished, and I, at least, feel that they have done this convincingly. Does this, however, establish their date of March 1, 49, in full possession of the field ? For myself this does not seem to be the case, and the reasons given by the Germans for holding that the command of Caesar terminated in 50 appear to have great weight. Some points, at least, have emerged from the discussion that seem to be very solidly established, either admitted by all sides to the controversy, or proved beyond much doubt. These points may be briefly summarized as follows :

1. The *lex Vatinia* conferred the governorship of Gaul on Caesar for five years beginning March 1, 59. Under this law Caesar's term would expire March 1, 54.

2. The *lex Pompeia-Licinia* extended his *imperium* for a second period of five years.

3. This law contained a clause forbidding any discussion of a successor to Caesar till after March 1, 50. As long as the Sempronian law remained in force this clause made it impossible to assign the Gauls as consular provinces and supersede Caesar there before 48, when he intended to be consul in Rome.

4. In pursuance of the design implied in 3, Caesar demanded and Pompey helped to pass a special law in 52 by which Caesar was allowed the privilege of being elected consul without a personal canvass for the office.

5. But Pompey, who had begun to fear Caesar and to ally himself with the senate, also passed a law in 52 which repealed the Sempronian law and made it possible for the senate to supersede Caesar as soon as his legal term expired.

6. Taking 4 and 5 together, it seems reasonable to conclude that the right of Caesar to be elected consul in his absence had been definitely agreed upon at the conference at Luca, and that in allowing the law of the ten tribunes to be passed Pompey was simply keeping his word to his partner. Having kept his promise according to the strict letter, Pompey tried by repealing the whole Sempronian law to render the concession which he found himself obliged to make quite worthless for the purpose for which it was intended.

7. Whatever the precise date when Caesar's legal term in Gaul would expire, there was a considerable interval between that date and the time when Caesar could be elected consul and a still longer

interval before he could assume office if elected. If he were superseded during this time he would become a private citizen, and as such he would be open to a prosecution in the courts for any illegal act he had committed. Such a prosecution some of his enemies were determined to bring against him, and he was equally determined to avoid.

8. The only way in which he could avoid prosecution was to remain proconsul of Gaul up to the very time when he would assume the consulship. It was, therefore, necessary that he should hold his province for a considerable time after his legal term expired. The only way in which he could do this was by preventing the appointment of a successor to take over the command until the beginning of his second consulship on January 1, 48.

9. Under the Sempronian law Caesar was amply safeguarded and could continue in Gaul for the required time. After Pompey repealed the Sempronian law this was wholly doubtful ; the senate now had the power to supersede him before he had been elected consul, or afterwards before he had actually taken office.

10. Caesar, as his one means of safety, strove to prevent the appointment of a successor and found in the veto of the tribunes an effective weapon for his purpose. Under the Sempronian law the tribunes had been deprived of the veto in connexion with the assignment of the consular provinces. When Pompey repealed the Sempronian law he inadvertently repealed this restriction on the veto along with the rest of the law. Curio made use of this fact to block all action in the senate, and Pompey was able to break the resulting deadlock only by methods of dubious legality.

Of these points only the second has been seriously questioned. Here it seems to me that the advocates of Mommsen's view have proved their case completely, and that the language of Cicero leaves practically no doubt that the *lex Pompeia-Licinia* extended Caesar's proconsulship for a definite period of five years. The orator frequently refers to Caesar's term in Gaul as lasting for ten years [1] and he states explicitly that it was prolonged for five years.[2] The suggestion has been put forward that Caesar meant to stand for the consulship in 50 and to hold that office in 49,[3] or at least that he was eligible to do so.[4] This seems to me untenable ;

---

[1] *Att.*, vii. 5, 7, 9, for example.   [2] *Att.*, vii. 6.

[3] Hirschfeld maintained this view in his articles.

[4] Mispoulet, *La vie parlementaire à Rome*, 353–4, offers this suggestion. The instances which he cites, however, seem to me wholly inconclusive.

the whole course of the negotiations appears to show clearly that the older view is correct on this point.

The principal question that is left open is that of the precise date at which Caesar's command, as extended by the *lex Pompeia-Licinia*, terminated. I am inclined to think, though tentatively, that the weight of the evidence available tends to show that it expired in 50 and probably early in the year. The issue really narrows down to the single question of when the second *quinquennium* began. Did it start, as Mommsen held, with the end of the first, that is with March 1, 54 ; or with the end of 55, as Judeich maintains ; or with the actual passage of the *lex Pompeia-Licinia* ? In the first case Caesar's command would end March 1, 49 ; in the second, December 29, 50 ; in the third, in the early part of 50, though on what precise day is uncertain.[1] This last conclusion seems to me the most probable of the three for the reasons which follow.

1. At Luca it was determined to give each of the triumvirs a province and an army. This would place the three upon an ostensibly equal footing, since each of them would now be invested with a great command. Moreover it was agreed that these commands should all be held for the same length of time ; Crassus and Pompey, therefore, were assigned the provinces of Syria and Spain for five years, and Caesar's proconsulship in Gaul was prolonged for the same period. Now it seems clear that the command of Crassus in Syria and that of Pompey in Spain began at once on the passage of the law (*lex Trebonia*) conferring these provinces upon them.[2] It would be natural, under these circum-

They are all cases of second consulships that occurred before the time of Sulla, who revived an old law requiring a ten-year interval. The only ground for thinking that Caesar had any intention of becoming a candidate in 50 is an expression in a letter of Caelius Rufus to Cicero, for which see the final note at the close of this section.

[1] The *lex Trebonia* and the *lex Pompeia-Licinia* were passed with no great interval between them, and from a letter of Cicero (*Att.*, iv. 9) it is clear that the first of these had been passed, or at least published, by April 27, 55. The view of Meyer (*Caesars Monarchie*, 158, note 1) is the same as the one here accepted.

[2] Judeich bases his theory on the supposition that the terms of Crassus and Pompey began January 1, 54 ; this he says there is no reason to doubt. In reply Hardy points out that Crassus left Rome for Syria early in November (*Att.*, iv. 13). The answer seems to me conclusive and to prove that the *lex Trebonia*, like the *lex Vatinia*, made the proconsulships begin

stances, that Caesar's command should be prolonged in such a way that it would not appear on the surface to outlast the others. This would be accomplished if his second five years were counted in the same way as those of his colleagues, namely from the date of the passage of the law extending his term. But while willing to put himself on a footing of nominal equality with his partners, Caesar was determined to safeguard his second consulship. To do this without making any obvious distinction between the three he inserted the special clause forbidding any discussion of a successor before March 1, 50, and very probably exacted a pledge that at a later time he should be given permission to stand for the consulship *in absentia*. While the Sempronian law stood, this arrangement safeguarded Caesar's interests perfectly, though rather indirectly. The only reason for such indirectness that I can see is the desire to avoid as far as possible the appearance of giving Caesar any more than was given to his partners. If his *imperium* would outlast theirs by practically a year the whole arrangement seems useless, since the clause forbidding discussion of a successor before March 1, 50 was quite unnecessary if Caesar's term was prolonged till March 1, 49 ; the fractional part of a year would prevent his being superseded during the remainder of 49 in any case. The speech of Cicero shows that the Gauls could not be assigned to any of the magistrates for 50, because they could only be given provinces of which they could take immediate possession.[1] Thus the Gauls could only be assigned to one of the magistrates for 49, who could not take over their provinces till January 1, 48. If Caesar's term expired in 50, however, the clause was necessary to prevent the Gauls being assigned to the consuls for 50, who would be able to take over the provinces at the beginning of 49, a full year before Caesar meant to leave. The presence of this special clause in the bill seems to me, therefore, a strong argument in favour of 50. It seems to me that the supporters of 49 are bound either to deny the presence of this clause in the law, which they agree in admitting although it cannot be said to be entirely certain,[2] or to furnish some explanation of its purpose.

immediately. Cicero makes it clear that the Romans would not have tolerated the idea of a proconsul wandering about the empire for nearly two months waiting for a province to become vacant, possessed of the *imperium* but unable to exercise it anywhere.

[1] *On the Consular Provinces*, 15.

[2] The existence of the clause is based on *Letters*, ii. 78 ; *Fam.*, viii. 8.

2. The only explicit statements which we have in ancient writers as to the time when Caesar's command expired point to 50 as the year. Dio gives this date and is so sure of it that he shortens the second *quinquennium* to three years to make it fit.[1] This shortening is made necessary by an error of two years in Dio's computation. He counts Caesar's first five years as beginning with his actual arrival in Gaul (March, 58) and not from the true date of a year earlier (March, 59). The second five years is then reckoned from the end of the first, so that if it expired in 50 it could have had a duration of only three years. Dio is plainly aware that the statement had been made that Caesar's term was renewed for a second five years, but he sets this aside because of his certainty that his term did in fact end in 50. The language of Appian is in accord with that of Dio, though it is not quite so explicit ; in his narrative of the events of 51 he says that Caesar's term was about to expire,[2] which is strange if it had more than a year still to run. The other writers use language which it seems to me will fit either date. It is a fact that ought not to be ignored, however, that the only two writers who make definite statements as to the date both affirm that it was 50, and that there is no equally clear statement of 49 to be found anywhere.

3. The contemporary evidence of the letters of Cicero and those of his friend Caelius Rufus seems to me to imply 50. The expressions to be found here can be, and have been, interpreted to fit the date of 49, but such an interpretation involves a rather forced construction and compels the conclusion that the writers did not say what they meant. It will be sufficient to cite one or two of the most important passages, and I take those that seem to me the most decisive.

During 50, while Cicero was in Cilicia, Caelius wrote to him : ' As for politics, every controversy centres on one point—the provinces. In this matter Pompey as yet seems to have thrown all his weight on the side of the senate's wish that Caesar should leave his province on the 13th of November . . . The situation turns entirely on this : Pompey, professing not to be attacking Caesar, but to be making an arrangement which he considers fair to him, says that Curio is deliberately seeking pretexts for strife. How-

The language of Caelius seems to me to make the presence of such a clause highly probable, but his words might perhaps be otherwise interpreted.

[1] Dio, xxxix. 33 ; xl. 59. Guiraud has shown clearly how Dio gets his three years.　　　　　　　　　　　　[2] Appian, ii. 26, 27.

ever, he is strongly against, and evidently alarmed at, the idea of Caesar becoming consul-designate before handing over his army and province.' ' Quod ad rem publicam attinet, in unam causam omnis contentio conlecta est de provinciis ; in quam adhuc incubuisse cum senatu Pompeius videtur, ut Caesar Id. Nov. decedat ; ... Scaena rei totius haec : Pompeius, tamquam Caesarem non inpugnet, sed, quod illi aequum putet, constituat, ait Curionem quaerere discordias, valde autem non vult et plane timet Caesarem cos. desig. prius quam exercitum et provinciam tradiderit.' ¹ As the date stands it would mean November 13, 50, and the proposal favoured by Pompey was that Caesar should be superseded on that date. If Caesar's term had not then legally ended it would seem impossible that such a proposition could be represented as fair in any sense of the words. Hardy, following Mommsen, maintains that the date should be November 13, 49, and that Caelius writing in haste did not take the trouble to make this clear, knowing that Cicero would not be in the slightest doubt as to what year he meant. This sounds reasonable in itself, but it makes nonsense of the last sentence of the passage quoted. If the November in question was in 49, what about the fears attributed to Pompey ? In November, 49, Caesar would already have been elected consul while still holding his army. Hardy meets this difficulty by assuming that the final sentence indicates Pompey's real feelings and not his professions. That is to say, Pompey is pretending to support the proposal of the senate that Caesar shall stay in Gaul till November, 49, but in reality he is opposed to it because he is afraid of Caesar's becoming consul while still retaining his army. But this is not what Caelius says ; the Latin reads quite clearly and in a different sense. Its obvious meaning is that Pompey supports the proposal of the senate and pretends that he is trying to be fair to Caesar, but in his heart he is afraid to let Caesar be elected until he has given up his army. In the clause beginning *valde autem* the *autem* connects what follows with what precedes, not with what comes several lines before. If we take the passage as it stands and read it in the natural sense of the Latin it is fatal to the date of 49. Pompey could not pretend that it was fair to supersede Caesar before his legal term had expired, but, if it had already expired in the early part of 50, then he could very well represent a date which allowed

---

¹ *Letters*, ii. 176-7 ; *Fam.*, viii. 11.

Caesar several months extra as a fair and even friendly arrangement. It will be noted that the language of Caelius is just as fatal to the theory of Judeich as to that of Mommsen.

In his letters written during 50 Cicero also uses language that seems on the face of it to imply that Caesar's term has expired. In December of that year he wrote to Atticus concerning Caesar's demands, ' Could anything be more impudent ? You have held a province for ten years, a time not granted you by the senate, but assumed by yourself with the help of violence and sedition : this period—not assigned by the law, but by your own caprice—has passed. Let us, however, grant that it was by the law : a decree is made for naming your successor : you cry halt and say, " Take my candidature into consideration." Rather do you take us into consideration. Are you to have an army (against the will of the senate) longer than the vote of the people gave it you ? ' ' Nam quid impudentius ? Tenuisti provinciam per annos decem, non tibi a senatu, sed a te ipso per vim et per factionem datos ; praeteriit tempus non legis, sed libidinis tuae, fac tamen legis ; ut succedatur decernitur ; impedis et ais : " Habe meam rationem." Habe tu nostram. Exercitum tu habeas diutius quam populus iussit, invito senatu ? '[1] It has been argued that here Cicero is placing himself in imagination in the near future, and is picturing what will happen two or three months hence. This seems possible, but the context suggests rather that he is speaking of the past and present ; the demands are those that Caesar was then making, and all that Cicero says was true of the past ; the senate *had* tried to pass a decree providing a successor for Caesar, and Caesar *had* objected on the ground that in granting him the right to be a candidate *in absentia* the people had extended his term by implication. It is therefore possible that in the whole passage Cicero meant exactly what he said, and if he did it is clear that Caesar's term had expired at the time he wrote. An argument in favour of 49 has been based on the expression, both in this passage and elsewhere, of ten years as the length of Caesar's term. It seems to me, however, that such language is wholly natural and need not be taken too literally ; Gaul was granted to Caesar for five years by the Vatinian law and then for a second five years by the law of Pompey and Crassus.

---

[1] *Letters*, ii. 232–3 ; *Att.*, vii. 9. Shuckburgh omits the *invito senatu* which I have inserted in parentheses.

This being so, if Cicero wished to speak of the entire term for which Caesar held his province it would be very natural for him to add the two grants together and describe the command of Caesar under the two laws as for ten years. Moreover, as Caesar had then held the province for almost nine years and ten months Cicero might very well speak in round numbers and call it ten years in a hasty letter.

Another passage to which reference should be made is found in a letter to Atticus written in January, 49, after Caesar had invaded Italy. Cicero is boiling over with indignation against Caesar, and he writes, after mentioning the news of his advance, ' Madman ! Miserable wretch, that has never seen even a shadow of virtue ! And he says that he is doing all this " to support his honour " ! How can there be any " honour " where there is no moral right ? Can it be morally right to have an army without commission from the state ? To seize cities inhabited by one's fellow citizens, as a means of attacking one's own country ? To be contriving abolition of debts, restoration of exiles, hundreds of other crimes . . .? ' The Latin of the critical part of this passage reads : ' Atque haec ait omnia facere se dignitatis causa. Ubi est autem dignitas nisi ubi honestas ? Honestum igitur habere exercitum nullo publico consilio, occupare urbes civium, quo facilior sit aditus ad patriam . . .? ' [1] Here Cicero seems to say clearly that Caesar has no right to have an army. But if his command did not end till March 1, 49, he did at that time have a perfect legal right to it. It is true that he had no right to bring his army into Italy, and perhaps this was what Cicero meant, but if so he failed to say this in his excitement. If Caesar's term had expired some time in 50 and if Caesar had since that date been holding on in Gaul by blocking the action of the senate through his tribunes, then Cicero wrote exactly what he meant. To him it seemed preposterous for Caesar to talk about his honour being involved when he was trying to retain possession of something to which he had no legal right.

One more passage in Cicero's letters should be cited because it has been made to figure in the controversy. In December, 50, Cicero wrote : ' Well then ! Do I approve of votes being taken for a man who is retaining an army beyond the legal day ? For my part, I say *no* ; nor in his absence either. But when the

[1] *Letters*, ii. 241 ; *Att.*, vii. 11.

former was granted him, so was the latter.' ' Quid ergo ? exercitum retinentis, cum legis dies transierit, rationem haberi placet ? Mihi vero ne absentis quidem ; sed, cum id datum est, illud una datum est.' [1] For my part I do not see that much can be made of this. Cicero is clearly thinking of Caesar as a candidate, and the passage may mean : Do I approve of giving a special privilege to a man who is now (50) holding an army beyond his legal term ? or it may equally well mean : Do I approve of letting a man receive votes who will be keeping an army then (when he becomes a candidate, in 49) ?

The passages cited above seem to me the decisive ones. If it is held that these passages will fit the date of March 1, 49, I cannot see any difficulty in construing the other expressions to be found in the correspondence of Cicero to fit it. If it be assumed that Caesar's term ended in 50, it does not seem to me that there is anything in the language of Cicero that conflicts with it, at least on the surface, except his reference to the ten years of Caesar's proconsulship. Whatever theory is adopted, there will remain a few expressions whose interpretation will offer some difficulty, but these expressions fail to fit any theory and the difficulty is no greater for one than for the other.

4. Finally, it seems to me that the policy of Pompey becomes more readily intelligible if the date be taken as 50. There seems no adequate reason for bringing up the question of appointing a successor to Caesar in March, 50, if his term had still a year to run. Hardy explains this by assuming that it was still doubtful whether or not Pompey's new law in regard to the provincial governors had actually repealed the Sempronian law,[2] and Meyer holds that the provisions of the latter remained in force which required the assignment of the consular provinces to take place eighteen months before the governor appointed took possession.[3] Both writers seem to have overlooked the fact that the Sempronian law was ignored at the assignment of the provinces in 51. Cicero was then given the province of Cilicia and he left Rome for the East in May, 51. He could not possibly have received this province eighteen months before, since this would have been before the law of Pompey was passed, and under the Sempronian law he was not eligible for a proconsulship. It is evident from

---

[1] *Letters*, ii. 228 ; *Att.*, vii. 7.
[2] Hardy, *Jour. of Phil.*, xxxiv. 178.     [3] Meyer, 256, note 2.

this that at the beginning of 51 the whole Sempronian law was regarded as repealed, and if this was true, there seems no very good reason for taking up the matter of the succession to the Gauls so long in advance of the possibility of effective action. Taken in connexion with Pompey's pretence of fairness in supporting the proposal to extend Caesar's term till November 13, the whole matter is most readily understandable on the supposition that Caesar's term expired early in 50. The date of March 1, 49, not only leaves us in the dark as to why the question should have been brought forward so early, but also forces us to set aside the obvious and natural meaning of the language of Caelius.

To sum up briefly my own impressions of the controversy, the explicit statement of Dio that Caesar's term expired in 50, which is supported by the testimony of Appian, seems evidence not to be lightly set aside. In this case it is reinforced by contemporary testimony. The letters of Caelius Rufus confirm Dio strongly, and can only be made to fit any other date by a rather strained interpretation. Cicero is somewhat less definite, but he too uses language which, if read according to its obvious natural meaning, implies that Caesar's term had expired in 50. Unless his words as to the ten years of Caesar's government are thought to imply 49, Cicero never uses language which on the face of it points to that date. Under these circumstances I can see no adequate reason for rejecting the authority of Dio—though he was certainly far from infallible—and for interpreting the language of Caelius and Cicero in any other than the obvious and natural way. This conclusion seems all the more reasonable because the date thus given is one which might be expected *a priori* from the conditions under which the triumvirate was renewed at Luca, and because it is strongly implied by what we know of the peculiar clause forbidding the discussion of a successor before March 1, 50, and lastly because this date fits the details of the diplomatic struggle between Pompey and Caesar at least as well as any other, if not better.

Whatever date is accepted, it does not appear to me to make any great difference. Caesar certainly meant to retain his command in Gaul after his legal term had expired, and Pompey certainly was determined that he should be superseded between that date (whenever it was) and the time when he would take office as consul in Rome at the beginning of 48. To make this possible, Pompey repealed the Sempronian law, and to ward off the new danger thus created, Caesar made use of the veto of his tribunes. In this way Caesar was able to hold Pompey in check and to prevent any decisive action by the senate. Unable to overcome these tactics by any other means, Pompey at length resorted to force and precipitated the civil war. Whether Caesar's term had actually expired, or whether Pompey was simply trying to take such steps that he could be superseded immediately after it should expire, is after all a question which can hardly affect materially our judgement of the actors.

In conclusion it may be well to notice two special points that have figured in the controversy but to which I am unable to attach any decisive importance. One of these is a passage in the eighth book of the Gallic War, written by Caesar's friend Hirtius, and the other is a passage in a letter of Caelius Rufus.

In describing the siege of Uxellodunum, Hirtius says of Caesar that on learning the steadfast purpose of the townsfolk—' though he disregarded their small numbers, he judged nevertheless that their obstinacy must be visited with a severe punishment, for he feared that the Gauls as a whole might suppose that what had been lacking in them for resisting the Romans was not strength, but resolution ; and that the rest of the states might follow this example and rely on any advantage offered by strong positions to reassert their liberty. All the Gauls were aware, as he knew, that there was one more summer season in his term of office, and that, if they could hold out for that, they had no further danger to fear.' ' Quorum etsi paucitatem contemnebat, tamen pertinaciam magna poena esse adficiendam iudicabat, ne universa Gallia non sibi vires defuisse ad resistendum Romanis, sed constantiam putaret, neve hoc exemplo ceterae civitates locorum opportunitate fretae se vindicarent in libertatem, cum omnibus Gallis notum esse sciret reliquam esse unam aestatem suae provinciae, quam si sustinere potuissent, nullum ultra periculum vererentur.[1] Hirschfeld makes the *unam aestatem* refer to that summer, namely the summer of 51. Holmes denies the possibility of this since only a part of the summer was then left and in another connexion Caesar speaks of a part of a summer as *exigua parte aestatis* (Gallic War, iv. 20). This does not seem to

---

[1] Caesar, *Gallic War*, viii. 39. I have taken the translation from that of Edwards in the *Loeb Library* edition, since he interprets the passage in the same fashion as Holmes and thinks that the *unam aestatem* refers to the summer of 50.

me very conclusive. In the first place, Hirtius is not Caesar, and his use of words might differ from that of his friend.[1] In the second place, the context is quite different in the two cases and would in itself explain a different form of expression. Lastly, the sense of the passage seems much better if Hirschfeld's interpretation is followed. Caesar made an example in this case for fear that the other Gauls would prolong their resistance, since they knew that that summer was the last of his term. If they thought that they had only to hold out a few months, one can readily understand the matter, but if the summer referred to is that of 50, as Holmes holds, it does not seem so clear ; they would in this case have to hold out not only for the rest of that summer but for the whole summer of 50 as well. Under these circumstances it would hardly seem that their knowledge of the date when Caesar's proconsulship ended can have had much influence on their conduct unless they felt sure that the course of Roman politics would keep Caesar in Cisalpine Gaul during the summer of 50. As Caesar's army must have known something of his plans and of Pompey's opposition to them, a calculation on the part of the Gauls that Caesar would be unable to undertake serious military operations in 50, whether his term expired then or early in 49, does not seem incredible. In short I do not see that this passage, however interpreted, is decisive for either side.

In a letter of Caelius Rufus, written in October, 51, he tells Cicero among other things that Caesar has made up his mind not to be a candidate this next year, ' neque hoc anno sua ratio habeatur '.[2] If this passage stood alone we should have no hesitation in deciding that *hoc anno* meant 50. An attempt has been made on the basis of it to maintain that Caesar meant to be a candidate in that year, and hence meant to hold the consulship in 49. I cannot think that this attempt has met with any success, and it must, I believe, be taken as established that Caesar did not mean to be a candidate in 50. But what then are we to do with the remark of Caelius ? Two explanations of it have been suggested,

---

[1] To me the force of Holmes's argument from the usage of Caesar is very greatly weakened, if not entirely destroyed, by his admission that Caesar never uses the word *provincia* in the sense here given to it. If Hirtius did not use single words in the same sense as Caesar, I really cannot see why he was bound to use phrases in the same way. See Holmes, *Caesar de Bello Gallico*, 389 note.

[2] *Letters*, ii. 78 ; *Fam.*, viii. 8.

one by Hardy and the other by Meyer. Hardy thinks that the words *hoc anno* should be understood to mean ' this year ', that is, the year that we both have in mind. Meyer thinks that the passage probably refers to some compromise proposal that had been put forward of which one provision was that Caesar should be given a special dispensation to permit of his election as consul in 50. So far as I can see the words of Caelius are equally difficult for all theories, and therefore nothing can be made of them in favour of any one.

## LAQUEUR'S THEORY

Since the publication of the first edition my attention has been called to the theory of Laqueur,[1] with which at the time of writing the above I was not familiar. In brief, he holds that Caesar's proconsulship in Gaul began on January 1, 59, and was only limited in point of time by a clause in the Vatinian law which provided that no successor should be appointed till after March 1, 55. The *lex Pompeia-Licinia* simply moved this date forward to March 1, 50. As to the first point it seems to me that the criticism of Holmes [2] is conclusive and that it must be rejected. Like Judeich, Laqueur takes Cicero's expression ' you have had a province for ten years ' literally, and thinks that Cicero could not have written thus if the ten years lacked two months of being complete. Yet on his own showing the ten years lacked four or five days of being complete, and, if Cicero wrote with mathematical exactness, Caesar's term began on December 26 or 27, 60, and not on January 1, 59 as he supposes. As to the second point, it seems to me untenable in the face of Cicero's words that Caesar is ' retaining an army beyond the legal day (*legis dies* )'. According to Laqueur there was no legal day when Caesar's proconsulship ended, and we are thus required to believe that, while Cicero could not write ten years when the words were only approximately correct, he could write other phrases which were absolutely false. To me the reverse seems clearly the case, and I can readily imagine Cicero writing ten years when the time was only nine years and ten months, while I find it very difficult

---

[1] R. Laqueur, in *Neue Jahrbücher für das klassische Altertum*, xlv (1920), xlvii (1921).

[2] Holmes, *The Roman Republic*, ii. 300, note 5.

to believe that he would. have written the expression *legis dies* if he knew that there was no such thing.

If these two contentions of Laqueur are rejected, the only point of interest that remains is his theory as to the law of the ten tribunes. This plebiscite we know authorized Caesar to be a candidate for the consulship in his absence. Laqueur assumes that it must have provided expressly that he could be a candidate while proconsul of Gaul, and that this provision could be interpreted in two ways. Under Sulla's law Caesar could not be a candidate till 49, as he could not hold the consulship again till 48, and he argued that the plebiscite extended his term till July 49. On the other hand Pompey might argue that the plebiscite authorized him to stand in 50 before his legal term in Gaul had expired, or as soon after that as possible. Against this theory is the fact that Cicero apparently never heard of the argument attributed by Laqueur to Pompey, for he refers to Caesar's candidacy in 49 as legal, and this without any qualification.[1] Still the theory of Laqueur may furnish an explanation of the *hoc anno* of Caelius. In 51 some of the friends of Caesar in Rome may have suggested that the plebiscite could be construed to authorize his candidacy in 50, and this suggestion may have been rejected. This may have been the compromise proposal which Meyer suspects. In any case the language of Cicero seems to show that the point was not again brought forward, and that, therefore, Laqueur is wrong in his contention that the ambiguity of the plebiscite was the *Rechtsfrage* at issue in the civil war. There was no such *Rechtsfrage* so far as I can see. Pompey wished to supersede Caesar as soon as his term expired, or at least before he became consul, and Caesar fought this by the veto of his tribunes. These last, I think, used Caesar's interpretation of the plebiscite as a justification of their veto, but that was all.

[1] *Letters*, ii. 228 and 231-2 ; *Att.*, vii. 7 and 9.

## III. THE INTENTIONS OF CAESAR AND THE DIARCHY OF AUGUSTUS [1]

IN discussing the probable plans of Caesar as to the government of the Roman world modern historians seem to me to have failed to grasp the full significance of his increase in the number of the magistrates. Unless this measure was merely a temporary expedient, it points clearly to the conclusion that he had in mind no such system as was set up by Augustus. A brief consideration of this matter may not be without interest.

Both Caesar and his adopted son had to provide for the administration of some twenty provinces. For this purpose the old republican machinery with two consuls and eight praetors was plainly inadequate. Caesar solved the difficulty by an increase in the number of the magistrates, which would automatically increase the size of the senate and the number of the noble families at the same time. Augustus carefully avoided tampering with the traditional machinery of the republic and found another solution. His method, known to moderns as the diarchy, consisted in its essence of a division of the empire into two parts. The old republic was restored and left to govern about as many provinces as it could manage, while those remaining were handed over to Augustus, who governed them at first largely through his relatives without much help from the senatorial nobility. Thus the diarchy, by creating a dual system of provincial administration, enabled Augustus to avoid any serious readjustment of the old republican forms. That Caesar undertook such changes in the number of the magistrates in spite of the fact that he must have known that it would cause bitter resentment, seems to show that he intended to establish a single administrative system for the whole Roman world. In making this decision he had come to the parting of the ways, and he made his choice sufficiently clear to his contemporaries. A uniform administrative system meant

[1] This appendix consists mainly of portions of an article entitled ' The Roman Aristocracy and the Death of Caesar', which appeared in the *Classical Journal* in 1925. For permission to make use of it I am indebted to the courtesy of the editors.

neither more nor less than an autocracy, and excluded all hope of a restoration of the republic in any form which the Roman nobles could, or would, accept. It was by the device of the diarchy that Augustus was able to restore the republic, and it was this restoration which made it possible for the aristocracy to accept his government. It will need only a brief consideration to bring out these points clearly.

That the emperor could not safely relax his control over the frontier provinces where the bulk of the army was stationed is obvious. If Caesar meant to intrust the government of the provinces to the ex-magistrates on any uniform system, he would be compelled to exercise a rigid control over the elections and over the assignment of the provinces. It would have been insanity to allow the people to elect some noble hostile to Caesar to the consulship and then permit him to draw by lot one of the important provinces which would place him at the head of a great army. Augustus was able to permit a certain show of freedom because all the provinces that really mattered had been handed over to him at the start. Caesar seems to have realized the situation perfectly, since he appointed the governors without the use of the lot [1] ; and in view of his expected absence during the Parthian war he took the power to name a large proportion of the magistrates for some years in advance. Had he returned victorious from the East and had he continued to administer the provinces on any uniform system, this control must have been established as a permanent part of the government.

Caesar's increase in the number of the magistrates would, therefore, seem to indicate that he had no idea of dividing the responsibility with the senate. The administrative need for the increase points rather toward a centralized system of government with himself as head exercising a practically complete control over the whole republican machine. If Caesar contemplated any other arrangement, he must have viewed the increase as a purely temporary expedient. Of this there is no evidence, and his contemporaries seem to have had no suspicion that the changes were merely provisional. A part of their resentment may have been due precisely to the fact that they saw clearly that these changes pointed definitely away from any plan to restore the old republic.

That the existing aristocracy was not adequate for the adminis-

[1] Dio, xliii. 47.

tration of the empire may have been true, and yet this consideration may not have gone far to reconcile the nobility to a rapid and sweeping increase in their number. Slight and gradual changes they might have endured, even if they did not approve, but Caesar's methods of reform may have seemed merely a first step toward discarding them altogether. This was to touch the nobles to the quick, for one of the things for which they had fought most persistently was their monopoly of office. This passionate determination of the aristocracy to keep the administration of the Roman world in their own hands lay behind much of their talk of liberty and the republic. A careful reading of Cicero's letters will show that to him the republic was identical with the senate. Throughout this period, however, the senate is simply the instrument of the nobility, so that government by the senate meant, in fact, the control of public affairs by the ring of noble families which formed the Roman aristocracy. This oligarchy, though unaccustomed to a master, might have submitted to a monarchy which left them to enjoy undisturbed the spoils of office and which respected their social prestige. But Caesar took no pains to do either of these things. Not only did the old families see their monopoly of office broken down, but the increase in the number of the magistrates would soon result in a very real change in the character of the aristocracy. In the near future the members of the great republican houses would find themselves lost amid a crowd of new men whom Caesar's favour had exalted. Such a prospect was intolerable to the nobles, and they could readily persuade themselves that in resisting Caesar and his reforms they were the champions of something more than their own selfish interests. In their class were gathered up the traditions of Roman law and government, and its too rapid transformation might be a dangerous matter. We of to-day may think that any change was likely to be for the better, but the Roman nobles could hardly be expected to see themselves through our eyes. When men like Cicero and Cato could still believe in the essential, if not divine, right of the nobility to rule the world, the aristocracy itself was not likely to be disturbed by any doubts as to its mission.

These phases of the problem seem to have been clearly realized by Augustus, more so perhaps than by the greater Julius, and in his final settlement he gave up entirely the policy that Caesar had foreshadowed. He took care to placate the nobility and abandoned the idea of any extensive creation of new peers. He brought back the number of the magistrates to approximately the old figures and this served as a pledge that he would respect the character of the old aristocracy. The gaps caused by the proscriptions and the civil wars he did indeed fill, but very largely by promotions from the lower ranks of the old nobility. In the early days of his reign he seems to have advanced comparatively few new men, at any rate to the consulship. To the aristocracy as thus reconstituted, in such a manner as to offend as little as possible against its exclusive spirit, he made over as large a share of the empire as it was capable of administering under the old system, while he relieved it from the burden of such additional regions as would have necessitated any considerable increase in the number of the nobles. Seen from this point of view, the principate solved the problem with a minimum of friction, and it may well have been the solution most agreeable to the old aristocracy. Their social prestige was unimpaired, and in Rome and the senatorial provinces the average noble could look forward to much the same career as under the republic.

If Caesar had lived and returned victorious from the East, he might have organized a permanent government on the foundations he had laid. A new and broader aristocracy would have supplied a governing class, but, without some such arrangement as the diarchy, Caesar must have held a position of far more open sovereignty than did his adopted son. He might have transacted all public business in the senate and chosen his officers from the nobility, but it would have been in a new senate and from a new nobility. Even had Caesar pledged himself to this, it would have done little to placate the aristocracy, since no future respect for senate or nobility had any value unless both were left substantially unchanged. The murder of Caesar may be regarded as a desperate attempt of the Roman nobles to preserve their privileges and to save their class from such a wholesale creation of new peers as would have profoundly modified its character. On the surface the murder was a tragic failure, but, when we note how carefully Augustus treated the surviving families of the old aristocracy, we may wonder whether, in some sense, it was not successful after all.

# IV. LIST OF BOOKS REFERRED TO IN THE NOTES

IN the following list no attempt has been made to enumerate all the works which have been used in the preparation of this book, still less to make a complete bibliography of the subject. All that has been intended is to give adequate information concerning the works referred to in the notes, and by this means to avoid frequent repetition of titles without inconveniencing the reader who may wish to verify a statement.

## THE SOURCES

As the sources referred to have all been published in numerous editions an enumeration of them is unnecessary, and it will be sufficient to say that all references to Appian are to the books on the *Civil Wars* and all those to Tacitus are to the *Annals*. Where references have been made to any particular edition this has been included in the list below under the name of the editor or translator.

## MODERN WORKS

Boak, A. E. R.—*A History of Rome to A.D. 565.* New York, 1921.

Bleckmann, F.—*Die erste syrische Statthalterschaft des F. Sulpicius Quirinius* in *Klio*, xvii, Leipzig, 1921.

Bouché-Leclercq, A.—*Histoire des Lagides.* 4 vols. Paris, 1903–7.

Caspari, M. O. B.—*On the Iuratio Italiae of 32 B.C.* in the *Classical Quarterly*, v. London and Boston, 1911.

Dessau, H.—*Geschichte der römischen Kaiserzeit. Erster Band; Bis zum ersten Thronwechsel.* Berlin, 1924.

Destarac, J.—*La Brigue électorale à Rome à la fin de la république.* Toulouse, 1908.

Dodge, T. A.—*Caesar.* New York, 1894.

Drumann, W.—*Geschichte Roms.* 2nd edition, edited by P. Groebe. Vols. i–iv, Berlin, 1899; vol. v, Leipzig, 1919.

Edwards, H. J.—*Caesar, The Gallic War.* Text and English translation in the *Loeb Library*. London and New York, 1917.

Ferguson, W. S.—*Greek Imperialism*. New York, 1913.

Ferrero, G.—*The Greatness and Decline of Rome*. 5 vols. London, 1907–9.

Ferrero, G.—*La Ruine de la civilisation antique*. Paris, 1921.

Frank, T.—*Roman Imperialism*. New York, 1914.

Frank, T.—*An Economic History of Rome to the End of the Republic*. Baltimore, 1920.

Frank, T.—*The Inscriptions of the Imperial Domains of Africa* in the *American Journal of Philology*, xlvii. Baltimore, 1926.

Gardthausen, V.—*Augustus und seine Zeit*. 3 vols. Leipzig, 1891–1904.

Gelzer, M.—*Die Nobilität der römischen Republik*. Leipzig, 1912.

Goyau, G.—*Chronologie de l'empire romain*. Paris, 1891.

Greenidge, A. H. J.—*A History of Rome during the Later Republic and Early Principate*. New York, 1905.

Groebe.—See Drumann.

Guiraud, P.—*Le Différend entre César et le sénat*. Paris, 1878.

Hardy, E. G.—*The Catilinarian Conspiracy in its Context : A Restudy of the Evidence*. Oxford, 1924.

Hardy, E. G.—*Caesar's Legal Position in Gaul 52 to 49 B.C.* in *Some Problems in Roman History*. Oxford, 1924.

Hardy, E. G.—*The Monumentum Ancyranum*. Oxford, 1923.

Hardy, E. G.—*Studies in Roman History*. 2 vols. Vol. i, 2nd edition. London, 1909–10.

Hartmann, L. M. and Kromayer, J.—*Römische Geschichte (Hartmanns Weltgeschichte in gemeinverständlicher Darstellung)*. Gotha, 1919.

Heitland, W. E.—*The Roman Republic*. 3 vols. Cambridge, 1909.

Hirschfeld, O.—Articles in *Klio*, iv and v. Leipzig, 1904–5.

Holmes, T. R.—*Caesar de Bello Gallico*. Oxford, 1914.

Holmes, T. R.—*Caesar's Conquest of Gaul*. 2nd edition. Oxford, 1911.

Holmes, T. R.—*Hirschfeld and Judeich on the Lex Pompeia-Licinia* in the *Classical Quarterly*, x. London and Boston, 1916.

Holmes, T. R.—*The Roman Republic*. 3 vols. Oxford, 1923.

Holzapfel, L.—Article in *Klio*, v. Leipzig, 1905.

Judeich, W.—*Das Ende von Caesars gallischer Statthalterschaft und der Ausbruch des Bürgerkrieges* in the *Rheinisches Museum für Philologie*, lxviii. Frankfurt, 1913.

Jullian, C.—*Histoire de la Gaule.* 6 vols., the first three in the 3rd edition. Paris, 1914–20.

Klebs, Dessau, and de Rohden.—*Prosopographia.* See that title.

Klein, J.—*Fasti Consulares inde a Caesaris nece usque ad imperium Diocletiani.* Leipzig, 1881.

Kromayer, J.—*Die Vorgeschichte des Kriegs von Actium* in *Hermes,* xxxiii and xxxiv. Berlin, 1898–9.

Lange, L.—*Römische Altertümer.* 3 vols. 2nd edition. Berlin, 1863–76.

Laqueur, R.—*Cäsars gallische Statthalterschaft und der Ausbruch des Bürgerkrieges,* in *Neue Jahrbücher für klassisches Altertum,* xlv and xlvii. Leipzig, 1920–1.

*Letters of Cicero.* See Shuckburgh, E. S.

Liebenam, W.—*Fasti Consulares Imperii Romani.* Bonn, 1909.

Liebenam, W.—*Forschungen zur Verwaltungsgeschichte des römischen Kaiserreichs.* I. *Die Legaten in den römischen Provinzen von Augustus bis Diocletian.* Leipzig, 1888.

McFayden, D.—*The Princeps and the Senatorial Provinces* in *Classical Philology,* xvi. Chicago, 1921.

Mahaffy, J. P.—*A History of Egypt under the Ptolemaic Dynasty.* London and New York, 1899.

Marquardt, J.—*Römische Staatsverwaltung.* 4 vols. in Marquardt and Mommsen, *Handbuch der römischen Altertümer.* 2nd edition. Leipzig, 1881–6.

Marsh, F. B.—*The Roman Aristocracy and the Death of Caesar* in the *Classical Journal,* xx. Chicago, 1925.

Meyer, E.—*Caesars Monarchie und das Principat des Pompeius.* 2nd edition. Stuttgart and Berlin, 1919.

Meyer, E.—*Kleine Schriften.* Halle, 1910.

Mispoulet, J. B.—*La Vie parlementaire à Rome sous la république.* Paris, 1899.

Mommsen, T.—*The History of Rome.* New edition. New York, 1903.

Mommsen, T.—*Die Rechtsfrage zwischen Caesar und dem Senat.* Breslau, 1857.

Pelham, H. F.—*Essays on Roman History.* Oxford, 1911.

Pocock, L. G.—*Publius Clodius and the Acts of Caesar* in the *Classical Quarterly,* xviii. London, 1924.

*Prosopographia Imperii Romani.* Vol. i, edited by E. Klebs. Vol. ii, edited by H. Dessau. Vol. iii, edited by P. de Rohden and H. Dessau. Berlin, 1897–8.

Reinach, T.—*Mithridate Eupator, roi de Ponte.* Paris, 1890.

Sage, E. T.—*The Date of the Vatinian Law,* in the *American Journal of Philology,* xxxix. Baltimore, 1918.

Salvioli, G.—*Le Capitalisme dans le monde antique.* Paris, 1906.

Schwartz, E.—*Die Vertheilung der römischen Provinzen nach Cäsars Tod* in *Hermes,* xxxiii. Berlin, 1898.

Shuckburgh, E. S.—*The Letters of Cicero.* Translated into English by E. S. Shuckburgh. 4 vols. in the *Bohn Library.*

Smith, W. (editor). *Dictionary of Greek and Roman Biography and Mythology.* 3 vols. London, 1880.

Strachan-Davidson, J. L.—*Cicero and the Fall of the Roman Republic* in the *Heroes of the Nations* series. London and New York, 1894.

Strack, M. L.—*Kleopatra* in the *Historische Zeitschrift,* cxv. Munich and Berlin, 1916.

White, H.—*Appian's Roman History.* Text and English translation in the *Loeb Library.* 4 vols. London and New York, 1912–13.

Willems, P.—*Le Droit public romain.* 7th edition. Louvain, 1910.

Willems, P.—*Le Sénat de la république romaine, sa composition et ses attributions.* 2 vols. Vol. i, 2nd edition. Louvain, 1883–85.

Winstedt, E. O.—*Cicero, Letters to Atticus.* Text and English translation in the *Loeb Library.* 3 vols. New York, 1912–18.

# INDEX